Second Edition

Great Jobs

for

Foreign Language Majors

Julie DeGalan
Stephen Lambert

AKIRA TOKI
MIDDLE SCHOOL LMC

MADISON
METROPOLITAN
SCHOOL DISTRICT
LMC

VGM Career Books
NTC/Contemporary Publishing Group

Library of Congress Cataloging-in-Publication Data

DeGalan, Julie.
    Great jobs for foreign language majors / Julie DeGalan & Stephen Lambert.—
2nd ed.
        p.   cm.
    Includes index.
    ISBN 0-658-00453-0
    1. Language and languages—Vocational guidance.   2. Job hunting.   3.
College graduates—Employment.   I. Lambert, Stephen.
II. Title.
P60 .D4 2000
650.14—dc21   99-43251
                                                                 CIP

To Barbara, Carolyn, Craig, Joyce, and Rip, with love

Published by VGM Career Books
A division of NTC/Contemporary Publishing Group, Inc.
4255 West Touhy Avenue, Lincolnwood (Chicago), Illinois 60712-1975 U.S.A.
Printed in the United States of America
International Standard Book Number: 0-658-00453-0
    04 05 06 LB 15 14 13 12 11 10 9 8 7 6 5 4 3 2

CONTENTS

TM

FOREIGN LANGUAGES AND THE EDUCATED PERSON

*D*efining the "educated person" is very difficult to do. However, although pundits disagree on many of the attributes that make someone truly educated, most would agree that the knowledge of at least one other language would be an important item on the list. If we review the history of the study of languages, we find that the study of Latin and Greek was, for many centuries, necessary for any scholar. As late as the middle of the nineteenth century, an educated person could read in their original form the works of great writers and thinkers, both ecclesiastical and secular. Virgil's *Aeneid*, Homer's *Iliad*, Aristotle's *Politics*, and Lady Murasaki Shikibu's *Tale of Genji* were all initially read and studied in their language of origin.

By the latter part of the nineteenth century, individual disciplines in the Arts and Sciences such as chemistry, botany, and geology began to evolve. Specialization in particular fields, including modern languages such as French and German, became necessary because it was no longer possible for an individual to be well read in many subject areas and stay current on rapid developments in industry, science, and medicine.

The study of European languages was brought to this country as part of a classic education. One could read and approach the literature, art, and architectural heritage of Europe more closely with an appreciation for, if not fluency in, one of the European languages. The "Grand Tour" of Europe was part of the finishing process of a certain class of young men and women, and a knowledge of one of the Romance tongues was certainly helpful in that respect. Here we are talking about the late eighteenth and early nineteenth centuries; however, vestiges of this custom remain in junior year programs of study abroad or the simple desire of a new graduate to go abroad before settling down to a career. There was a strong feeling that simply to have been exposed to foreign languages was a hallmark of good scholarship and a "proper" education.

Even the somewhat crude jibe leveled against the French student of old that "at least you'll be able to order a good meal" had an element of truth. Much fine dining was continental and French. More important, the worlds of art, fashion, decorating, and the theater were and still are filled with the linguistic heritage of their origin. The French word *matinée* for the afternoon theatrical performance or the word *loge* for the upper boxes in the theater are typical examples of the pervasiveness of this European heritage.

Studying a foreign language was often done out of strong social pressures to be appropriate, to know the correct things, to have a well-rounded education, to be well read, and to be worldly. As actual contact with these cultures was apt to be filtered and rather narrow, one would find it difficult to make a case that language study was for communication. It was done rather for self-improvement, often even for self-aggrandizement, and most often for social reasons.

Whatever the motivation might be for language study early in our academic history, except for language scholars, there was not a rationale to support a tradition of extended foreign language study. Language study was principally a college occupation; it was not a lifelong occupation or concern but rather a requirement or a set of courses to accomplish.

TODAY A BRIDGE TO UNDERSTANDING

Language Displays a Culture

When you study another language, you gain the understanding of language, not only the one being learned, but also of your own. Foreign language study brings home the impact, the sensitivity, and the limitations of our native language. It teaches volumes about the culture that uses the language being studied. Developing an understanding of a simple phrase in another language can explode the imagination. No mere translation can convey the true meaning of the phrase you understand in its original expression.

In examining the Eskimo language, you'll find just one word for a motorized vehicle, meaning both an automobile and a motorcycle. You cannot distinguish between the two different machines by vocabulary, because historically the Eskimo culture was seldom confronted with motorized vehicles. On the other hand, these people, who live in what others see as an almost monochromatic world of ice, have a multitude of words for snow. Wet snow, big snowflakes, dry dusty snow, intermittent spitting snow, snow that falls so fast there is no visibility—all have a term. Each culture reflects what is important to it in the language that it uses. Vocabulary teaches you far more than the correct word choice; it also betrays significance and cultural weight.

Americans are sometimes referred to as being culturally isolated but, like many blanket statements, this simply is not accurate. The United States is made up of citizens from countless nations, many of whom continue to speak their native language in the home and with friends. We even have communities of native speakers, so you might find a large cluster of Koreans in Los Angeles and an equally dense population of Cambodians in Lowell, Massachusetts. We are, in fact, a polyglot nation, and a careful look at our citizens would indicate that.

Our so-called English language is also interwoven with non-English words, although most of us don't realize it. *Dungaree* is an Indian word; *kindergarten* is, of course, a German word. We use a number of French words, too: *croissant, esprit de corps, maitre d', hors d'oeuvres, chateaubriand*. We constantly use imports from many languages.

However, it is true that Americans do not have a good reputation for learning foreign languages, certainly not to the extent of other countries. Part of this is our size and physical isolation from neighbors speaking a foreign tongue. There are some exceptions, however. In Vermont, New Hampshire, and Maine, bordering the Canadian province of Quebec, where French is spoken, many Americans of French-Canadian extraction speak French. In the Southwest, along the border of Mexico, Spanish is an important language.

Outside of these regions, unlike in Europe and Asian countries, which are in close proximity to other countries and whose citizens therefore learn several languages, Americans are isolated from other languages. Add to that the growing dominance of English in international business, and some Americans can justifiably feel less urgency about learning a foreign language. No matter where we go, we think that somebody who can speak some English will always be right around the corner.

French, German, and Spanish: In Classic Trio

French has been in our curriculums for almost 150 years, and, because of its associations with art, architecture, literature, cooking, and the world of diplomacy, it has remained a popular language option. Even though the number of French-speaking citizens is far smaller than the number of Germans or Italians, for example, French has remained a prominent language. Helping this dominance may be the fact that French literature remains a vital arena, as does French film. The French continue to play an important international role in other areas, as well, including medicine, pharmacology, and science. Add to that the French zest for life and love of their own tongue, including vigorous efforts to preserve its purity, and you can understand the language's staying power in this country.

German, the language traditionally associated with science, precision, and the military, has enjoyed some recent resurgence of popularity. Since the nineteenth century, it has been part of a good education. World War I and World War II did much to diminish the popularity of the study of German, and there still may be some residual feelings in older generations. Nevertheless, with the reunification of East and West Germany and Germany's participation in the European Community structure, it is anticipated that German will continue to be popular in foreign language training.

Spanish now reigns as the most popular language, in terms of enrollment, being taught in this country. Spanish language training often begins in the earliest grades. In some parts of the United States, notably Florida, California, and the Southwest, there has been some controversy over the use of Spanish in public school systems. General debate continues in the media over what some see as a growing threat to the dominance of English in these parts of the country. A judge has even awarded U.S. citizenship to a group of Americans who took the oath in Spanish.

Because of the large numbers of Spanish-speaking households in the United States, many different types of businesses are trying to service these bilingual customers. For example, newspapers, ATMs, magazines, and TV and radio stations have targeted residents of certain communities by using languages other than English. Government agencies are also responding. Signage in some areas is in both English and Spanish.

This trio of French, German, and Spanish—hardly begins to define the breadth of foreign language study being offered in this country. You can major in Swedish, Estonian, or Tibetan, and there are programs in Thai, Cantonese, Czech, Hebrew, Japanese, Chinese, Greek, or Laotian. And this list could go on and on. Language studies are alive and well in the United States.

Foreign Languages Are Useful and Needed

The exciting fact here is that foreign language study is needed now more than ever. For both the students and the teachers of foreign languages comes the bonus that experiencing the language, using the language, and hearing and seeing it used are no longer confined to the classroom. Nor does it take a trip abroad. The world has grown closer and smaller, and that makes learning a language not just more meaningful, but also imperative.

The need for foreign language skills confronts you daily. In the political arena, world leaders often cannot retire alone to discuss important matters face to face and confidentially; interpreters must relay their communications. In equally significant arenas of economics, joint military operations, medicine, and science, global sharing is imperative and can be seriously impeded by the need for translation services. Each day the world community becomes ever more entwined in economic, political, social, and military combinations of states and countries. All work to do the best for their individual interests and at the same time make a contribution to overall harmony. The breakdown of the Berlin Wall, the growing influence of the European Community, the increasing acceptance in Japan of foreign investment, the development of the Chinese marketplace, the increasing openness of the Russian economy to entrepreneurship, foreign investment, and democratization all suggest exchange, movement, contact, and, above all else, a need for understanding.

The Internet has created a world at our fingertips. It allows us to tour the Louvre without leaving home, and we can even appropriate one of the great paintings in the galleries to display on our computer desktop! Sites in many other countries offer the option of various languages with which to navigate their Web pages. We can now receive Italian television in our homes via satellite dishes, we can phone Thailand as easily as calling out of state, and we can correspond instantaneously using a fax machine with anyone in the world who has a machine to receive our message. The author recently planned a trip to Paris and with a few phone calls (in French) made hotel reservations, booked theater tickets, and even listened to a prerecorded listing (in English) of upcoming events in the City of Light. Our stores are filled with products from around the world, many in the original packaging. Our cities abound with restaurants, coffeehouses, newspapers, radio and TV stations, and social centers for groups that are built around other languages. With so many dramatic examples of cultural interchange, it's easy to see why we need skilled foreign language graduates.

Early language exposure invigorates the awareness of foreign language study by exposing students earlier to the process of acquiring another tongue. It extends the reach of skills acquisition by starting early in the educational process and by demanding that high school and college language programs provide increasing challenges and sophistication. The employment opportunities provided by the additional years of possible study are obvious. There would be gains in fluency, in text reading capability, and in transcription and translation skills.

Japanese, for example, requires considerable years of study to master not only the spoken language but the 1,600 *kanji* (pictographs) necessary for basic literacy. There are tens of thousands more needed for advanced reading. Beginning Japanese study in elementary school and continuing through high school and college could result in a verbal fluency and a mastery of written and printed Japanese not currently achieved by students who begin their Japanese studies in college.

Because the Japanese educational system requires twelve years of English study, there are far more native Japanese than American bilingual English/Japanese interpreters and translators. With an earlier start on the language, this would become a more competitive employment situation. The same holds true for other languages.

The Foreign Service of the United States uses an interesting definition of "useful" in categorizing language skill. For them it is the ability to handle everyday speech, to read a newspaper, and to read and discuss a technical article in one particular field. Those skills are obvious, certainly, and can be gained through language institutes, preparation for graduate reading exams, or trade schools. They permit us to begin to make the real "connections" with people who speak that language and not our own. Important as that is, for many students of foreign languages it is not the most crucial. Many would say the real advantage of knowing a foreign language is the liberation of your mind.

Not Just Language Training, But Understanding

The growing interrelationships among the members of the world community call for sensitivity and understanding and not just of an emotive, affectionate nature. A sensitivity that is born out of an understanding and appreciation for another culture can best be achieved by knowing the language. Language gives us clues about how a people think and what a people value. While it is often mistakenly said that Japanese has no personal pronouns, it is true that Japanese is remarkably (and for students, frustratingly) free of references to personal pronouns. Who is speaking and to whom is determined by the degree of honorific in the verb endings, and those degrees are many and subtle.

What do we learn from that? We certainly get the suggestion that aggressive self-promotion would be out of keeping with the Japanese character as would assertive references to others. Individuals in Japan approach each other delicately and subtly; they allow lots of maneuvering room for changes in tone, intention, and definitiveness. The implications for Americans interested in doing business with the Japanese are quite clear. We need people, both

Japanese and American, who can help us bridge those differences and forge a relationship of meaning.

Without the foundation of some common language, communication is either crude gesture and pantomime or clinical data transfer devoid of any warmth, humor, or compassion. With shared language, we reach across enormous cultural boundaries. It is certainly a skill and an art that are well worth the many hours of study, language lab practice, travel, and reading to attain.

LOOKING AHEAD: A MUST FOR OUR WORLD COMMUNITY

The story of foreign language study has been one of shifting and deepening focus. Learning someone else's language is no longer some personal cultural adornment, but rather a signal of membership in and stewardship of the world community, which impacts us now with increasing frequency and urgency. The ground is shifting under our feet, and we will continue to see dramatic changes in the numbers of people learning foreign languages, in the use of and exposure to foreign languages in our own country, and, most important, in public opinion about the value and place of foreign language study.

The early indications of this shift have been mostly commercial. We are seeing a number of foreign languages used in American TV commercials, and the public is accepting it and enjoying it. Northwest Airlines has advertised in English over a duplicate copy of the ad in Japanese. It may be a background singer performing in French, it may be a German baker extolling an American product with subtitles, but whatever the use, it is no longer a shock to the formerly isolated English speakers of the United States to hear other languages being spoken and to see them in print. All of this serves to make us comfortable with what once was unusual and incomprehensible.

With the introduction of language studies to elementary school children, we can expect earlier foreign language acquisition and a greater number of languages learned in a lifetime. This is comparable to what has been happening in Europe for many generations, where inhabitants of small countries with relatively free border crossings found it imperative to learn several languages. Now, at least metaphorically, and with the aid of technology (television, telephones, facsimiles, and transportation), our own proximity to other peoples, cultures, and languages has become much closer. We need to cross those borders more frequently and with greater understanding.

And it is not just the so-called traditional languages that are being introduced so early. Of course, Spanish, French, and German are popular, but so are Japanese, Chinese, Russian, and Italian. Computer technology is supporting these young language learners by speeding up the learning process.

In addition, books and other aids will continue to become available for teaching and learning any number of languages at every educational level.

Technology is currently being developed that will have a significant impact on world interactions and language learning. Translators of both Japanese and Chinese, two complex ideogram-based languages that use extensive pictographic vocabularies, are developing computer programs that will "read" text or convert simpler syllabary text into pictographic symbols. Current government standards of literacy require knowledge of 1,600 Japanese ideograms. However, some intellectuals are said to be able to recognize ten times that many characters, and there are many, many more that are possible in infinite combinations.

Ideogram-based languages have made international correspondence difficult. We still do not have an easily accessible Japanese or Chinese typewriter that will print characters, although software has been developed for word processors. Consequently, publishing books and newspapers or writing correspondence are time-consuming activities and much transcription is still done by hand. Computer technology will be valuable for solving some of these issues and will save time and money in the process. We may find that we can "read" another language by scanning the text and having it translated for us by computer.

Untold riches of art, literature, and tradition await as the growing mutual understanding of languages unfolds. We need this cultural interchange and the ideas it provides. Although U.S. culture, especially popular culture, is known the world over, how many of us can name the most popular Indian movie stars? Not many. That is particularly sad when we find out that the Indian movie industry is the largest in the world. And the same lack of knowledge exists about contemporary French novelists, Vietnamese poets, African artists, and countless other nations and their peoples' output. All of this will be available to us in a world that shares languages.

Ultimately, we need to make the individual connections, whether it is two powerful leaders adjourning for some private conversation or a tourist and native sharing a cup of tea together. Each will find differences really not so vast as we once supposed when communication was obscured by the veil of a language we did not understand. The arenas may change; they may be political, social, economic, military, artistic, educational, or recreational, but the underlying need for individuals to understand each other does not change. Nothing can make those connections faster or more human than sharing a common language.

PART ONE

THE JOB SEARCH

CHAPTER ONE

THE
SELF-ASSESSMENT

Self-assessment is the process by which you begin to acknowledge your own particular blend of education, experiences, values, needs, and goals. It provides the foundation for career planning and the entire job search process. Self-assessment involves looking inward and asking yourself what can sometimes prove to be difficult questions. This self-examination should lead to an intimate understanding of your personal traits, your personal values, your consumption patterns and economic needs, your longer-term goals, your skill base, your preferred skills, and your underdeveloped skills.

You come to the self-assessment process knowing yourself well in some of these areas, but you may still be uncertain about other aspects. You may be well aware of your consumption patterns, but have you spent much time specifically identifying your longer-term goals or your personal values as they relate to work? No matter what level of self-assessment you have undertaken to date, it is now time to clarify all of these issues and questions as they relate to the job search.

The knowledge you gain in the self-assessment process will guide the rest of your job search. In this book, you will learn about all of the following tasks:

- Writing resumes
- Exploring possible job titles
- Identifying employment sites
- Networking
- Interviewing
- Following up
- Evaluating job offers

In each of these steps, you will rely on and often return to the understanding gained through your self-assessment. Any individual seeking employment must be able and willing to express these facets of his or her personality to recruiters and interviewers throughout the job search. This communication allows you to show the world who you are so that together with employers you can determine whether there will be a workable match with a given job or career path.

HOW TO CONDUCT A SELF-ASSESSMENT

The self-assessment process goes on naturally all the time. People ask you to clarify what you mean, you make a purchasing decision, or you begin a new relationship. You react to the world and the world reacts to you. How you understand these interactions and any changes you might make because of them are part of the natural process of self-discovery. There is, however, a more comprehensive and efficient way to approach self-assessment with regard to employment.

Because self-assessment can become a complex exercise, we have distilled it into a seven-step process that provides an effective basis for undertaking a job search. The seven steps include the following:

1. Understanding your personal traits

2. Identifying your personal values

3. Calculating your economic needs

4. Exploring your longer-term goals

5. Enumerating your skill base

6. Recognizing your preferred skills

7. Assessing skills needing further development

As you work through your self-assessment, you might want to create a worksheet similar to the one shown in Exhibit 1.1 starting on the following page. Or you might want to keep a journal of the thoughts you have as you undergo this process. There will be many opportunities to revise your self-assessment as you start down the path of seeking a career.

STEP 1 Understanding Your Personal Traits

Each person has a unique personality that he or she brings to the job search process. Gaining a better understanding of your personal traits can help you

Exhibit 1.1

Self-Assessment Worksheet

STEP 1.　Understand Your Personal Traits
　　　　　The personal traits that describe me are:
　　　　　(Include all of the words that describe you.)

　　　　　The ten personal traits that most accurately describe
　　　　　me are: *(List these ten traits.)*

STEP 2.　Identify Your Personal Values
　　　　　Working conditions that are important to me include:
　　　　　*(List working conditions that would have to exist for
　　　　　you to accept a position.)*

　　　　　The values that go along with my working conditions
　　　　　are:
　　　　　*(Write down the values that correspond to each
　　　　　working condition.)*

　　　　　Some additional values I've decided to include are:
　　　　　*(List those values you identify as you conduct this job
　　　　　search.)*

STEP 3.　Calculate Your Economic Needs
　　　　　My estimated minimum annual salary requirement is:
　　　　　*(Write the salary you have calculated based on your
　　　　　budget.)*

　　　　　Starting salaries for the positions I'm considering are:
　　　　　*(List the name of each job you are considering and
　　　　　the associated starting salary.)*

STEP 4.　Explore Your Longer-Term Goals
　　　　　My thoughts on longer-term goals right now are:
　　　　　*(Jot down some of your longer-term goals as you
　　　　　know them right now.)*

STEP 5. Enumerate Your Skill Base

The general skills I possess are:
(List the skills that underlie tasks you are able to complete.)

The specific skills I possess are:
(List more technical or specific skills that you possess and indicate your level of expertise.)

General and specific skills that I want to promote to employers for the jobs I'm considering are:
(List general and specific skills for each type of job you are considering.)

STEP 6. Recognize Your Preferred Skills

Skills that I would like to use on the job include:
(List skills that you hope to use on the job, and indicate how often you'd like to use them.)

STEP 7. Assess Skills Needing Further Development

Some skills that I'll need to acquire for the jobs I'm considering include:
(Write down skills listed in job advertisements or job descriptions that you don't currently possess.)

I believe I can build these skills by:
(Describe how you plan to acquire these skills.)

evaluate job and career choices. Identifying these traits and then finding employment that allows you to draw on at least some of them can create a rewarding and fulfilling work experience. If potential employment doesn't allow you to use these preferred traits, it is important to decide whether you can find other ways to express them or whether you would be better off not considering this type of job. Interests and hobbies pursued outside of work hours can be one way to use personal traits you don't have an opportunity to draw on in your work. For example, if you consider yourself an outgoing person and the kinds of jobs you are examining allow little contact with other people, you may be able to achieve the level of interaction that is comfortable for you outside of your work setting. If such a compromise seems impractical or otherwise unsatisfactory, you probably should explore only jobs that provide the interaction you want and need on the job.

Many young adults who are not very confident about their attractiveness to employers will downplay their need for income. They will say, "Money is not all that important if I love my work." But if you begin to document exactly what you need for housing, transportation, insurance, clothing, food, and utilities, you will begin to understand that some jobs cannot meet your financial needs and it doesn't matter how wonderful the job is. If you have to worry each payday about bills and other financial obligations, you won't be very effective on the job. Begin now to be honest with yourself about your needs.

Inventorying Your Personal Traits. Begin the self-assessment process by creating an inventory of your personal traits. Using the list in Exhibit 1.2, decide which of these personal traits describe you.

Exhibit 1.2

Personal Traits

Accurate	Cool	Feeling
Active	Cooperative	Firm
Adaptable	Courageous	Flexible
Adventurous	Critical	Formal
Affectionate	Curious	Friendly
Aggressive	Daring	Future-oriented
Ambitious	Decisive	Generous
Analytical	Deliberate	Gentle
Appreciative	Detail-oriented	Good-natured
Artistic	Determined	Helpful
Brave	Discreet	Honest
Businesslike	Dominant	Humorous
Calm	Eager	Idealistic
Capable	Easygoing	Imaginative
Caring	Efficient	Impersonal
Cautious	Emotional	Independent
Cheerful	Empathetic	Individualistic
Clean	Energetic	Industrious
Competent	Excitable	Informal
Confident	Expressive	Innovative
Conscientious	Extroverted	Intellectual
Conservative	Fair-minded	Intelligent
Considerate	Farsighted	Introverted

Intuitive	Persuasive	Sensible
Inventive	Pleasant	Sensitive
Jovial	Poised	Serious
Just	Polite	Sincere
Kind	Practical	Sociable
Liberal	Precise	Spontaneous
Likable	Principled	Strong
Logical	Private	Strong-minded
Loyal	Productive	Structured
Mature	Progressive	Subjective
Methodical	Quick	Tactful
Meticulous	Quiet	Thorough
Mistrustful	Rational	Thoughtful
Modest	Realistic	Tolerant
Motivated	Receptive	Trusting
Objective	Reflective	Trustworthy
Observant	Relaxed	Truthful
Open-minded	Reliable	Understanding
Opportunistic	Reserved	Unexcitable
Optimistic	Resourceful	Uninhibited
Organized	Responsible	Verbal
Original	Reverent	Versatile
Outgoing	Sedentary	Wholesome
Patient	Self-confident	Wise
Peaceable	Self-controlled	
Personable	Self-disciplined	

Focusing on Selected Personal Traits. Of all the traits you identified from the list in Exhibit 1.2, select the ten you believe most accurately describe you. If you are having a difficult time deciding, think about which words people who know you well would use to describe you. Keep track of these ten traits.

Considering Your Personal Traits in the Job Search Process. As you begin exploring jobs and careers, watch for matches between your personal traits and the job descriptions you read. Some jobs will require many personal traits you know you possess, and others will not seem to match those traits.

....

A translator's work, for example, requires self-discipline, motivation, and an acute understanding of the text he or she is working with. Translators usually work alone, often at home, with limited opportunities to interact with others. An interpreter, on the other hand, interacts constantly with others. Interpreters need strong interpersonal and verbal skills and must be able to work under intense pressure. They must enjoy being up in front of groups and must not mind interacting with individuals highly placed in government or business.

....

Your ability to respond to changing conditions, your decision-making ability, productivity, creativity, and verbal skills all have a bearing on your success in and enjoyment of your work life. To better guarantee success, be sure to take the time needed to understand these traits in yourself.

STEP 2   Identifying Your Personal Values

Your personal values affect every aspect of your life, including employment, and they develop and change as you move through life. Values can be defined as principles that we hold in high regard, qualities that are important and desirable to us. Some values aren't ordinarily connected to work (love, beauty, color, light, relationships, family, or religion), and others are (autonomy, cooperation, effectiveness, achievement, knowledge, and security). Our values determine, in part, the level of satisfaction we feel in a particular job.

Defining Acceptable Working Conditions. One facet of employment is the set of working conditions that must exist for someone to consider taking a job.

Each of us would probably create a unique list of acceptable working conditions, but items that might be included on many people's lists are the amount of money you would need to be paid, how far you are willing to drive or travel, the amount of freedom you want in determining your own schedule, whether you would be working with people or data or things, and the types of tasks you would be willing to do. Your conditions might include statements of working conditions you will *not* accept; for example, you might not be willing to work at night or on weekends or holidays.

If you were offered a job tomorrow, what conditions would have to exist for you to realistically consider accepting the position? Take some time and make a list of these conditions.

Realizing Associated Values. Your list of working conditions can be used to create an inventory of your values relating to jobs and careers you are exploring. For example, if one of your conditions stated that you wanted to earn at least $30,000 per year, the associated value would be financial gain. If

---

Exhibit 1.3

Work Values

Achievement	Development	Physical activity
Advancement	Effectiveness	Power
Adventure	Excitement	Precision
Attainment	Fast pace	Prestige
Authority	Financial gain	Privacy
Autonomy	Helping	Profit
Belonging	Humor	Recognition
Challenge	Improvisation	Risk
Change	Independence	Security
Communication	Influencing others	Self-expression
Community	Intellectual stimulation	Solitude
Competition	Interaction	Stability
Completion	Knowledge	Status
Contribution	Leading	Structure
Control	Mastery	Supervision
Cooperation	Mobility	Surroundings
Creativity	Moral fulfillment	Time freedom
Decision making	Organization	Variety

---

another condition was that you wanted to work with a friendly group of people, the value that went along with that might be belonging or interaction with people. Exhibit 1.3 provides a list of commonly held values that relate to the work environment; use it to create your own list of personal values.

Relating Your Values to the World of Work. As you read the job descriptions in this book and in other suggested resources, think about the values associated with each position.

· ·

For example, the duties of a translator would include reading for complete comprehension in several languages, writing, and editing. Associated values are imagination, intellectual stimulation, and a desire for clear, accurate communication.

· ·

If you were thinking about a career in this field, or any other field you're exploring, at least some of the associated values should match those you extracted from your list of working conditions. Take a second look at any values that don't match up. How important are they to you? What will happen if they are not satisfied on the job? Can you incorporate those personal values elsewhere? Your answers need to be brutally honest. As you continue your exploration, be sure to add to your list any additional values that occur to you.

STEP 3 Calculating Your Economic Needs

Each of us grew up in an environment that provided for certain basic needs, such as food and shelter, and, to varying degrees, other needs that we now consider basic, such as cable TV, E-mail, or an automobile. Needs such as privacy, space, and quiet, which at first glance may not appear to be monetary needs, may add to housing expenses and so should be considered as you examine your economic needs. For example, if you place a high value on a large, open living space for yourself, it would be difficult to satisfy that need without an associated high housing cost, especially in a densely populated city environment.

As you prepare to move into the world of work and become responsible for meeting your own basic needs, it is important to consider the salary you will need to be able to afford a satisfying standard of living. The three-step process outlined here will help you plan a budget, which in turn will allow you to evaluate the various career choices and geographic locations you are considering. The steps include (1) developing a realistic budget, (2) examining starting salaries, and (3) using a cost-of-living index.

Developing a Realistic Budget. Each of us has certain expectations for the kind of lifestyle we want to maintain. In order to begin the process of defining your economic needs, it will be helpful to determine what you expect to spend on routine monthly expenses. These expenses include housing, food, transportation, entertainment, utilities, loan repayments, and revolving charge accounts. A worksheet that details many of these expenses is shown in Exhibit 1.4. You may not currently spend anything for certain items, but you probably will have to once you begin supporting yourself. As you develop this budget, be generous in your estimates, but keep in mind any items that could be reduced or

---

Exhibit 1.4

Estimated Monthly Expenses Worksheet

		Could Reduce Spending? (Yes/No)
Cable	$ _____	_____
Child care	_____	_____

		Could Reduce Spending? (Yes/No)
Clothing	$ _____	_____
Educational loan repayment	_____	_____
Entertainment	_____	_____
Food		
At home	_____	_____
Meals out	_____	_____
Gifts	_____	_____
Housing		
Rent/mortgage	_____	_____
Insurance	_____	_____
Property taxes	_____	_____
Medical insurance	_____	_____
Reading materials		
Newspapers	_____	_____
Magazines	_____	_____
Books	_____	_____
Revolving loans/charges	_____	_____
Savings	_____	_____
Telephone	_____	_____
Transportation		
Auto payment	_____	_____
Insurance	_____	_____
Parking	_____	_____
Gasoline	_____	_____
or		
Cab/train/bus fare	_____	_____
Utilities		
Electric	_____	_____
Gas	_____	_____
Water/sewer	_____	_____
Vacations	_____	_____
Miscellaneous expense 1	_____	_____
Expense: _____		
Miscellaneous expense 2	_____	_____
Expense: _____		
Miscellaneous expense 3	_____	_____
Expense: _____		
TOTAL MONTHLY EXPENSES:	_____	

YEARLY EXPENSES (Monthly expenses × 12): _____

INCREASE TO INCLUDE TAXES (Yearly expenses × 1.35): ____ =

MINIMUM ANNUAL SALARY REQUIREMENT: _____

eliminated. If you are not sure about the cost of a certain item, talk with family or friends who would be able to give you a realistic estimate.

If this is new or difficult for you, start to keep a log of expenses right now. You may be surprised at how much you actually spend each month for food or stamps or magazines. Household expenses and personal grooming items can often loom very large in a budget, as can auto repairs or home maintenance.

Income taxes must also be taken into consideration when examining salary requirements. State and local taxes vary by location, so it is difficult to calculate exactly the effect of taxes on the amount of income you need to generate. To roughly estimate the gross income necessary to generate your minimum annual salary requirement, multiply the minimum salary you have calculated (see Exhibit 1.4) by a factor of 1.35. The resulting figure will be an approximation of what your gross income would need to be, given your estimated expenses.

Examining Starting Salaries. Starting salaries for each of the career tracks are provided throughout this book. These salary figures can be used in conjunction with the cost-of-living index (discussed in the next section) to determine whether you would be able to meet your basic economic needs in a given geographic location.

Using a Cost-of-Living Index. If you are thinking about trying to get a job in a geographic region other than the one where you now live, understanding differences in the cost of living will help you come to a more informed decision about making a move. By using a cost-of-living index, you can compare salaries offered and the cost of living in different locations with what you know about the salaries offered and the cost of living in your present location.

Many variables are used to calculate the cost-of-living index. Often included are housing, groceries, utilities, transportation, health care, clothing, and entertainment expenses. Right now you do not need to worry about the details associated with calculating a given index. The main purpose of this exercise is to help you understand that pay ranges for entry-level positions may not vary greatly, but the cost of living in different locations *can* vary tremendously.

....

If you lived in Cleveland, Ohio, for example, and you were interested in working as a human resources generalist, you would plan on earning $29,053 annually. But let's say you're also thinking about moving to New York,

Los Angeles, or Houston. You know you can live on $29,053 in Cleveland, but you want to be able to equal that salary in the other locations you're considering. How much will you have to earn in those locations to do this? Determining the cost of living for each city will show you.

There are many websites like Home Fair's (www .homefair.com/cmr/salcalc.html) that can assist you as you undertake this research. Use any search engine and enter the keywords *cost of living index*. Several choices will appear. Choose one site and look for options like cost-of-living analysis or cost-of-living comparator. Some sites will ask you to register and/or pay for the information, but most sites are free. Follow the instructions provided and you will be able to create a table of information like the one shown below.

Job: Human Resources Generalist		
City	Base Amount	Equivalent Salary
Cleveland, OH	$29,053	
New York, NY		$32,772
Los Angeles, CA		$35,795
Minneapolis, MN		$31,738

At the time this comparison was done, you would have needed to earn $32,772 in New York, $35,795 in Los Angeles, and $31,738 in Minneapolis to match the buying power of $29,053 in Cleveland.

If you would like to determine whether it's financially worthwhile to make any of these moves, one more piece of information is needed: the salaries of human resources generalists in these other cities. One example of a website that contains job descriptions and salary information is WageWeb (www.wageweb.com). This site focuses information and services on the following fields: human resources, administration, finance, information management, engineering, health care, sales/marketing, and manufacturing. WageWeb reports the following average actual lowest salary paid for the cities being considered. These figures reflect entry-level salaries.

City	Actual Lowest Salary	Equivalent Salary Needed	Change in Buying Power
New York, NY	$33,301	$32,772	+ $529
Los Angeles, CA	$36,465	$35,795	+ $670
Minneapolis, MN	$30,895	$31,738	− $843

If you moved to New York City and secured employment as a human resources generalist you would be able to maintain a lifestyle similar to the one you lead in Cleveland. In fact, you would be able to enhance your lifestyle very modestly given the slight increase in buying power. The same would be true with a move to Los Angeles. Moving to Minneapolis from Cleveland, however, would modestly decrease your buying power. Remember, these figures change all the time, so be sure to undertake your own calculations. If you would like to see the formula used, you can visit a website like Deloitte & Touche (www.dtonline.com/tip/1997/tip0728.htm).

. . . .

You can work through a similar exercise for any type of job you are considering and for many locations when current salary information is available. It will be worth your time to undertake this analysis if you are seriously considering a relocation. By doing so you will be able to make an informed choice.

STEP 4 Exploring Your Longer-Term Goals

There is no question that when we first begin working, our goals are to use our skills and education in a job that will reward us with employment, income, and status relative to the preparation we brought with us to this position. If we are not being paid as much as we feel we should for our level of education, or if job demands don't provide the intellectual stimulation we had hoped for, we experience unhappiness and as a result often seek other employment.

Most jobs we consider "good" are those that fulfill our basic "lower-level" needs of security, food, clothing, shelter, income, and productive work. But even when our basic needs are met and our jobs are secure and productive, we as individuals are constantly changing. As we change, the demands and expectations we place on our jobs may change. Fortunately, some jobs grow and change with us, and this explains why some people are happy throughout many years in a job.

But more often people are bigger than the jobs they fill. We have more goals and needs than any job could fulfill. These are "higher-level" needs of self-esteem, companionship, affection, and an increasing desire to feel we are employing ourselves in the most effective way possible. Not all of these higher-level needs can be fulfilled through employment, but for as long as we are employed, we increasingly demand that our jobs play their part in moving us along the path to fulfillment.

Another obvious but important fact is that we change as we mature. Although our jobs also have the potential for change, they may not change as frequently or as markedly as we do. There are increasingly fewer one-job, one-employer careers; we must think about a work future that may involve voluntary or forced moves from employer to employer. Because of that very real possibility, we need to take advantage of the opportunities in each position we hold to acquire skills and competencies that will keep us viable and attractive as employees in a job market that is not only technology/computer dependent, but also is populated with more and more small, self-transforming organizations rather than the large, seemingly stable organizations of the past.

It may be difficult in the early stages of the job search to determine whether the path you are considering can meet these longer-term goals. Reading about career paths and individual career histories in your field can be very helpful in this regard. Meeting and talking with individuals further along in their careers can be enlightening as well. Older workers can provide valuable guidance on "self-managing" your career, which will become an increasingly valuable skill in the future. Some of these ideas may seem remote as you read this now, but you should be able to appreciate the need to ensure that you are growing, developing valuable new skills, and researching other employers who might be interested in your particular skills package.

· ·

**If you are considering a position in translating for the
State Department, you would gain a far better perspective**

of this career if you could talk to an entry-level translator, a more senior and experienced department head, and, finally, a senior foreign service officer with a significant work history. Each will have a different perspective, unique concerns, and an individual set of value priorities.

....

STEP 5 Enumerating Your Skill Base

In terms of the job search, skills can be thought of as capabilities that can be developed in school, at work, or by volunteering and then used in specific job settings. Many studies have documented the kinds of skills that employers seek in entry-level applicants. For example, some of the most desired skills for individuals interested in the teaching profession include the ability to interact effectively with students one on one, to manage a classroom, to adapt to varying situations as necessary, and to get involved in school activities. Business employers have also identified important qualities, including enthusiasm for the employer's product or service, a businesslike mind, the ability to follow written or verbal instructions, the ability to demonstrate self-control, the confidence to suggest new ideas, the ability to communicate with all members of a group, an awareness of cultural differences, and loyalty, to name just a few. You will find that many of these skills are also in the repertoire of qualities demanded in your college major.

In order to be successful in obtaining any given job, you must be able to demonstrate that you possess a certain mix of skills that will allow you to carry out the duties required by that job. This skill mix will vary a great deal from job to job; to determine the skills necessary for the jobs you are seeking, you can read job advertisements or more generic job descriptions, such as those found later in this book. If you want to be effective in the job search, you must directly show employers that you possess the skills needed to be successful in filling the position. These skills will initially be described on your resume and then discussed again during the interview process.

Skills are either general or specific. General skills are those that are developed throughout the college years by taking classes, being employed, and getting involved in other related activities such as volunteer work or campus organizations. General skills include the ability to read and write, to perform computations, to think critically, and to communicate effectively. Specific skills are also acquired on the job and in the classroom, but they allow you to complete tasks that require specialized knowledge. Computer programming, drafting, language translating, and copyediting are just a few examples of specific skills that may relate to a given job.

In order to develop a list of skills relevant to employers, you must first identify the general skills you possess, then list specific skills you have to offer, and, finally, examine which of these skills employers are seeking.

Identifying Your General Skills. Because you possess or will possess a college degree, employers will assume that you can read and write, perform certain basic computations, think critically, and communicate effectively. Employers will want to see that you have acquired these skills, and they will want to know which additional general skills you possess.

One way to begin identifying skills is to write an experiential diary. An experiential diary lists all the tasks you were responsible for completing for each job you've held and then outlines the skills required to do those tasks. You may list several skills for any given task. This diary allows you to distinguish between the tasks you performed and the underlying skills required to complete those tasks. Here's an example:

Tasks	Skills
Answering telephone	Effective use of language, clear diction, ability to direct inquiries, ability to solve problems
Waiting on tables	Poise under conditions of time and pressure, speed, accuracy, good memory, simultaneous completion of tasks, sales skills

For each job or experience you have participated in, develop a worksheet based on the example shown here. On a resume, you may want to describe these skills rather than simply listing tasks. Skills are easier for the employer to appreciate, especially when your experience is very different from the employment you are seeking. In addition to helping you identify general skills, this experiential diary will prepare you to speak more effectively in an interview about the qualifications you possess.

Identifying Your Specific Skills. It may be easier to identify your specific skills because you can definitely say whether you can speak other languages, program a computer, draft a map or diagram, or edit a document using appropriate symbols and terminology.

Using your experiential diary, identify the points in your history where you learned how to do something very specific and decide whether you have a beginning, intermediate, or advanced knowledge of how to use that particular skill. Right now, be sure to list *every* specific skill you have, and don't consider whether you like using the skill. Write down a list of specific skills you have acquired and the level of competence you possess—beginning, intermediate, or advanced.

Relating Your Skills to Employers. You probably have thought about a couple of different jobs you might be interested in obtaining, and one way to begin relating the general and specific skills you possess to a potential employer's needs is to read actual advertisements for these types of positions (see Part Two for resources listing actual job openings).

· ·

For example, you might be interested in working as a media coordinator. A typical job listing might read, "Enter data, including program and commercial formats, into computer to prepare daily schedules and program log. Compose stay-tuned announcements using computer. Requires 1–2 years of experience." If you then used any one of a number of general sources of information that describe the job of media coordinator, you would find additional information. Media coordinators also review overnight television ratings, provide for clearance and rotation of spot commercials, and perform related clerical duties.

Begin building a comprehensive list of required skills with the first job description you read. Exploring advertisements for and descriptions of several types of related positions will reveal an important core of skills that are necessary for obtaining the type of work you're interested in. In building this list, include both general and specific skills.

Following is a sample list of skills needed to be successful as a media coordinator. These items were extracted from both general resources and actual job listings.

Job: Media Coordinator

General Skills	Specific Skills
Perform clerical duties	Prepare daily schedules
Gather information	
Conduct research	Prepare program logs
Enter data into computer	Compose stay-tuned announcements
Work in hectic environment	

Meet deadlines	Review overnight TV
Work in noisy environment	ratings
Work varying hours	Provide for clearance
including nights	and rotation of spot
and weekends	commercials
Exhibit precision	Ensure time separation
Exhibit drive	between advertised
Collaborate on projects	products of similar nature
	Schedule announcers

On separate sheets of paper, try to generate a comprehensive list of required skills for at least one job you are considering.

The list of general skills that you develop for a given career path will be valuable for any number of jobs you might apply for. Many of the specific skills would also be transferable to other types of positions. For example, preparing daily schedules is a required specific skill for some media coordinators, and it also would be required for some advertising research positions.

• •

Now review the list of skills you developed and check off those skills that *you know you possess* and that are required for jobs you are considering. You should refer to these specific skills on the resume that you write for this type of job. See Chapter 2 for details on resume writing.

STEP 6   Recognizing Your Preferred Skills

In the previous section you developed a comprehensive list of skills that relate to particular career paths that are of interest to you. You can now relate these to skills that you prefer to use. We all use a wide range of skills (some researchers say individuals have a repertoire of about 500 skills), but we may not be particularly interested in using all of them in our work. There may be some skills that come to us more naturally or that we use successfully time and time again and that we want to continue to use; these are best described as our preferred skills. For this exercise use the list of skills that you developed for the previous section and decide which of them you are *most interested in using* in future work and how often you would like to use them. You might be interested in using some skills only occasionally, while others you would like to use more regularly. You probably also have skills that you hope you can use constantly.

As you examine job announcements, look for matches between this list of preferred skills and the qualifications described in the advertisements. These skills should be highlighted on your resume and discussed in job interviews.

STEP 7 Assessing Skills Needing Further Development

Previously you developed a list of general and specific skills required for given positions. You already possess some of these skills; those that remain to be developed are your underdeveloped skills.

If you are just beginning the job search, there may be gaps between the qualifications required for some of the jobs you're considering and skills you possess. The thought of having to admit to and talk about these underdeveloped skills, especially in a job interview, is a frightening one. One way to put a healthy perspective on this subject is to target and relate your exploration of underdeveloped skills to the types of positions you are seeking. Recognizing these shortcomings and planning to overcome them with either on-the-job training or additional formal education can be a positive way to address the concept of underdeveloped skills.

On your worksheet or in your journal, make a list of up to five general or specific skills required for the positions you're interested in that you *don't currently possess.* For each item list an idea you have for specific action you could take to acquire that skill. Do some brainstorming to come up with possible actions. If you have a hard time generating ideas, talk to people currently working in this type of position, professionals in your college career services office, trusted friends, family members, or members of related professional associations.

If, for example, you are interested in a job for which you don't have some specific required experience, you could locate training opportunities such as classes or workshops offered through a local college or university, community college, or club or association that would help you build the level of expertise you need for the job.

You will notice in this book that many excellent positions for your major demand computer skills. While basic word processing has been something you've done all through college, you may be surprised at the additional computer skills required by employers. Many positions for college graduates will ask for some familiarity with spreadsheet programming, and frequently some database-management software familiarity is a job demand as well. Desktop publishing software, graphics programs, and basic Web-page design also pop up frequently in job ads for college graduates. If your degree program hasn't introduced you to a wide variety of computer applications, what are your options? If you're still in college, take what computer courses you can before you graduate. If you've already graduated, look at evening programs, continuing education courses, or tutorial programs that may be available commercially. Developing a modest level of expertise will encourage you to be more confident in suggesting to potential employers that you can continue to add to your skill base on the job.

In Chapter 5 on interviewing, we will discuss in detail how to effectively address questions about underdeveloped skills. Generally speaking, though, employers want genuine answers to these types of questions. They want you to reveal "the real you," and they also want to see how you answer difficult questions. In taking the positive, targeted approach discussed above, you show the employer that you are willing to continue to learn and that you have a plan for strengthening your job qualifications.

USING YOUR SELF-ASSESSMENT

Exploring entry-level career options can be an exciting experience if you have good resources available and will take the time to use them. Can you effectively complete the following tasks?

1. Understand and relate your personality traits to career choices

2. Define your personal values

3. Determine your economic needs

4. Explore longer-term goals

5. Understand your skill base

6. Recognize your preferred skills

7. Express a willingness to improve on your underdeveloped skills

If so, then you can more meaningfully participate in the job search process by writing a more effective resume, finding job titles that represent work you are interested in doing, locating job sites that will provide the opportunity for you to use your strengths and skills, networking in an informed way, participating in focused interviews, getting the most out of follow-up contacts, and evaluating job offers to find those that create a good match between you and the employer. The remaining chapters in Part One guide you through these next steps in the job search process. For many job seekers, this process can take anywhere from three months to a year to implement. The time you will need to put into your job search will depend on the type of job you want and the geographic location where you'd like to work. Think of your effort as a job in itself, requiring you to set aside time each week to complete the needed work. Carefully undertaken efforts may reduce the time you need for your job search.

CHAPTER TWO

THE RESUME AND COVER LETTER

The task of writing a resume may seem overwhelming if you are unfamiliar with this type of document, but there are some easily understood techniques that can and should be used. This section was written to help you understand the purpose of the resume, the different types of resume formats available, and how to write the sections of information traditionally found on a resume. We will present examples and explanations that address questions frequently posed by people writing their first resume or updating an old resume.

Even within the formats and suggestions given, however, there are infinite variations. True, most resumes follow one of the outlines suggested, but you should feel free to adjust the resume to suit your needs and make it expressive of your life and experience.

WHY WRITE A RESUME?

The purpose of a resume is to convince an employer that you should be interviewed. Whether you're mailing, faxing, or E-mailing this document, you'll want to present enough information to show that you can make an immediate and valuable contribution to an organization. A resume is not an in-depth historical or legal document; later in the job search process you may be asked to document your entire work history on an application form and attest to its validity. The resume should, instead, highlight relevant information pertaining directly to the organization that will receive the document or to the type of position you are seeking.

We will discuss four types of resumes in this chapter: the chronological resume, functional resume, targeted resume, and the digital resume. The reasons for using one type of resume over another and the typical format for each are addressed in the following sections.

THE CHRONOLOGICAL RESUME

The chronological resume is the most common of the various resume formats and therefore the format that employers are most used to receiving. This type of resume is easy to read and understand because it details the chronological progression of jobs you have held. (See Exhibit 2.1.) It begins with your most recent employment and works back in time. If you have a solid work history or have experience that provided growth and development in your duties and responsibilities, a chronological resume will highlight these achievements. The typical elements of a chronological resume include the heading, a career objective, educational background, employment experience, activities, and references.

The Heading

The heading consists of your name, address, telephone number, and other means of contact. This may include a fax number, E-mail address, and your home-page address. If you are using a shared E-mail account or a parent's business fax, be sure to let others who use these systems know that you may receive important professional correspondence via these systems. You wouldn't want to miss a vital E-mail or fax! Likewise, if your resume directs readers to a personal home page on the Web, be certain it's a *professional* personal home page designed to be viewed and appreciated by a prospective employer. This may mean making substantial changes in the home page you currently mount on the Web.

We suggest that you spell out your full name in your resume heading and type it in all capital letters in bold type. After all, you are the focus of the resume! If you have a current as well as a permanent address and you include both in the heading, be sure to indicate until what date your current address will be valid. The two-letter state abbreviation should be the only abbreviation that appears in your heading. Don't forget to include the zip code with your address and the area code with your telephone number.

The Objective

As you formulate the wording for this part of your resume, keep the following points in mind.

Exhibit 2.1

Chronological Resume

SAMANTHA WELSH

Tulip Tree Apartments #35   36 Chase Court
University of Georgia   Martinez, GA 30693
Athens, GA 30602   (404) 555-6666
(404) 555-5555
swelsh@xxx.com
(until May 2004)

OBJECTIVE

To obtain a position as assistant director of international student affairs

EDUCATION

Bachelor of Arts in Spanish
University of Georgia, Athens
May 2004
Minor: Human Relations

HONORS/AWARDS

President's List, Fall Semester 2002, 2003
Who's Who Among Universities and Colleges, 2002–2004
Phi Kappa Phi National Honor Society

RELATED COURSES

Group Counseling   Multiculturalism
Speech   Marketing

EXPERIENCE

Night Secretary: Gordon Research Conference, Augusta, Georgia, 2003–2004
  Provided administrative support for conference evening activities. Extensive international telephone work, some in Spanish, and international fax transmissions. Daily contact with international community of scientists. Received meritorious bonus each year.

Student Assistant: Dean of Student Affairs Office, University of Georgia, 2001–2004

A recurring financial aid award position. Each year I added new duties and responsibilities, including booking appointments, touring guests around campus, assisting the dean with research, contacting students, and resolving problems. Constant contact with international students and their concerns.

Projectionist: Gordon Research Conference, Augusta, Georgia, 2000–2001

Summer position for world-renowned conference of international scientists. Provided all audiovisual setups for speakers from many different countries.

ACTIVITIES

Spanish Club, active member four years.
International Student Society sponsor. Helped a different international student each year meet friends and learn the campus.

REFERENCES

Both personal and professional references are available upon request.

The Objective Focuses the Resume. Without a doubt this is the most challenging part of the resume for most resume writers. Even for individuals who have quite firmly decided on a career path, it can be difficult to encapsulate all they want to say in one or two brief sentences. For job seekers who are unfocused or unclear about their intentions, trying to write this section can inhibit the entire resume writing process.

Recruiters tell us, time and time again, that the objective creates a frame of reference for them. It helps them see how you express your goals and career focus. In addition, the statement may indicate in what ways you can immediately benefit an organization. Given the importance of the objective, every point covered in the resume should relate to it. If information doesn't relate, it should be omitted. You'll file a number of resume variations in your computer. There's no excuse for not being able to tailor a resume to individual employers or specific positions.

Choose an Appropriate Length. Because of the brevity necessary for a resume, you should keep the objective as short as possible. Although objectives of only four or five words often don't show much direction, objectives that take three full lines could be viewed as too wordy and might possibly be ignored.

Consider Which Type of Objective Statement You Will Use. There are many ways to state an objective, but generally there are four forms this statement can take: (1) a very general statement; (2) a statement focused on a specific position; (3) a statement focused on a specific industry; or (4) a summary of your qualifications. In our contacts with employers, we often hear that many resumes don't exhibit any direction or career goals, so we suggest avoiding general statements when possible.

1. General Objective Statement. General objective statements look like the following:

- ❑ An entry-level educational programming coordinator position
- ❑ An entry-level marketing position

This type of objective would be useful if you know what type of job you want but you're not sure which industries interest you.

2. Position-Focused Objective. Following are examples of objectives focusing on a specific position:

- ❑ To obtain the position of conference coordinator at State College
- ❑ To obtain a position as assistant editor at *Time* magazine

When a student applies for an advertised job opening, this type of focus can be very effective. The employer knows that the applicant has taken the time to tailor the resume specifically for this position.

3. Industry-Focused Objective. Focusing on a particular industry in an objective could be stated as follows:

- ❑ To begin a career as a sales representative in the cruise line industry

4. Summary of Qualifications Statement. The summary of qualifications can be used instead of an objective or in conjunction with an objective. The purpose of this type of statement is to highlight relevant qualifications gained through a variety of experiences. This type of statement is often used by individuals with extensive and diversified work experience. An example of a qualifications statement follows:

....

A degree in French and four years of progressively increasing job responsibility within the hospitality industry have prepared me to begin a career as a hotel manager trainee with an organization that values hard work and dedication.

....

Support Your Objective. A resume that contains any one of these types of objective statements should then go on to demonstrate why you are qualified to get the position. Listing academic degrees can be one way to indicate qualifications. Another demonstration would be in the way previous experiences, both volunteer and paid, are described. Without this kind of documentation in the body of the resume, the objective looks unsupported. Think of the resume as telling a connected story about you. All the elements should work together to form a coherent picture that ideally should relate to your statement of objective.

Education

This section of your resume should indicate the exact name of the degree you will receive or have received, spelled out completely with no abbreviations. The degree is generally listed after the objective, followed by the institution name and address, and then the month and year of graduation. This section could also include your academic minor, grade point average (GPA), and appearance on the Dean's List or President's List.

If you have enough space, you might want to include a section listing courses related to the field in which you are seeking work. The best use of a "related courses" section would be to list some course work that is not traditionally associated with the major. Perhaps you took several computer courses outside your degree that will be helpful and related to the job prospects you are entertaining. Several education section examples are shown here:

....

- ❑ Bachelor of Arts in Interdisciplinary Studies, a self-designed program concentrating in Spanish and Graphic Design, State College, Columbus, OH, May 2004

- ❑ Bachelor of Science Degree in French Education, State College, Plymouth, NH, December 2003
  Minor: Art

❏ **Bachelor of Arts Degree in German, State College, San Francisco, CA, May 2004**

An example of a format for a related courses section follows:

RELATED COURSES

Desktop Publishing	Advanced Composition
Computer Graphics	Creative Writing
Software Systems Design	Technical Writing

Experience

The experience section of your resume should be the most substantial part and should take up most of the space on the page. Employers want to see what kind of work history you have. They will look at your range of experiences, longevity in jobs, and specific tasks you are able to complete. This section may also be called "work experience," "related experience," "employment history," or "employment." No matter what you call this section, some important points to remember are the following:

1. **Describe your duties** as they relate to the position you are seeking.

2. **Emphasize major responsibilities** and indicate increases in responsibility. Include all relevant employment experiences: summer, part-time, internships, cooperative education, or self-employment.

3. **Emphasize skills**, especially those that transfer from one situation to another. The fact that you coordinated a student organization, chaired meetings, supervised others, and managed a budget leads one to suspect that you could coordinate other things as well.

4. **Use descriptive job titles** that provide information about what you did. A "Student Intern" should be more specifically stated as, for example, "Magazine Operations Intern." "Volunteer" is also too general; a title such as "Peer Writing Tutor" would be more appropriate.

5. **Create word pictures** by using active verbs to start sentences. Describe *results* you have produced in the work you have done.

A limp description would say something like the following: "My duties included helping with production, proofreading, and editing. I used a word-processing package to alter text." An action statement would be stated as follows: "Coordinated and assisted in the creative marketing of brochures and seminar promotions, becoming proficient in Word."

Remember, an accomplishment is simply a result, a final measurable product that people can relate to. A duty is not a result, it is an obligation—every job holder has duties. For an effective resume, list as many results as you can. To make the most of the limited space you have and to give your description impact, carefully select appropriate and accurate descriptors from the list of action words in Exhibit 2.2.

Exhibit 2.2

Resume Action Verbs

Achieved	Demonstrated	Initiated
Acted	Designed	Innovated
Administered	Determined	Instituted
Advised	Developed	Instructed
Analyzed	Directed	Integrated
Assessed	Documented	Interpreted
Assisted	Drafted	Introduced
Attained	Edited	Learned
Balanced	Eliminated	Lectured
Budgeted	Ensured	Led
Calculated	Established	Maintained
Collected	Estimated	Managed
Communicated	Evaluated	Mapped
Compiled	Examined	Marketed
Completed	Explained	Met
Composed	Facilitated	Modified
Conceptualized	Finalized	Monitored
Condensed	Generated	Negotiated
Conducted	Handled	Observed
Consolidated	Headed	Obtained
Constructed	Helped	Operated
Controlled	Identified	Organized
Converted	Illustrated	Participated
Coordinated	Implemented	Performed
Corrected	Improved	Planned
Created	Increased	Predicted
Decreased	Influenced	Prepared
Defined	Informed	Presented

continued

continued

Processed	Reinforced	Solved
Produced	Reported	Staffed
Projected	Represented	Streamlined
Proposed	Researched	Studied
Provided	Resolved	Submitted
Qualified	Reviewed	Summarized
Quantified	Scheduled	Systematized
Questioned	Selected	Tabulated
Realized	Served	Tested
Received	Showed	Transacted
Recommended	Simplified	Updated
Recorded	Sketched	Verified
Reduced	Sold	

Here are some traits that employers tell us they like to see:

- ❏ Teamwork
- ❏ Energy and motivation
- ❏ Learning and using new skills
- ❏ Demonstrated versatility
- ❏ Critical thinking
- ❏ Understanding how profits are created
- ❏ Displaying organizational acumen
- ❏ Communicating directly and clearly, in both writing and speaking
- ❏ Risk taking
- ❏ Willingness to admit mistakes
- ❏ Manifesting high personal standards

SOLUTIONS TO FREQUENTLY ENCOUNTERED PROBLEMS

Repetitive Employment with the Same Employer

EMPLOYMENT: The Foot Locker, Portland, Oregon. Summer 2001, 2002, 2003. Initially employed in high school as salesclerk. Due to successful performance, asked to return next two summers at higher pay with added responsibility. Ranked as the #2 salesperson the first summer and #1 the next two summers. Assisted in arranging eye-catching retail displays; served as manager of other summer workers during owner's absence.

A Large Number of Jobs

EMPLOYMENT: Recent Hospitality Industry Experience: Affiliated with four upscale hotel/restaurant complexes (September 2001–February 2004), where I worked part- and full-time as a waiter, bartender, disc jockey, and bookkeeper to produce income for college.

Several Positions with the Same Employer

EMPLOYMENT: Coca-Cola Bottling Co., Burlington, VT, 2001–2004. In four years, I received three promotions, each with increased pay and responsibility.

Summer Sales Coordinator: Promoted to hire, train, and direct efforts of add-on staff of fifteen college-age route salespeople hired to meet summer peak demand for product.

Sales Administrator: Promoted to run home office sales desk, managing accounts and associated delivery schedules for professional sales force of ten people. Intensive phone work, daily interaction with all personnel, and strong knowledge of product line required.

Route Salesperson: Summer employment to travel and tourism industry sites that use Coke products. Met specific schedule demands, used good communication skills with wide variety of customers, and demonstrated strong selling skills. Named salesperson of the month for July and August of that year.

QUESTIONS RESUME WRITERS OFTEN ASK

How Far Back Should I Go in Terms of Listing Past Jobs?

Usually, listing three or four jobs should suffice. If you did something back in high school that has a bearing on your future aspirations for employment, by all means list the job. As you progress through your college career, high school jobs may be replaced on the resume by college employment.

Should I Differentiate Between Paid and Nonpaid Employment?

Most employers are not initially concerned about how much you were paid. They are anxious to know how much responsibility you held in your past employment. There is no need to specify that your work was as a volunteer if you had significant responsibilities.

How Should I Represent My Accomplishments or Work-Related Responsibilities?

Succinctly, but fully. In other words, give the employer enough information to arouse curiosity, but not so much detail that you leave nothing to the imagination. Besides, some jobs merit more lengthy explanations than others. Be sure to convey any information that can give an employer a better understanding of the depth of your involvement at work. Did you supervise others? How many? Did your efforts result in a more efficient operation? How much did you increase efficiency? Did you handle a budget? How much? Were you promoted in a short time? Did you work two jobs at once or fifteen hours per week after high school? Where appropriate, quantify.

Should the Work Section Always Follow the Education Section on the Resume?

Always lead with your strengths. If your education closely relates to the employment you now seek, put this section after the objective. Or, if you are weak on the academic side but have a surplus of good work experiences, consider reversing the order of your sections to lead with employment, followed by education.

How Should I Present My Activities, Honors, Awards, Professional Societies, and Affiliations?

This section of the resume can add valuable information for an employer to consider if used correctly. The rule of thumb for information in this section is to include only those activities that are in some way relevant to the objective stated on your resume. If you can draw a valid connection between your activities and your objective, include them; if not, leave them out.

Granted, this is hard to do. Playing center on the championship basketball team or serving as coordinator of the biggest homecoming parade ever held are roles that have meaning for you and represent personal accomplishments you'd like to share. But the resume is a brief document, and the information you provide on it should help the employer make a decision about your job eligibility. Including personal details can be confusing and could hurt your candidacy. Limiting your activity list to a few very significant experiences can be very effective.

If you are applying for a position as a safety officer, your certificate in Red Cross lifesaving skills or CPR would be related and valuable. You would want to include it. If, however, you are applying for a job as a junior account executive in an advertising agency, that information would be unrelated and superfluous. Leave it out.

Professional affiliations and honors should *all* be listed; especially important are those related to your job objective. Social clubs and activities need not be a part of your resume unless you hold a significant office or you are looking for a position related to your membership. Be aware that most prospective employers' principal concerns are related to your employability, not your social life. If you have any, publications can be included as an addendum to your resume.

The focus of the resume is your experience and education. It is not necessary to describe your involvement in activities. However, if your resume needs to be lengthened, this section provides the freedom either to expand on or mention only briefly the contributions you have made. If you have made significant contributions (e.g., an officer of an organization or a particularly long tenure with a group), you may choose to describe them in more detail. It is not always necessary to include the dates of your memberships with your activities the way you would include job dates.

There are a number of different ways in which to present additional information. You may give this section a number of different titles. Assess what you want to list, and then use an appropriate title. Do not use "extracurricular activities." This terminology is scholastic, not professional, and therefore not appropriate. The following are two examples:

❑ ACTIVITIES: Society for Technical Communication, Student
                Senate, Student Admissions Representative, Senior
                Class Officer

❑ ACTIVITIES:
   • Society for Technical Communication Member
   • Student Senator
   • Student Admissions Representative
   • Senior Class Officer

The position you are looking for will determine what you should or should not include. *Always* look for a correlation between the activity and the prospective job.

How Should I Handle References?

The use of references is considered a part of the interview process, and they should never be listed on a resume. You would always provide references to a potential employer if requested to, so it is not even necessary to include this section on the resume if room does not permit. If space is available, it is acceptable to include one of the following statements:

❑ REFERENCES: Furnished upon request.

❑ REFERENCES: Available upon request.

Individuals used as references must be protected from unnecessary contacts. By including names on your resume, you leave your references unprotected. Overuse and abuse of your references will lead to less-than-supportive comments. Protect your references by giving out their names only when you are being considered seriously as a candidate for a given position.

THE FUNCTIONAL RESUME

The functional resume departs from a chronological resume in that it organizes information by specific accomplishments in various settings: previous jobs, volunteer work, associations, and so forth. This type of resume permits you to stress the substance of your experiences rather than the position titles you have held. (See Exhibit 2.3.) You should consider using a functional resume if you have held a series of similar jobs that relied on the same skills or abilities.

Exhibit 2.3

Functional Resume

JOYCE JOHNSON

Student Apartment 12
Cleveland State University
Cleveland, OH 44115
(216) 555-5555
Fax (216) 555-9999
jjohnson@xxx.com
(until May 2003)

12 Cornwall Street
Rocky River, OH 44116
(215) 555-6666

OBJECTIVE
An entry-level research assistant position that allows me to use my problem-solving, computing, and communication skills.

CAPABILITIES
- Analytical problem solver
- Experienced software and hardware user
- Effective communicator

SELECTED ACCOMPLISHMENTS
PROBLEM SOLVING: Researched current and accurate sources of information for ongoing research projects. Developed methods and systems for processing survey data results for 23 different projects. Established processing priorities for several overlapping projects; answered questions and resolved problems for library patrons.

COMPUTING: Used SPSS and SAS software packages to process data; manipulated digitizers, plotters, and graphics software to create graphics for reports; utilized mainframe and personal computing hardware; helped implement library security system.

COMMUNICATING: Assisted in writing and editing project reports; conducted telephone and door-to-door surveys in the local community; coordinated writing, editing, and computer assignments with three other research assistants; presented survey findings to several audiences. Helped library patrons locate needed materials.

AWARDS
Awarded outstanding part-time employee of the year certificate
Graduated with honors in German
Nominated to National Honor Society

EMPLOYMENT HISTORY
Research Assistant, Center for Urban Studies, Cleveland State University, Cleveland, OH. Summers 2001–2003
Library Worker, Cleveland State University Library, Cleveland, OH 2001–2002

EDUCATION
Bachelor of Arts in German
Cleveland State University, Cleveland, OH
May 2003

REFERENCES
Provided upon request

The Objective

A functional resume begins with an objective that can be used to focus the contents of the resume.

Specific Accomplishments

Specific accomplishments are listed on this type of resume. Examples of the types of headings used to describe these capabilities might include research, computer skills, teaching, communication, production, management, marketing, or writing. The headings you choose will directly relate to your experience and the tasks that you carried out. Each accomplishment section contains statements related to your experience in that category, regardless of when or where it occurred. Organize the accomplishments and the related tasks you describe in their order of importance as related to the position you seek.

Experience or Employment History

Your actual work experience is condensed and placed after the specific accomplishments section. It simply lists dates of employment, position titles, and employer names.

Education

The education section of a functional resume is identical to that of the chronological resume, but it does not carry the same visual importance because it is placed near the bottom of the page.

References

Because actual reference names are never listed on a resume, a statement of reference availability is optional if space does not permit.

THE TARGETED RESUME

The targeted resume focuses on specific work-related capabilities you can bring to a given position within an organization. (See Exhibit 2.4.) It should be sent to an individual within the organization who makes hiring decisions about the position you are seeking.

The Objective

The objective on this type of resume should be targeted to a specific career or position. It should be supported by the capabilities, accomplishments, and achievements documented in the resume.

Exhibit 2.4

Targeted Resume

VAL DeVOSS

Student Apartment 104B
University of Denver
Denver, CO 80201
(303) 555-5555
Fax (303) 555-5556
vdevoss@xxx.com
(until May 2004)

12 West 80th Avenue
Denver, CO 80201
(303) 555-6666

JOB TARGET
Planning assistant with a state or regional planning agency

CAPABILITIES
- Provide technical and administrative support
- Work under broad direction of chief planner
- Review and revise reports and planning documents
- Collect and analyze data
- Use a variety of software and hardware

ACHIEVEMENTS
- Edited prize-winning university literary review
- Researched background material for campus author
- Ran successful house-painting business
- Maintained an A average throughout college

WORK HISTORY

2003–present
(part-time)
Research Assistant, City of Denver Planning Board
- Analyze data to report to city planner

2001–present
Editor, THE CLARION, campus newspaper
- Responsible for editing entire newspaper

2001–2002
Tutor, Foreign Language Department
- Tutored students in Spanish and French

2000
Laborer, Facility Services, University of Denver
- Member of grounds maintenance crew

continued

continued

EDUCATION

Bachelor of Arts in Spanish, 2004
University of Denver
Minor: Geography

Capabilities

Capabilities should be statements that illustrate tasks you believe you are capable of based on your accomplishments, achievements, and work history. Each should relate to your targeted career or position. You can stress your qualifications rather than your employment history. This approach may require research to obtain an understanding of the nature of the work involved and the capabilities necessary to carry out that work.

Accomplishments/Achievements

This section relates the various activities you have been involved in to the job market. These experiences may include previous jobs, extracurricular activities at school, internships, and part-time summer work.

Experience

Your work history should be listed in abbreviated form and may include position title, employer name, and employment dates.

Education

Because this type of resume is directed toward a specific job target and an individual's related experience, the education section is not prominently located at the top of the resume as is done on the chronological resume.

DIGITAL RESUMES

Today's employers have to manage an enormous number of resumes. One of the most frequent complaints the writers of this series hear from students is the failure of employers to even acknowledge the receipt of a resume and cover letter. Frequently, the reason for this poor response or nonresponse is the volume of applications received for every job. In an attempt to better manage the considerable labor investment involved in processing large numbers of resumes, many employers are requiring digital submission of resumes. There are two types of digital resumes: those that can be E-mailed or posted to a website, called *electronic resumes,* and those that can be "read" by a computer, commonly called *scannable resumes.* Though the format may be a bit different than the traditional "paper" resume, the goal of both types of digital resumes is the same—to get you an interview! These resumes must be designed to be "technologically friendly." What that basically means to you is that they should be free of graphics and fancy formatting.

Electronic Resumes

Sometimes referred to as plain-text resumes, electronic resumes are designed to be E-mailed to an employer or posted to a commercial Internet database such as CareerMosaic.com, America's Job Bank (www.ajb.dni.us), or Monster.com.

Some technical considerations:

- Electronic resumes must be written in American Standard Code for Information Interchange (ASCII), which is simply a plain-text format. These characters are universally recognized so that every computer can accurately read and understand them. To create an ASCII file of your current resume, open your document, then save it as a text or ASCII file. This will eliminate all formatting. Edit as needed using your computer's text editor application.

- Use a standard-width typeface. Courier is a good choice because it is the font associated with ASCII in most systems.

- Use a font size of 11 to 14 points. A 12-point font is considered standard.

- Your margin should be left-justified.

- Do not exceed sixty-five characters per line, because the word-wrap function doesn't operate in ASCII.

- Do not use boldface, italics, underlining, bullets, and various font sizes. Instead, use asterisks, plus signs, and all capital letters when you want to emphasize something.

- Avoid graphics and shading.

- Use as many "keywords" as you possibly can. These are words or phrases usually relating to skills or experience that are either specifically used in the job announcement or are popular buzzwords in the industry.

- Minimize abbreviations. One exception is B.S. or B.A. for your degree.

- Your name should be the first line of text.

- Conduct a "test run" by E-mailing your resume to yourself and a friend before you send it to the employer. See how it transmits, and make any changes you need to. Continue to test it until it's exactly how you want it to look.

- Unless an employer specifically requests that you send the resume in the form of an attachment, don't. Employers can encounter problems opening a document as an attachment, and there are always viruses to consider.

- Don't forget your cover letter. Send it along with your resume as a single message.

Scannable Resumes

Some companies are relying on technology to narrow the candidate pool for available job openings. Electronic Applicant Tracking uses imaging to scan, sort, and store resume elements in a database. Then, through OCR (Optical Character Recognition) software, the computer scans the resumes for keywords and phrases. To have the best chance at getting an interview, you want to increase the number of "hits"—matches of your skills, abilities, experience, and education to those the computer is scanning for—your resume will get. You can see how critical using the right keywords is for this type of resume.

Technical considerations include:

- Again, do not use boldface (newer systems may read this OK, but many older ones won't), italics, underlining, bullets, shading, graphics, and multiple font sizes. Instead, for emphasis, use asterisks, plus signs, and all capital letters. Minimize abbreviations.

- Use a popular typeface such as Courier, Helvetica, Ariel, or Palatino. Avoid decorative fonts.

- Font size should be between 11 and 14 points.

- Do not compress the spacing between letters.

- Use horizontal and vertical lines sparingly; the computer may misread them as the letters L or I.

- Left-justify the text.

- Do not use parentheses or brackets around telephone numbers, and be sure your phone number is on its own line of text.

- Your name should be the first line of text and on its own line. If your resume is longer than one page, be sure to put your name on the top of all pages.

- Use a traditional resume structure. The chronological format may work best.

- Use nouns that are skill-focused, such as *management, writer,* and *programming.* This is different from traditional paper resumes, which use action-oriented verbs.

- Laser printers produce the finest copies. Avoid dot-matrix printers.

- Use standard, light-colored paper with text on one side only. Since the higher the contrast the better, your best choice is black ink on white paper.

- Always send original copies. If you must fax, set the fax on fine mode, not standard.

- Do not staple or fold your resume. This can confuse the computer.

- Before you send your scannable resume, be certain the employer uses this technology. If you can't determine this, you may want to send two versions (scannable and traditional) to be sure your resume gets considered.

Exhibit 2.5

DIGITAL RESUME

SARAH MCDOUGLE ←——————— Put your name at the top
117 Stetson Avenue   on its own line.
Small School, MA 02459 ——— Put your phone number
859-425-5478 ←——————————— on its own line.
saramc@xxx.com ←————————— Use a standard-width
                                   typeface—like Courier.

KEYWORD SUMMARY
B.S. Computer Science, 2002, C++, Visual
Basic, Assemble, FORTRAN, TUTOR,   Keywords make your
HTML, CAD, PATRAN, Oracle, MS Office,   resume easier to find in a
IBM 630-670, Windows NT, UNIX,   database.
Programmer

EDUCATION ←——————————— Capital letters emphasize
Bachelor of Science, Computer Science,   headings.
2002
Small State College, Small School,
Massachusetts

continued

continued

Minor: Graphic Design

G.P.A.: 3.0/4.0

Related Courses

Database Design, Compiler Design,

System Architecture, Operating Systems,

Data Structures

No line should exceed sixty-five characters.

COMPUTER SKILLS

Languages: C/C++, Visual Basic, Assembly,
FORTRAN, TUTOR, HTML

Software: CAD, PATRAN, Oracle, MS
Office

Systems: IBM 360/370, Windows NT,
UNIX

EXPERIENCE

Support desk, Small State College, 2001–02

End each line by hitting the ENTER key.

* Maintained computer systems in
computer lab
* Installed application and performed
troubleshooting
* Instructed students on application and
systems

Programmer (intern), Large Company, 2001

* Wrote instructional programs using
TUTOR language
* Corrected errors in prewritten
programs using C++

Use a space between asterisk and text.

* Altered existing programs to fit user
needs

Data-entry clerk, XYZ Sales, Winter 2000

* Updated inventory and sales data

COMMUNICATION SKILLS

Served as a vice president of Computer Science Society

Received As in technical writing and speech class

REFERENCES

Available upon request

++ Willing to relocate ++

Asterisks and plus signs replace bullets.

RESUME PRODUCTION AND OTHER TIPS

An ink-jet printer is the preferred option for printing your resume. Begin by printing just a few copies. You may find a small error or you may simply want to make some changes, and this is less frustrating and less expensive if you print in small batches.

Resume paper color should be carefully chosen. You should consider the types of employers who will receive your resume and the types of positions for which you are applying. Use white or ivory paper for traditional or conservative employers or for higher-level positions.

Black ink on sharp, white paper can be harsh on the reader's eyes. Think about an ivory or cream paper that will provide less contrast and be easier to read. Pink, green, and blue tints should generally be avoided.

Many resume writers buy packages of matching envelopes and cover sheet stationery that, although not absolutely necessary, do convey a professional impression.

If you'll be producing many cover letters at home, be sure you have high quality printing equipment. Learn standard envelope formats for business and retain a copy of every cover letter you send out. You can use the copies to take notes of any telephone conversations that may occur.

If attending a job fair, either carry a briefcase or place your resume in a nicely covered legal-size pad holder.

THE COVER LETTER

The cover letter provides you with the opportunity to tailor your resume by telling the prospective employer how you can be a benefit to the organization. It will allow you to highlight aspects of your background that are not already discussed in your resume and that might be especially relevant to the organization you are contacting or to the position you are seeking. Every resume should have a cover letter enclosed when you send it out. Unlike the resume, which may be mass-produced, a cover letter is most effective when it is individually typed and focused on the particular requirements of the organization in question.

A good cover letter should supplement the resume and motivate the reader to review the resume. The format shown in Exhibit 2.6 is only a suggestion to help you decide what information to include in writing a cover letter.

Begin the cover letter with your street address twelve lines down from the top. Leave three to five lines between the date and the name of the person to whom you are addressing the cover letter. Make sure you leave one blank line between the salutation and the body of the letter and between paragraphs.

After typing "Sincerely," leave four blank lines and type your name. This should leave plenty of room for your signature. A sample cover letter is shown in Exhibit 2.7.

Exhibit 2.6

Cover Letter Format

Your Name
Your Street Address
Your Town, State, Zip
Phone Number
Fax Number
E-mail

Date

Name
Title
Organization
Address

Dear _____:

First Paragraph. In this paragraph state the reason for the letter, name the specific position or type of work you are applying for, and indicate from which resource (career services office, website, newspaper, contact, employment service) you learned of this opening. The first paragraph can also be used to inquire about future openings.

Second Paragraph. Indicate why you are interested in this position, the company, its products or services, and what you can do for the employer. If you are a recent graduate, explain how your academic background makes you a qualified candidate. Try not to repeat the same information found in the resume.

Third Paragraph. Refer the reader to the enclosed resume for more detailed information.

Fourth Paragraph. In this paragraph say what you will do to follow up on your letter. For example, state that you will call by a certain date to set up an interview or to find out if the company will be recruiting in your area. Finish by indicating your willingness to answer any questions they may have. Be sure you have provided your phone number.

Sincerely,

Type your name

Enclosure

The following guidelines will help you write good cover letters:

1. Be sure to type your letter; ensure there are no misspellings.

2. Avoid unusual typefaces, such as script.

Exhibit 2.7

Sample Cover Letter

143 Random Way
Shreveport, LA 71130
(318) 555-5555
Fax (318) 555-5556
jsmith@xxx.com
November 29, 2002

Kimberly Crane
Director of Personnel
Acme Distributors
279 Main Street
Shreveport, LA 71130

Dear Ms. Crane:

In May of 2003 I will graduate from Louisiana State University with a bachelor of arts degree in French. I read of your sales opening on *The Times* website, and I am very interested in the possibilities it offers. I am writing to explore the opportunity for employment with your company.

The ad indicated that you were looking for enthusiastic individuals with exceptional communication skills. I believe that I

continued

continued

possess those qualities. Through my job as a waitress at a busy diner, I have learned the importance of having high energy and maintaining a positive attitude toward customers. In addition to the various marketing classes in my academic program, I felt it important to enroll in some communication courses, such as human communication skills, interpersonal communication, and public speaking. These courses helped me to become comfortable in my interactions with other people, and they taught me how to communicate clearly. These characteristics will help me to represent Acme in a professional and enthusiastic manner.

As you will see by my enclosed resume, I was an admissions representative for three years of college. This position provided me with sales experience in that campus tours involved a certain degree of persuasive presentation of the college and its features to prospective students.

I would like to meet with you to discuss how my education and experience would be consistent with your needs. I will contact your office next week to discuss the possibility of an interview. In the meantime, if you have any questions or require additional information, please contact me at home, (318) 555-5555.

Sincerely,

Jennifer Smith

Enclosure

3. Address the letter to an individual, using the person's name and title. To obtain this information, call the company. If answering a blind newspaper advertisement, address the letter "To Whom It May Concern" or omit the salutation.

4. Be sure your cover letter directly indicates the position you are applying for and tells why you are qualified to fill it.

5. Send the original letter, not a photocopy, with your resume. Keep a copy for your records.

6. Make your cover letter no more than one page.

7. Include a phone number where you can be reached.

8. Avoid trite language and have someone read the letter over to react to its tone, content, and mechanics.

9. For your own information, record the date you send out each letter and resume.

CHAPTER THREE

RESEARCHING CAREERS

· ·

One common question a career counselor encounters is "What can I do with my degree?" Foreign language majors often struggle with this problem because, unlike their fellow students in more applied fields, such as accounting, computer science, or health and physical education, there is real confusion about just what kinds of jobs they can do with their degree and what kinds of organizations hire for those positions. An accounting major becomes an accountant. A computer science major can apply for a job as a data analyst. But what does a foreign language major become?

· ·

WHAT DO THEY CALL THE JOB YOU WANT?

There is every reason to be unaware. One reason for confusion is perhaps a mistaken assumption that a college education provides job training. In most cases it does not. Of course, applied fields such as engineering, management, or education provide specific skills for the workplace, whereas most liberal arts degrees simply provide an education. A liberal arts education exposes you to numerous fields of study and teaches you quantitative reasoning, critical thinking, writing, and speaking, all of which can be successfully applied to a number of different job fields. But it still remains up to you to choose a job field and to learn how to articulate the benefits of your education in a way the employer will appreciate.

As indicated in Chapter 1 on self-assessment, your first task is to understand and value what parts of that education you enjoyed and were good at and would continue to enjoy in your life's work. Did your writing courses encourage you in your ability to express yourself in writing? Did you enjoy the research process, and did you find your work was well received? Did you enjoy any of your required quantitative subjects such as algebra or calculus?

The answers to questions such as these provide clues to skills and interests you bring to the employment market over and above the credential of your degree. In fact, it is not an overstatement to suggest that most employers who demand a college degree immediately look beyond that degree to you as a person and your own individual expression of what you like to do and think you can do for them, regardless of your major.

Collecting Job Titles

The world of employment is a big place, and even seasoned veterans of the job hunt can be surprised about what jobs are to be found in what organizations. You need to become a bit of an explorer and adventurer and be willing to try a variety of techniques to begin a list of possible occupations that might use your talents and education. Once you have a list of possibilities that you are interested in and qualified for, you can move on to find out what kinds of organizations have these job titles.

....

Not every employer seeking to hire a translator may be equally desirable to you. Some employment environments may be more attractive to you than others. A foreign language major considering translating as a job title could do that in a major corporation, a government agency, a medical institution, a financial organization, or a court system. Each of these environments presents a different "culture" with associated norms in the pace of work, the subject matter of interest, and the backgrounds of its employees. Although the job titles may be the same, not all locations may present the same "fit" for you.

If you majored in foreign languages and enjoyed the in-class presentations you made as part of your degree and developed some good writing skills, you might naturally think law is a possibility for you. You're considering graduate school and a J.D. degree. But foreign language majors with these skills also become government managers, advertising executives, trainers, public relations practitioners, and bank officers. Each of these job titles can also be found in a number of different settings.

· ·

Take training, for example. Trainers write policy and procedural manuals and actively teach to assist all levels of employees in mastering various tasks and work-related systems. Trainers exist in all large corporations, banks, consumer goods manufacturers, medical diagnostic equipment firms, sales organizations, and any organization that has processes or materials that need to be presented to and learned by the staff.

In reading job descriptions or want ads for any of these positions, you would find your four-year degree a "must." However, the academic major might be less important than your own individual skills in critical thinking, analysis, report writing, public presentations, and interpersonal communication. Even more important than thinking or knowing you have certain skills is your ability to express those skills concretely and the examples you use to illustrate them to an employer.

The best beginning to a job search is to create a list of job titles you might want to pursue, learn more about the nature of the jobs behind those titles, and then discover what kinds of employers hire for those positions. In the following section we'll teach you how to build a job title directory to use in your job search.

Developing a Job Title Directory That Works for You

A job title directory is simply a complete list of all the job titles you are interested in, are intrigued by, or think you are qualified for. Combining the understanding gained through self-assessment with your own individual interests and the skills and talents you've acquired with your degree, you'll soon start to read and recognize a number of occupational titles that seem right for you. There are several resources you can use to develop your list, including computer searches, books, and want ads.

Computerized Interest Inventories. One way to begin your search is to identify a number of jobs that call for your degree and the particular skills and interests you identified as part of the self-assessment process. There are excellent interactive computer career guidance programs on the market to help you produce such selected lists of possible job titles. Most of these are available at high schools and colleges and at some larger town and city libraries.

Two of the industry leaders are SIGI and DISCOVER. Both allow you to enter interests, values, educational background, and other information to produce lists of possible occupations and industries. Each of the resources listed here will produce different job title lists. Some job titles will appear again and again, while others will be unique to a particular source. Investigate them all!

Reference Books. Books on the market that may be available through your local library, bookstore, or career counseling office also suggest various occupations related to a number of majors. The following are only two of the many good books on the market: *Occupational Outlook Handbook (OOH)* and *Occupational Projections and Training Data*, both put out annually by the U.S. Department of Labor, Bureau of Labor Statistics (www.bls.gov). The *OOH* describes hundreds of job titles under several broad categories such as Executive, Administrative, and Managerial Occupations and also identifies those jobs by their *Dictionary of Occupational Titles (DOT)* code. (See the following discussion.)

· ·

Many college and university career office Web pages offer some great information on what you can do with specific majors. Several of the best we've seen are from Florida State University (www.fsu.edu/~career/match_ match), Georgia Southern University (www2.gasou.edu/ sta/career), and the University of North Carolina at Wilmington (www.uncwil.edu/stuaff/career). In addition to potential job titles and/or employers, these sites will provide you with further related resources to explore, including websites.

· ·

Each job title deserves your consideration. Like the layers of an onion, the search for job titles can go on and on! As you spend time doing this activity, you are actually learning more about the value of your degree. What's important in your search at this point is not to become critical or selective, but rather to develop as long a list of possibilities as you can. Every source used will help you add new and potentially exciting jobs to your growing list.

Want Ads. It has been well publicized that newspaper want ads represent only about 10 to 15 percent of the current job market. However, with the current high state of employment as this book goes to press, the percentage of jobs advertised in the newspapers and on-line is rising dramatically, so don't ignore these sources.

Read the Sunday want ads in a major market newspaper for several Sundays in a row. Save any and all ads that interest you and seem to call for something close to your education and experience. Remember, because want ads are written for what an organization *hopes* to find, you don't have to meet absolutely every criterion. However, if certain requirements are stated as absolute minimums and you cannot meet them, it's best not to waste your time.

A recent examination of *The Boston Sunday Globe* (www.boston.com) reveals the following possible occupations for a liberal arts major with some computer skills and limited prior work experience. (This is only a partial list of what was available.)

❏ Admissions representative	❏ Technical writer
❏ Salesperson	❏ Personnel trainee
❏ Compliance director	❏ GED examiner
❏ Assistant principal gifts writer	❏ Direct mail researcher
❏ Public relations officer	❏ Associate publicist

After performing this exercise for a few Sundays, you'll find you have collected a new library of job titles.

The Sunday want ads exercise is important because these jobs are out in the marketplace. They truly exist, and people with your qualifications are being sought to apply. What's more, many of these advertisements describe the duties and responsibilities of the job advertised and give you a beginning sense of the challenges and opportunities such a position presents. Some will indicate salary, and that will be helpful as well. This information will better define the jobs for you and provide some good material for possible interviews in that field.

If you are able to be mobile in your job search, you may want to search other newspapers in other cities for their classified sections. This is now possible on-line. A good source for this search is the site called www.look smart.com. Using the keywords "newspaper classifieds" will lead you to their site where you can search by state alphabetically. It's an excellent source for want ads.

Exploring Job Descriptions

Once you've arrived at a solid list of possible job titles that interest you and for which you believe you are somewhat qualified, it's a good idea to do some research on each of these jobs. The preeminent source for such job information is the *Dictionary of Occupational Titles,* or *DOT* (www.wave .net/upg/immigration/dot_index.html). This directory lists every conceivable job and provides excellent up-to-date information on duties and responsibilities, interactions with associates, and day-to-day assignments and tasks. These descriptions provide a thorough job analysis, but they do not consider the possible employers or the environments in which a job may be performed. So, although a position as public relations officer may be well defined in terms of duties and responsibilities, it does not explain the differences in doing public relations work in a college or a hospital or a factory or a bank. You will need to look somewhere else for work settings.

Learning More About Possible Work Settings

After reading some job descriptions, you may choose to edit and revise your list of job titles once again, discarding those you feel are not suitable and keeping those that continue to hold your interest. Or you may wish to keep your list intact and see where these jobs may be located. For example, if you are interested in public relations and you appear to have those skills and the requisite education, you'll want to know what organizations do public relations. How can you find that out? How much income does someone in public relations make a year and what is the employment potential for the field of public relations?

To answer these and many other good questions about your list of job titles, we recommend you try any of the following resources: *Careers Encyclopedia,* a career information center site such as that provided by the American Marketing Association at www.amaboston.org/jobs.htm; *College to Career: The Guide to Job Opportunities*; and the *Occupational Outlook Handbook* (http://stats.bls.gov/ocohome.htm). Each of these resources, in a different way, will help to put the job titles you have selected into an employer context. *VGM's Handbook for Business and Management Careers* contains detailed career descriptions for more than fifty fields. Entries include complete information on duties and responsibilities for individual careers and detailed entry-level requirements. There is information on working conditions and promotional opportunities as well. Salary ranges and career outlook projections are also provided. Perhaps the most extensive discussion is found in the *Occupational Outlook Handbook,* which gives a thorough presentation of the nature of the work, the working conditions, employment statistics, training, other qualifications, and advancement possibilities as well as job outlook and earnings. Related occupations are also detailed, and a select bibliography is provided to help you find additional information.

Continuing with our public relations example, your search through these reference materials would teach you that the public relations jobs you find attractive are available in larger hospitals, financial institutions, most corporations (both consumer goods and industrial goods), media organizations, and colleges and universities.

Networking to Get the Complete Story

You now have not only a list of job titles but also, for each of these job titles, a description of the work involved and a general list of possible employment settings in which to work. You'll want to do some reading and keep talking to friends, colleagues, teachers, and others about the possibilities. Don't neglect to ask if the career office at your college maintains some kind of alumni network. Often such alumni networks will connect you with another graduate from the college who is working in the job title or industry you are seeking information about. These career networkers offer what assistance they can. For some it is a full day "shadowing" the alumnus as he or she goes about the job. Others offer partial-day visits, tours, informational interviews, resume reviews, job postings, or, if distance prevents a visit, telephone interviews. As fellow graduates, they'll be frank and informative about their own jobs and prospects in their field.

Take them up on their offer and continue to learn all you can about your own personal list of job titles, descriptions, and employment settings. You'll probably continue to edit and refine this list as you learn more about the realities of the job, the possible salary, advancement opportunities, and supply and demand statistics.

In the next section we'll describe how to find the specific organizations that represent these industries and employers so that you can begin to make contact.

WHERE ARE THESE JOBS, ANYWAY?

Having a list of job titles that you've designed around your own career interests and skills is an excellent beginning. It means you've really thought about who you are and what you are presenting to the employment market. It has caused you to think seriously about the most appealing environments to work in, and you have identified some employer types that represent these environments.

The research and the thinking that you've done thus far will be used again and again. They will be helpful in writing your resume and cover letters, in talking about yourself on the telephone to prospective employers, and in answering interview questions.

Now is a good time to begin to narrow the field of job titles and employment sites down to some specific employers to initiate the employment contact.

Finding Out Which Employers Hire People Like You

This section will provide tips, techniques, and specific resources for developing an actual list of specific employers that can be used to make contacts. It is only an outline that you must be prepared to tailor to your own particular needs and according to what you bring to the job search. Once again, it is important to stress the need to communicate with others along the way exactly what you're looking for and what your goals are for the research you're doing. Librarians, employers, career counselors, friends, friends of friends, business contacts, and bookstore staff will all have helpful information on geographically specific and new resources to aid you in locating employers who'll hire you.

Identifying Information Resources

Your interview wardrobe and your new resume may have put a dent in your wallet, but the resources you'll need to pursue your job search are available for free (although you might choose to copy materials on a machine instead of taking notes by hand). The categories of information detailed here are not hard to find and are yours for the browsing.

Numerous resources described in this section will help you identify actual employers. Use all of them or any others that you identify as available in your geographic area. As you become experienced in this process, you'll quickly figure out which information sources are helpful and which are not. If you live in a rural area, a well-planned day trip to a major city that includes a college career office, a large college or city library, state and federal employment centers, a chamber of commerce office, and a well-stocked bookstore can produce valuable results.

There are many excellent resources available to help you identify actual job sites. They are categorized into employer directories (usually indexed by product lines and geographic location), geographically based directories (designed to highlight particular cities, regions, or states), career-specific directories (e.g., *Sports MarketPlace*, which lists tens of thousands of firms involved with sports), periodicals and newspapers, targeted job posting publications, and videos. This is by no means meant to be a complete list of resources, but rather a starting point for identifying useful resources.

Working from the more general references to highly specific resources, we will provide a basic list to help you begin your search. Many of these you'll find easily available. In some cases reference librarians and others will suggest even better materials for your particular situation. Start to create your own customized bibliography of job search references. Use copying services to save time and to allow you to carry away information about organizations' missions, locations, company officers, phone numbers, and addresses.

Employer Directories. There are many employer directories available to give you the kind of information you need for your job search. Some of our favorites are listed here, but be sure to ask the professionals you are working with to make additional suggestions.

- *America's Corporate Families* (www.apsu.edu/~careers/res3.htm), the website of Austin Peay State University in Clarksville, Tennessee, has an excellent directory of corporate affiliations, parent companies, and subsidiaries. It has several links for corporate families.

- *Million Dollar Directory: America's Leading Public and Private Companies* lists about 160,000 companies.

- *Moody's* (www.moodys.com) various manuals are intended as guides for investors, so they contain a history of each company. Each manual contains a classification of companies by industries and products.

- *Standard and Poor's Register of Corporations* (www.stockinfo.standardpoor.com) contains listings for 45,000 businesses, some of which are not listed in the *Million Dollar Directory.*

- *Job Seekers Guide to Private and Public Companies* (www.tomah.com/jobseeker) profiles 15,000 employers in four volumes, each covering a different geographic region. Company entries include contact information, business descriptions, and application procedures.

- *The Career Guide: Dun's Employment Opportunities Directory* includes more than 5,000 large organizations, including hospitals and local governments. Profiles include an overview and history of the employer as well as opportunities, benefits, and contact names. It contains geographic and industrial indexes and indexes by discipline or internship availability. This guide also includes a state-by-state list of professional personnel consultants and their specialties.

❑ *Professional's Job Finder/Government Job Finder/Non-Profits Job Finder* (http://einsys.einpgh.org) is the general website that will ultimately lead you to specific directories of job services, salary surveys, and periodical listings in which advertisements for jobs in the professional, government, or not-for-profit sector are found. Search under the icon "Title" for these directories.

❑ *The 100 Best Companies to Sell For* lists companies by industry and provides contact information and describes benefits and corporate culture.

❑ *The 100 Best Companies to Work for in America* rates organizations based on several factors including opportunities, job security, and pay.

❑ *Companies That Care* lists organizations that the authors believe are family-friendly. One index organizes information by state.

❑ *Infotrac CD-ROM Business Index* (http://infotrac.galegroup.com) covers business journals and magazines as well as newsmagazines and can provide information on public and private companies.

❑ *ABI/Inform on Disc* (CD-ROM) indexes articles from more than 800 journals.

Geographically Based Directories. The Job Bank series published by Bob Adams, Inc. (www.aip.com) contains detailed entries on each area's major employers, including business activity, address, phone number, and hiring contact name. Many listings specify educational backgrounds being sought in potential employees. Each volume contains a solid discussion of each city's or state's major employment sectors. Organizations are also indexed by industry. Job Bank volumes are available for the following places: Atlanta, Boston, Chicago, Denver, Dallas–Ft. Worth, Florida, Houston, Ohio, St. Louis, San Francisco, Seattle, Los Angeles, New York, Detroit, Philadelphia, Minneapolis, the Northwest, and Washington, D.C.

National Job Bank (www.careercity.com) lists employers in every state, along with contact names and commonly hired job categories. Included are many small companies often overlooked by other directories. Companies are also indexed by industry. This publication provides information on educational backgrounds sought and lists company benefits.

Career-Specific Directories. VGM (www.ntccpg.com) publishes a number of excellent series detailing careers for college graduates. In the Professional Career series are guides to careers in a range of fields, among them:

❑ Advertising

❑ Business

❑ Communications

❑ Computers

❑ Health Care

❑ High Tech

Each of these books is titled *Careers in . . .* and provides an excellent discussion of the industry, educational requirements for jobs, salary ranges, duties, and projected outlooks for the field.

Another VGM series, *Opportunities in . . .* , has an equally wide range of titles relating to specific majors, such as the following:

❑ *Opportunities in Education Careers*

❑ *Opportunities in Film Careers*

❑ *Opportunities in Insurance Careers*

❑ *Opportunities in Journalism Careers*

❑ *Opportunities in Law Careers*

❑ *Opportunities in Nursing Careers*

❑ *Opportunities in Government Careers*

❑ *Opportunities in Teaching Careers*

❑ *Opportunities in Technical Writing Careers*

Sports MarketPlace (Sportsguide) lists organizations by sport. It also describes trade/professional associations, college athletic organizations, multisport publications, media contacts, corporate sports sponsors, promotion/event/athletic management services, and trade shows.

Periodicals and Newspapers. Several sources are available to help you locate which journals or magazines carry job advertisements in your field. Other resources help you identify opportunities in other parts of the country.

❑ *The Helping Professions: A Career Sourcebook* contains a periodicals matrix organized by academic discipline and highlights periodicals containing job listings.

❏ *National Business Employment Weekly* (www.nbew.com) compiles want ads from four regional editions of the *Wall Street Journal* (http://interactive.wsj.com). Most are business and management positions.

❏ *National Ad Search* (www.nationaladsearch.com) reprints ads from seventy-five metropolitan newspapers across the country. Although the focus is on management positions, technical and professional postings are also included. *Caution:* Watch deadline dates carefully on listings because deadlines may have already passed by the time the ad is printed.

❏ The *Federal Jobs Digest* (www.jobsfed.com) and *Federal Career Opportunities* list government positions.

❏ *World Chamber of Commerce Directory* (www.chamberofcommerce.org) lists addresses for chambers worldwide, state boards of tourism, convention and visitors' bureaus, and economic development organizations.

This list is certainly not exhaustive; use it to begin your job search work.

Targeted Job Posting Publications. Although the resources that follow are national in scope, they are either targeted to one medium of contact (telephone), focused on specific types of jobs, or are less comprehensive than the sources previously listed.

❏ *Job Hotlines USA* (www.careers.org/topic/01_002.html) pinpoints more than 1,000 hard-to-find telephone numbers for companies and government agencies that use prerecorded job messages and listings. Very few of the telephone numbers listed are toll-free, and sometimes recordings are long, so callers beware!

❏ *The Job Hunter* (www.jobhunter.com) is a national biweekly newspaper listing business, arts, media, government, human services, health, community-related, and student services job openings.

❏ *Current Jobs for Graduates* (www.graduatejobs.com) is a national employment listing for liberal arts professions, including editorial positions, management opportunities, museum work, teaching, and nonprofit work.

❏ *Environmental Opportunities* (www.ecojobs.com) serves environmental job interests nationwide by listing administrative, marketing, and human resources positions along with education-related jobs and positions directly related to a degree in an environmental field.

❑ *Y National Vacancy List* (www.ymcahrm.ns.ca/employed/jobleads.html) shows YMCA professional vacancies, including development, administration, programming, membership, and recreation postings.

❑ *ARTSearch* is a national employment service bulletin for the arts, including administration, managerial, marketing, and financial management jobs.

❑ *Community Jobs* is an employment newspaper for the nonprofit sector that provides a variety of listings, including project manager, canvas director, government relations specialist, community organizer, and program instructor.

❑ *College Placement Council Annual: A Guide to Employment Opportunities for College Graduates* is an annual guide containing solid job-hunting information and, more important, displaying ads from large corporations actively seeking recent college graduates in all majors. Company profiles provide brief descriptions and available employment opportunities. Contact names and addresses are given. Profiles are indexed by organization name, geographic location, and occupation.

Videos. You may be one of the many job seekers who like to get information via a medium other than paper. Many career libraries, public libraries, and career centers in libraries carry an assortment of videos that will help you learn new techniques and get information helpful in the job search.

Locating Information Resources

An essay by John Case that appeared in the *Boston Globe* alerts both new and seasoned job seekers that the job market is changing, and the old guarantees of lifelong employment no longer hold true. Some of our major corporations, which were once seen as the most prestigious of employment destinations, are now laying off thousands of employees. Middle management is especially hard hit in downsizing situations. On the other side of the coin, smaller, more entrepreneurial firms are adding employees and realizing enormous profit margins. The geography of the new job market is unfamiliar, and the terrain is much harder to map. New and smaller firms can mean different kinds of jobs and new job titles. The successful job seeker will keep an open mind about where he or she might find employment and what that employment might be called.

In order to become familiar with this new terrain, you will need to undertake some research, which can be done at any of the following locations:

- ❑ Public libraries

- ❑ Business organizations

- ❑ Employment agencies

- ❑ Bookstores

- ❑ Career libraries

Each one of these places offers a collection of resources that will help you get the information you need.

As you meet and talk with service professionals at all these sites, be sure to let them know what you're doing. Inform them of your job search, what you've already accomplished, and what you're looking for. The more people who know you're job seeking, the greater the possibility that someone will have information or know someone who can help you along your way.

Public Libraries. Large city libraries, college and university libraries, and even well-supported town library collections contain a variety of resources to help you conduct a job search. It is not uncommon for libraries to have separate "vocational choices" sections with books, tapes, computer terminals, and associated materials relating to job search and selection. Some are now even making resume creation software available for use by patrons.

Some of the publications we name throughout this book are expensive reference items that are rarely purchased by individuals. In addition, libraries carry a wide range of newspapers and telephone Yellow Pages as well as the usual array of books. If resources are not immediately available, many libraries have loan arrangements with other facilities and can make information available to you relatively quickly.

Take advantage not only of the reference collections, but also the skilled and informed staff. Let them know exactly what you are looking for, and they'll have their own suggestions. You'll be visiting the library frequently, and the reference staff will soon come to know who you are and what you're working on. They'll be part of your job search network!

Business Organizations. Chambers of Commerce, Offices of New Business Development, Councils on Business and Industry, Small Business Administration

(SBA) offices, and professional associations can all provide geographically specific lists of companies and organizations that have hiring needs. They also have an array of other available materials, including visitors' guides and regional fact books that provide additional employment information.

These agencies serve to promote local and regional businesses and ensure their survival and success. Although these business organizations do not advertise job openings or seek employees for their members, they may be very aware of staffing needs among their member firms. In your visits to each of these locations, spend some time with the personnel, getting to know who they are and what they do. Let them know of your job search and your intentions regarding employment. You may be surprised and delighted at the information they may provide.

Employment Agencies. Employment agencies (including state and federal employment offices), professional "headhunters" or executive search firms, and some private career counselors can provide direct leads to job openings. Don't overlook these resources. If you are mounting a complete job search program and want to ensure that you are covering the potential market for employers, consider the employment agencies in your territory. Some of these organizations work contractually with several specific firms and may have access that is unavailable to you. Others may be particularly well-informed about supply and demand in particular industries or geographic locations.

In the case of professional (commercial) employment agencies, which include those executive recruitment firms labeled "headhunters," you should be cautious about entering into any binding contractual agreement. Before doing so, be sure to get the information you need to decide whether their services can be of use to you. Questions to ask include the following: Who pays the fee when employment is obtained? Are there any other fees or costs associated with this service? What is their placement rate? Can you see a list of previous clients and can you talk to any for references? Do they typically work with entry-level job seekers? Do they tend to focus on particular kinds of employment or industries?

A few cautions are in order, however, when you work with professional agencies. Remember, the professional employment agency is, in most cases, paid by the hiring organization. Naturally, their interest and attention is largely directed to the employer, not to the candidate. Of course, they want to provide good candidates to guarantee future contracts, but they are less interested in the job seeker than the employer.

For teacher candidates there are a number of good placement firms that charge the prospective teacher, not the employer. This situation has evolved over time as a result of supply and demand and financial structuring of most school systems, which cannot spend money on recruiting teachers. Usually these firms charge a nonrefundable administrative fee and, upon successful placement, require a fee based on a percentage of salary, which may range from 10 to 20 percent of annual compensation. Often, this can be repaid over a number of months. Check your contract carefully.

State and federal employment offices are no-fee services that maintain extensive "job boards" and can provide detailed specifications for each job advertised and help with application forms. Because government employment application forms are detailed, keep a master copy along with copies of all additional documentation (resumes, educational transcripts, military discharge papers, proof of citizenship, and so forth). Successive applications may require separate filings. Visit these offices as frequently as you can because most deal with applicants on a "walk-in" basis and will not telephone prospective candidates or maintain files of job seekers. Check your telephone book for the address of the nearest state and federal offices.

The Web is also a great source of job listings for teachers, especially for entry-level positions. A good search tactic on the Web is to use a "metaengine" that combines several search engines in one. Dogpile.com is an example of a metasearch engine. Using search string descriptors such as "teacher recruitment," "teacher supply," or "K12 jobs," you will discover job boards with current postings. At the time of publication, three excellent sites were: www.teachersatwork.com, www.K12jobs.com/jobfinder, and www.edweek .org, which has listings by region.

One type of employment service that causes much confusion among job seekers is the outplacement firm. Their advertisements tend to suggest they will put you in touch with the "hidden job market." They use advertising phrases such as "We'll work with you until you get that job" or "Maximize your earnings and career opportunities." In fact, if you read the fine print on these ads, you will notice these firms must state they are "Not an employment agency." These firms are, in fact, corporate and private outplacement counseling agencies whose work involves resume editing, counseling to provide leads for jobs, interview skills training, and all the other aspects of hiring preparation. They do this for a fee, sometimes in the thousands of dollars range, which is paid by you, the client. Some of these firms have good reputations and provide excellent materials and techniques. Most, however, provide a service you as a college student or graduate can receive free from your alma mater or through a reciprocity agreement between your college and a college or university located closer to your current address.

Bookstores. Any well-stocked bookstore will carry some job search books that are worth buying. Some major stores will even have an extensive section devoted to materials, including excellent videos, related to the job search process. You will also find copies of local newspapers and business magazines.

The one advantage that is provided by resources purchased at a bookstore is that you can read and work with the information in the comfort of your own home and do not have to conform to the hours of operation of a library, which can present real difficulties if you are working full-time as you seek employment. A few minutes spent browsing in a bookstore might be a beneficial break from your job search activities and turn up valuable resources.

Career Libraries. Career libraries, which are found in career centers at colleges and universities and sometimes within large public libraries, contain a unique blend of the job search resources housed in other settings. In addition, career libraries often purchase a number of job listing publications, each of which targets a specific industry or type of job. You may find job listings specifically for entry-level positions for your specific major. Ask about job posting newsletters or newspapers specifically focused on careers in the area that most interests you. Each center will be unique, but you are certain to discover some good sources of jobs.

Most college career libraries now hold growing collections of video material on specific industries and on aspects of your job search process, including dress and appearance, how to manage the luncheon or dinner interview, how to be effective at a job fair, and many other specific titles. Some larger corporations produce handsome video materials detailing the variety of career paths and opportunities available in their organizations.

Some career libraries also house computer-based career planning and information systems. These interactive computer programs help you to clarify your values and interests and will combine that with your education to provide possible job titles and industry locations. Some even contain extensive lists of graduate school programs.

One specific kind of service a career library will be able to direct you to is computerized job search services. These services, of which there are many, are run by private companies, individual colleges, or consortiums of colleges. They attempt to match qualified job candidates with potential employers. The candidate submits a resume (or an application) to the service. This information (which can be categorized into hundreds of separate "fields" of data) is entered into a computer database. Your information is then compared with the information from employers about what they desire in a prospective employee. If there is a "match" between what they want and what you have indicated you can offer, the job search service or the employer will contact you directly to continue the process.

Computerized job search services can complement an otherwise complete job search program. They are *not*, however, a substitute for the kinds of activities described in this book. They are essentially passive operations that are random in nature. If you have not listed skills, abilities, traits, experiences, or education *exactly* as an employer has listed its needs, there is simply no match.

Consult with the staff members at the career libraries you use. These professionals have been specifically trained to meet the unique needs you present. Often you can just drop in and receive help with general questions, or you may want to set up an appointment to speak one-on-one with a career counselor to gain special assistance.

Every career library is different in size and content, but each can provide valuable information for the job search. Some may even provide limited counseling. If you have not visited the career library at your college or alma mater, call and ask if these collections are still available for your use. Be sure to ask about other services that you can use as well.

If you are not near your own college as you work on your job search, call the career office and inquire about reciprocal agreements with other colleges that are closer to where you live. Very often, your own alma mater can arrange for you to use a limited menu of services at another school. This typically would include access to a career library and job posting information and might include limited counseling.

CHAPTER FOUR

NETWORKING

*N*etworking is the process of deliberately establishing relationships to get career-related information or to alert potential employers that you are available for work. Networking is critically important to today's job seeker for two reasons: it will help you get the information you need, and it can help you find out about *all* of the available jobs.

Getting the Information You Need

Networkers will review your resume and give you feedback on its effectiveness. They will talk about the job you are looking for and give you a candid appraisal of how they see your strengths and weaknesses. If they have a good sense of the industry or the employment sector for that job, you'll get their feelings on future trends in the industry as well. Some networkers will be very forthcoming about salaries, job-hunting techniques, and suggestions for your job search strategy. Many have been known to place calls right from the interview desk to friends and associates who might be interested in you. Each networker will make his or her own contribution, and each will be valuable.

Because organizations must evolve to adapt to current global market needs, the information provided by decision makers within various organizations will be critical to your success as a new job market entrant. For example, you might learn about the concept of virtual organizations from a networker. Virtual organizations coordinate economic activity to deliver value to customers using resources outside the traditional boundaries of the organization. This concept is being discussed and implemented by chief executive officers of many organizations, including Ford Motor, Dell, and IBM.

Networking can help you find out about this and other trends currently affecting the industries under your consideration.

Finding Out About All of the Available Jobs

Not every job that is available at this very moment is advertised for potential applicants to see. This is called the *hidden job market*. Only 15 to 20 percent of all jobs are formally advertised, which means that 80 to 85 percent of available jobs do not appear in published channels. Networking will help you become more knowledgeable about all the employment opportunities available during your job search period.

Although someone you might talk to today doesn't know of any openings within his or her organization, tomorrow or next week or next month an opening may occur. If you've taken the time to show an interest in and knowledge of their organization, if you've shown the company representative how you can help achieve organizational goals and that you can fit into the organization, you'll be one of the first candidates considered for the position.

Networking: A Proactive Approach

Networking is a proactive rather than a reactive approach. You, as a job seeker, are expected to initiate a certain level of activity on your own behalf; you cannot afford to simply respond to jobs listed in the newspaper. Being proactive means building a network of contacts that includes informed and interested decision makers who will provide you with up-to-date knowledge of the current job market and increase your chances of finding out about employment opportunities appropriate for your interests, experience, and level of education.

An old axiom of networking says, "You are only two phone calls away from the information you need." In other words, by talking to enough people, you will quickly come across someone who can offer you help. Start with your professors. Each of them probably has a wide circle of contacts. In their work and travel they might have met someone who can help you or direct you to someone who can.

Control and the Networking Process

In deliberately establishing relationships, the process of networking begins with you in control—*you* are contacting specific individuals. As your network expands and you establish a set of professional relationships, your search for information or jobs will begin to move outside of your total control. A part of the networking process involves others assisting you by gathering information for you or recommending you as a possible job candidate.

As additional people become a part of your networking system, you will have less knowledge about activities undertaken on your behalf; you will undoubtedly be contacted by individuals whom you did not initially approach. If you want to function effectively in surprise situations, you must be prepared at all times to talk with strangers about the informational or employment needs that motivated you to become involved in the networking process.

PREPARING TO NETWORK

In deliberately establishing relationships, maximize your efforts by organizing your approach. Five specific areas in which you can organize your efforts include reviewing your self-assessment, reviewing your research on job sites and organizations, deciding who it is you want to talk to, keeping track of all your efforts, and creating your self-promotion tools.

Review Your Self-Assessment

Your self-assessment is as important a tool in preparing to network as it has been in other aspects of your job search. You have carefully evaluated your personal traits, personal values, economic needs, longer-term goals, skill base, preferred skills, and underdeveloped skills. During the networking process you will be called upon to communicate what you know about yourself and relate it to the information or job you seek. Be sure to review the exercises that you completed in the self-assessment section of this book in preparation for networking. We've explained that you need to assess what skills you have acquired from your major that are of general value to an employer and to be ready to express those in ways employers can appreciate as useful in their own organizations.

Review Research on Job Sites and Organizations

In addition, individuals assisting you will expect that you'll have at least some background information on the occupation or industry of interest to you. Refer to the appropriate sections of this book and other relevant publications to acquire the background information necessary for effective networking. They'll explain how to identify not only the job titles that might be of interest to you, but also what kinds of organizations employ people to do that job. You will develop some sense of working conditions and expectations about duties and responsibilities—all of which will be of help in your networking interviews.

Decide Who It Is You Want to Talk To

Networking cannot begin until you decide who it is that you want to talk to and, in general, what type of information you hope to gain from your contacts. Once you know this, it's time to begin developing a list of contacts. Five useful sources for locating contacts are described here.

College Alumni Network. Most colleges and universities have created a formal network of alumni and friends of the institution who are particularly interested in helping currently enrolled students and graduates of their alma mater gain employment-related information.

. . . .

> **With the exception of the language teaching positions, persons with foreign language skills use their talents across a spectrum of possible employment settings. Just the diversity of employment within a list of your college's alumni who are using their foreign language degrees should be both encouraging and informative to you. Among such a diversified group, there are likely to be scores of people you would enjoy talking with and perhaps meeting.**

. . . .

It is usually a simple process to make use of an alumni network. You need only visit the alumni or career office at your college or university and follow the procedure that has been established. Often, you will simply complete a form indicating your career goals and interests and you will be given the names of appropriate individuals to contact. In many cases staff members will coach you on how to make the best use of the limited time these alumni contacts may have available for you.

Alumni networkers may provide some combination of the following services: day-long shadowing experiences, telephone interviews, in-person interviews, information on relocating to given geographic areas, internship information, suggestions on graduate school study, and job vacancy notices.

. . . .

> **What a valuable experience. Perhaps you are interested in working as an interpreter in a big city children's hospital but are unsure about your language skills or whether you'd like it or not. Spending a day with an alumnus in such a setting is a good way to resolve some of those questions. Asking your alumni contacts about their own academic preparation and the role of their foreign language**

education in their current jobs and observing firsthand the dynamics of their day on the job will be a far better decision criterion for you than any reading on the subject could possibly provide.

....

Present and Former Supervisors. If you believe you are on good terms with present or former job supervisors, they may be an excellent resource for providing information or directing you to appropriate resources that would have information related to your current interests and needs. Additionally, these supervisors probably belong to professional organizations that they might be willing to utilize to get information for you.

....

If, for example, you were interested in working abroad in the hospitality industry, perhaps for a major hotel chain, and you were currently working on the wait staff of a local restaurant, talk with your supervisor or the owner. He or she may belong to the local chamber of commerce, whose director would have information on members affiliated with large hotel operations in your area. You would probably be able to obtain the names and telephone numbers of these people, which would allow you to begin the networking process.

....

Employers in Your Area. Although you may be interested in working in a geographic location different from the one where you currently reside, don't overlook the value of the knowledge and contacts those around you are able to provide. Use the local telephone directory and newspaper to identify the types of organizations you are thinking of working for or professionals who have the kinds of jobs you are interested in. Recently, a call made to a local hospital's financial administrator for information on working in health-care financial administration yielded more pertinent information on training seminars, regional professional organizations, and potential employment sites than a national organization was willing to provide.

Employers in Geographic Areas Where You Hope to Work. If you are thinking about relocating, identifying prospective employers or informational contacts in the new location will be critical to your success. Here are some tips for on-line searching. First, use a "metasearch," engine to get the most out of your search. Metasearch engines combine several engines into one powerful tool. The authors frequently use www.dogpile.com and www.metasearch.com for this purpose. Try using the city and state as your keywords in a search. "New Haven, Connecticut" will bring you to the city's website with links to the chamber of commerce, member businesses, and other valuable resources. By using www.looksmart.com you can locate newspapers in any area and they, too, can provide valuable insight before relocating. Of course, both dogpile and metasearch can lead you to yellow and white page directories in areas you are considering.

Professional Associations and Organizations. Professional associations and organizations can provide valuable information in several areas: career paths that you may not have considered, qualifications relating to those career choices, publications that list current job openings, and workshops or seminars that will enhance your professional knowledge and skills. They can also be excellent sources for background information on given industries: their health, current problems, and future challenges.

There are several excellent resources available to help you locate professional associations and organizations that would have information to meet your needs. Two especially useful publications are the *Encyclopedia of Associations* and *National Trade and Professional Associations of the United States.*

Keep Track of All Your Efforts

It can be difficult, almost impossible, to remember all the details related to each contact you make during the networking process, so you will want to develop a record-keeping system that works for you. Formalize this process by using your computer to keep a record of the people and organizations you want to contact. You can simply record the contact's name, address, telephone number, and what information you hope to gain. Each entry might look something like this:

Contact Name	Address	Phone #	Purpose
Mr. Lee Perkins	13 Muromachi		Local market
Osaka Branch	Osaka-shi	73-8906	information

You could record this as a simple Word document and you could still use the "Find" function if you were trying to locate some data and could only recall the firm's name or the contact's name. If you're comfortable with database management and have some database software on your computer, then you can put information at your fingertips even if you have only the zip code! The point here is not technological sophistication but good record keeping.

Once you have created this initial list, it will be helpful to keep more detailed information as you begin to actually make the contacts. Using the Network Contact Record form in Exhibit 4.1 will help you keep good information on all your network contacts. They'll appreciate your recall of details of your meetings and conversations, and the information will help you to focus your networking efforts.

Exhibit 4.1

Network Contact Record

Name: Be certain your spelling is correct.

Title: Pick up a business card to be certain of the correct title.

Employing organization: Note any parent company or subsidiaries.

Business mailing address: This is often different from the street address.

Business E-mail address:

Business telephone number: Include area code and alternative numbers.

Business fax number:

Source for this contact: Who referred you, and what is their relationship to the contact?

Date of call or letter: Use plenty of space here to record multiple phone calls or visits, other employees you may have met, names of secretaries/ receptionists, and so forth.

Content of discussion: Keep enough notes here to remind you of the substance of your visits and telephone conversations in case some time elapses between contacts.

Follow-up necessary to continue working with this contact:
Your contact may request that you send him or her some materials or direct you to contact an associate. Note any such instructions or assignments in this space.

Name of additional networker: Here you would record the
Address: names and phone numbers of
E-Mail: additional contacts met at this
Phone: employer's site. Often you will
Fax: be introduced to many people,
Name of additional networker: some of whom may indicate
Address: a willingness to help in your
E-mail: job search.
Phone:
Fax:
Name of additional networker:
Address:
E-mail:
Phone:
Fax:

Date thank-you note written: May help to date your next contact.

Follow-up action taken: Phone calls, visits, additional notes.

Other miscellaneous notes: Record any other additional interaction you think may be important to remember in working with this networking client. You will want this form in front of you when telephoning or just before and after a visit.

Create Your Self-Promotion Tools

There are two types of promotional tools that are used in the networking process. The first is a resume and cover letter, and the second is a one-minute "infomercial," which may be given over the telephone or in person.

Techniques for writing an effective resume and cover letter are discussed in Chapter 2. Once you have reviewed that material and prepared these important documents, you will have created one of your self-promotion tools.

The one-minute infomercial will demand that you begin tying your interests, abilities, and skills to the people or organizations you want to network with. Think about your goal for making the contact to help you understand what you should say about yourself. You should be able to express yourself easily and convincingly. If, for example, you are contacting an alumnus of your institution to obtain the names of possible employment sites in a distant city, be prepared to discuss why you are interested in moving to that location, the types of jobs you are interested in, and the skills and abilities you possess that will make you a qualified candidate.

To create a meaningful one-minute infomercial, write it out, practice it as if it will be a spoken presentation, rewrite it, and practice it again if necessary until expressing yourself comes easily and is convincing.

Here's a simplified example of an infomercial for use over the telephone:

....

Hello, Ms. Regan? My name is Ruth Fowler. I am a recent graduate of Polytechnic University, and I want to enter the field of import/export. I was a French major and feel confident that I have many of the skills I understand are valued in import/export beyond my fluency in French. I have good computational skills, computer expertise, and I am confident of my writing and speaking abilities in English as well. What's more, I work well under pressure. I have read that can be a real advantage in your field!

Ms. Regan, I'm calling you because I still need more information about the import/export field. I'm hoping you'll have the time to sit down with me for about half an hour and discuss your perspective on import/export careers with me. There are so many possible industries that are involved in import/export, and I am seeking some advice on which of those settings might be the best for my particular combination of skills and experiences.

Would you be willing to do that for me? I would greatly appreciate it. I am available most mornings, if that's convenient for you.

....

It very well may happen that your employer contact wishes you to communicate by E-mail. The infomercial quoted above could easily be rewritten for an E-mail message. You should "cut and paste" your resume right into the E-mail text itself.

Other effective self-promotion tools include portfolios for those in the arts, writing professions, or teaching. Portfolios show examples of work, photographs of projects or classroom activities, or certificates and credentials that are job related. There may not be an opportunity to use the portfolio during an interview, and it is not something that should be left with the organization. It is designed to be explained and displayed by the creator. However, during some networking meetings, there may be an opportunity to illustrate a point or strengthen a qualification by exhibiting the portfolio.

BEGINNING THE NETWORKING PROCESS

Set the Tone for Your Contacts

It can be useful to establish "tone words" for any communications you embark upon. Before making your first telephone call or writing your first letter, decide what you want your contact to think of you. If you are networking to try to obtain a job, your tone words might include words such as *genuine, informed,* and *self-knowledgeable.* When trying to acquire information, your tone words may have a slightly different focus, such as *courteous, organized, focused,* and *well-spoken.* Use the tone words you establish for your contacts to guide you through the networking process.

Honestly Express Your Intentions

When contacting individuals, it is important to be honest about your reasons for making the contact. Establish your purpose in your own mind and be able and ready to articulate it concisely. Determine an initial agenda, whether it be informational questioning or self-promotion, present it to your contact, and be ready to respond immediately. If you don't adequately prepare before initiating your contacts, you may find yourself at a disadvantage if you're asked to immediately begin your informational interview or self-promotion during the first phone conversation or visit.

Start Networking Within Your Circle of Confidence

Once you have organized your approach—by utilizing specific researching methods, creating a system for keeping track of the people you will contact, and developing effective self-promotion tools—you are ready to begin networking. The best way to begin networking is by talking with a group of people you trust and feel comfortable with. This group is usually made up of your family, friends, and career counselors. No matter who is in this inner circle, they will have a special interest in seeing you succeed in your job search. In addition, because they will be easy to talk to, you should try taking some risks in terms of practicing your information-seeking approach. Gain confidence in talking about the strengths you bring to an organization and the underdeveloped skills you feel hinder your candidacy. Be sure to review the section on self-assessment for tips on approaching each of these areas. Ask for critical but constructive feedback from the people in your circle of confidence on the letters you write and the one-minute infomercial you have developed. Evaluate whether you want to make the changes they suggest, then practice the changes on others within this circle.

Stretch the Boundaries of Your Networking Circle of Confidence

Once you have refined the promotional tools you will use to accomplish your networking goals, you will want to make additional contacts. Because you will not know most of these people, it will be a less comfortable activity to undertake. The practice that you gained with your inner circle of trusted friends should have prepared you to now move outside of that comfort zone.

It is said that any information a person needs is only two phone calls away, but the information cannot be gained until you (1) make a reasonable guess about who might have the information you need and (2) pick up the telephone to make the call. Using your network list that includes alumni, instructors, supervisors, employers, and associations, you can begin preparing your list of questions that will allow you to get the information you need. Review the question list that follows and then develop a list of your own.

Questions You Might Want to Ask

1. In the position you now hold, what do you do on a typical day?

2. What are the most interesting aspects of your job?

3. What part of your work do you consider dull or repetitious?

4. What were the jobs you had that led to your present position?

5. How long does it usually take to move from one step to the next in this career path?

6. What is the top position to which you can aspire in this career path?

7. What is the next step in *your* career path?

8. Are there positions in this field that are similar to your position?

9. What are the required qualifications and training for entry-level positions in this field?

10. Are there specific courses a student should take to be qualified to work in this field?

11. What are the entry-level jobs in this field?

12. What types of training are provided to persons entering this field?

13. What are the salary ranges your organization typically offers to entry-level candidates for positions in this field?

14. What special advice would you give a person entering this field?

15. Do you see this field as a growing one?

16. How do you see the content of the entry-level jobs in this field changing over the next two years?

17. What can I do to prepare myself for these changes?

18. What is the best way to obtain a position that will start me on a career in this field?

19. Do you have any information on job specifications and descriptions that I may have?

20. What related occupational fields would you suggest I explore?

21. How could I improve my resume for a career in this field?

22. Who else would you suggest I talk to, both in your organization and in other organizations?

Questions You Might Have to Answer

In order to communicate effectively, you must anticipate questions that will be asked of you by the networkers you contact. Review the list below and see if you can easily answer each of these questions. If you cannot, it may be time to revisit the self-assessment process.

1. Where did you get my name, or how did you find out about this organization?

2. What are your career goals?

3. What kind of job are you interested in?

4. What do you know about this organization and this industry?

5. How do you know you're prepared to undertake an entry-level position in this industry?

6. What course work have you done that is related to your career interests?

7. What are your short-term career goals?

8. What are your long-term career goals?

9. Do you plan to obtain additional formal education?

10. What contributions have you made to previous employers?

11. Which of your previous jobs have you enjoyed the most and why?

12. What are you particularly good at doing?

13. What shortcomings have you had to face in previous employment?

14. What are your three greatest strengths?

15. Describe how comfortable you feel with your communication style.

General Networking Tips

Make Every Contact Count. Setting the tone for each interaction is critical. Approaches that will help you communicate in an effective way include politeness, being appreciative of time provided to you, and being prepared and thorough. Remember, *everyone* within an organization has a circle of influence, so be prepared to interact effectively with each person you encounter in the networking process, including secretarial and support staff. Many information or job seekers have thwarted their own efforts by being rude to some individuals they encountered as they networked because they made the incorrect assumption that certain persons were unimportant.

Sometimes your contacts may be surprised at their ability to help you. After meeting and talking with you, they might think they have not offered much in the way of help. A day or two later, however, they may make a contact that would be useful to you and refer you to it.

With Each Contact, Widen Your Circle of Networkers. Always leave an informational interview with the names of at least two more people who can help you get the information or job that you are seeking. Don't be shy about asking for additional contacts; networking is all about increasing the number of people you can interact with to achieve your goals.

Make Your Own Decisions. As you talk with different people and get answers to the questions you pose, you may hear conflicting information or get conflicting suggestions. Your job is to listen to these "experts" and decide what information and which suggestions will help you achieve *your* goals. Only implement those suggestions that you believe will work for you.

SHUTTING DOWN YOUR NETWORK

As you achieve the goals that motivated your networking activity—getting the information you need or the job you want—the time will come to inactivate all or parts of your network. As you do so, be sure to tell your primary supporters about your change in status. Call or write to each one of them and give them as many details about your new status as you feel is necessary to maintain a positive relationship.

Because a network takes on a life of its own, activity undertaken on your behalf will continue even after you cease your efforts. As you get calls or are contacted in some fashion, be sure to inform these networkers about your change in status, and thank them for assistance they have provided.

Information on the latest employment trends indicates that workers will change jobs or careers several times in their lifetime. Networking, then, will be a critical aspect in the span of your professional life. If you carefully and thoughtfully conduct your networking activities during your job search, you will have a solid foundation of experience when you need to network the next time around.

CHAPTER FIVE

INTERVIEWING

*C*ertainly, there can be no one part of the job search process more fraught with anxiety and worry than the interview. Yet seasoned job seekers welcome the interview and will often say, "Just get me an interview and I'm on my way!" They understand that the interview is crucial to the hiring process and equally crucial for them, as job candidates, to have the opportunity of a personal dialogue to add to what the employer may already have learned from a resume, cover letter, and telephone conversations.

Believe it or not, the interview is to be welcomed, and even enjoyed! It is a perfect opportunity for you, the candidate, to sit down with an employer and express yourself and display who you are and what you want. Of course, it takes thought and planning and a little strategy; after all, it *is* a job interview! But it can be a positive, if not pleasant, experience and one you can look back on and feel confident about your performance and effort.

For many new job seekers, a job, any job, seems a wonderful thing. But seasoned interview veterans know that the job interview is an important step for both sides—the employer and the candidate—to see what each has to offer and whether there is going to be a "fit" of personalities, work styles, and attitudes. And it is this concept of balance in the interview, that both sides have important parts to play, that holds the key to success in mastering this aspect of the job search strategy.

Try to think of the interview as a conversation between two interested and equal partners. You both have important, even vital, information to deliver and to learn. Of course, there's no denying the employer has some leverage, especially in the initial interview for recruitment or any interview scheduled by the candidate and not the recruiter. That should not prevent the interviewee from seeking to play an equal part in what should be a fair exchange of information. Too often the untutored candidate allows the interview to become one-sided. The employer asks all the questions and the candidate simply responds. The ideal would be for two mutually interested parties to sit down and discuss possibilities for each. This is a *conversation of significance,* and it requires pre-interview preparation, thought about the tone of the interview, and planning of the nature and details of the information to be exchanged.

PREPARING FOR THE INTERVIEW

Most initial interviews are about thirty minutes long. Given the brevity, the information that is exchanged ought to be important. The candidate should be delivering material that the employer cannot discover on the resume and, in turn, the candidate should be learning things about the employer that he or she could not otherwise find out. After all, if you have only thirty minutes, why waste time on information that is already published? The information exchanged is more than just factual, and both sides will learn much from what they see of each other, as well. How the candidate looks, speaks, and acts is important to the employer. The employer's attention to the interview and awareness of the candidate's resume, the setting, and the quality of information presented are important to the candidate.

Just as the employer has every right to be disappointed when a prospect is late for the interview, looks unkempt, and seems ill-prepared to answer fairly standard questions, the candidate may be disappointed with an interviewer who isn't ready for the meeting, hasn't learned the basic resume facts, and is constantly interrupted for telephone calls. In either situation there's good reason to feel let down.

There are many elements to a successful interview, and some of them are not easy to describe or prepare for. Sometimes there is just a chemistry between interviewer and interviewee that brings out the best in both, and a good exchange takes place. But there is much the candidate can do to pave the way for success in terms of his or her resume, personal appearance, goals, and interview strategy—each of which we will discuss. However, none of this preparation is as important as the time and thought the candidate gives to personal self-assessment.

Self-Assessment

Neither a stunning resume nor an expensive, well-tailored suit can compensate for candidates who do not know what they want, where they are going, or why they are interviewing with a particular employer. Self-assessment, the process by which we begin to know and acknowledge our own particular blend of education, experiences, needs, and goals, is not something that can be sorted out the weekend before a major interview. Of all the elements of interview preparation, this one requires the longest lead time and cannot be faked.

Because the time allotted for most interviews is brief, it is all the more important for job candidates to understand and express succinctly why they are there and what they have to offer. This is not a time for undue modesty (or for braggadocio either); it is a time for a compelling, reasoned statement of why you feel that you and this employer might make a good match. It means you have to have thought about your skills, interests, and attributes; related those to your life experiences and your own history of challenges and opportunities; and determined what that indicates about your strengths, preferences, values, and areas needing further development.

A common complaint of employers is that many candidates didn't take advantage of the interview time, didn't seem to know why they were there or what they wanted. When candidates are asked to talk about themselves and their work-related skills and attributes, employers don't want to be faced with shyness or embarrassed laughter; they need to know about you so they can make a fair determination of you and your competition. If you lose the opportunity to make a case for your employability, you can be certain the person ahead of you has or the person after you will, and it will be on the strength of those impressions that the employer will hire.

If you need some assistance with self-assessment issues, refer to Chapter 1. Included are suggested exercises that can be done as needed, such as making up an experiential diary and extracting obvious strengths and weaknesses from past experiences. These simple assignments will help you look at past activities as collections of tasks with accompanying skills and responsibilities. Don't overlook your high school or college career office. Many offer personal counseling on self-assessment issues and may provide testing instruments such as the Myers-Briggs Type Indicator (MBTI), the Harrington-O'Shea Career Decision-Making System (CDM), the Strong Interest Inventory (SII), or any of a wide selection of assessment tools that can help you clarify some of these issues prior to the interview stage of your job search.

The Resume

Resume preparation has been discussed in detail, and some basic examples of various types were provided. In this section we want to concentrate on how best to use your resume in the interview. In most cases the employer will have seen the resume prior to the interview, and, in fact, it may well have been the quality of that resume that secured the interview opportunity.

An interview is a conversation, however, and not an exercise in reading. So, if the employer hasn't seen your resume and you have brought it along to the interview, wait until asked or until the end of the interview to offer it. Otherwise, you may find yourself staring at the back of your resume and simply answering "yes" and "no" to a series of questions drawn from that document.

Sometimes an interviewer is not prepared and does not know or recall the contents of the resume and may use the resume to a greater or lesser degree as a "prompt" during the interview. It is for you to judge what that may indicate about the individual doing the interview or the employer. If your interviewer seems surprised by the scheduled meeting, relies on the resume to an inordinate degree, and seems otherwise unfamiliar with your background, this lack of preparation for the hiring process could well be a symptom of general management disorganization or may simply be the result of poor planning on the part of one individual. It is your responsibility as a potential employee to be aware of these signals and make your decisions accordingly.

. . . .

In any event, it is perfectly acceptable for you to get the conversation back to a more interpersonal style by saying something like, "Mr. Smith, you might be interested in some recent interpreting experience I gained in a volunteer position at our local hospital that is not detailed on my resume. May I tell you about it?" This can return the interview to two people talking to each other, not one reading and the other responding.

. . . .

By all means, bring at least one copy of your resume to the interview. Occasionally, at the close of an interview, an interviewer will express an interest in circulating a resume to several departments, and you could then offer the copy you brought. Sometimes, an interview appointment provides an opportunity to meet others in the organization who may express an interest in you and your background, and it may be helpful to follow up with a copy of your resume. Our best advice, however, is to keep it out of sight until needed or requested.

Appearance

Although many of the absolute rules that once dominated the advice offered to job candidates about appearance have now been moderated significantly, conservative is still the watchword unless you are interviewing in a fashion-related industry. For men, conservative translates into a well-cut dark suit with appropriate tie, hosiery, and dress shirt. A wise strategy for the male job seeker looking for a good but not expensive suit would be to try the men's department of a major department store. They usually carry a good range of sizes, fabrics, and prices; offer professional sales help; provide free tailoring; and have associated departments for putting together a professional look.

For women, there is more latitude. Business suits are still popular, but they have become more feminine in color and styling with a variety of jacket and skirt lengths. In addition to suits, better-quality dresses are now worn in many environments and, with the correct accessories, can be most appropriate. Company literature, professional magazines, the business section of major newspapers, and television interviews can all give clues about what is being worn in different employer environments.

Both men and women need to pay attention to issues such as hair, jewelry, and makeup; these are often what separates the candidate in appearance from the professional workforce. It seems particularly difficult for the young job seeker to give up certain hairstyles, eyeglass fashions, and jewelry habits, yet those can be important to the employer who is concerned with your ability to successfully make the transition into the organization. Candidates often find the best strategy is to dress conservatively until they find employment. Once employed and familiar with the norms within your organization, you can begin to determine a look that you enjoy, works for you, and fits your organization.

Choose clothes that suit your body type, fit well, and flatter you. Feel good about the way you look! The interview day is not the best for a new hairdo, a new pair of shoes, or any other change that will distract you or cause you to be self-conscious. Arrive a bit early to avoid being rushed, and ask the receptionist to direct you to a restroom for any last-minute adjustments of hair and clothes.

Employer Information

Whether your interview is for graduate school admission, an overseas corporate position, or a reporter position with a local newspaper, it is important to know something about the employer or the organization. Keeping in mind that the interview is relatively brief and that you will hopefully have other interviews with other organizations, it is important to keep your research in proportion. If secondary interviews are called for, you will have additional time to do further research. For the first interview, it is helpful to know the organization's mission, goals, size, scope of operations, and so forth. Your research may uncover recent areas of challenge or particular successes that may help to fuel the interview. Use the "What Do They Call the Job You Want?" section of Chapter 3, your library, and your career or guidance office to help you locate this information in the most efficient way possible. Don't be shy in asking advice of these counseling and guidance professionals on how best to spend your preparation time. With some practice, you'll soon learn how much information is enough and which kinds of information are most useful to you.

INTERVIEW CONTENT

We've already discussed how it can help to think of the interview as an important conversation—one that, as with any conversation, you want to find pleasant and interesting and to leave you with a good feeling. But because this conversation is especially important, the information that's exchanged is critical to its success. What do you want them to know about you? What do you need to know about them? What interview technique do you need to particularly pay attention to? How do you want to manage the close of the interview? What steps will follow in the hiring process?

Except for the professional interviewer, most of us find interviewing stressful and anxiety-provoking. Developing a strategy before you begin interviewing will help you relieve some stress and anxiety. One particular strategy that has worked for many and may work for you is interviewing by objective. Before you interview, write down three to five goals you would like to achieve for that interview. They may be technique goals: smile a little more, have a firmer handshake, be sure to ask about the next stage in the interview process before leaving. They may be content-oriented goals: find out about the company's current challenges and opportunities; be sure to speak of your recent research, writing experiences, or foreign travel. Whatever your goals, jot down a few of them as goals for each interview.

Most people find that, in trying to achieve these few goals, their interviewing technique becomes more organized and focused. After the interview, the most common question friends and family ask is "How did it go?" With this technique, you have an indication of whether you met *your* goals for the meeting, not just some vague idea of how it went. Chances are, if you accomplished what you wanted to, it improved the quality of the entire interview. As you continue to interview, you will want to revise your goals to continue improving your interview skills.

Now, add to the concept of the significant conversation the idea of a beginning, a middle, and a closing and you will have two thoughts that will give your interview a distinctive character. Be sure to make your introduction warm and cordial. Say your full name (and if it's a difficult-to-pronounce name, help the interviewer to pronounce it) and make certain you know your interviewer's name and how to pronounce it. Most interviews begin with some "soft talk" about the weather, chat about the candidate's trip to the interview site, or national events. This is done as a courtesy to relax both you and the interviewer, to get you talking, and to generally try to defuse the atmosphere of excessive tension. Try to be yourself, engage in the conversation, and don't try to second-guess the interviewer. This is simply what it appears to be—casual conversation.

Once you and the interviewer move on to exchange more serious information in the middle part of the interview, the two most important concerns become your ability to handle challenging questions and your success at asking meaningful ones. Interviewer questions will probably fall into one of three categories: personal assessment and career direction, academic assessment, and knowledge of the employer. The following are some examples of questions in each category:

Personal Assessment and Career Direction

1. How would you describe yourself?

2. What motivates you to put forth your best effort?

3. In what kind of work environment are you most comfortable?

4. What do you consider to be your greatest strengths and weaknesses?

5. How well do you work under pressure?

6. What qualifications do you have that make you think you will be successful in this career?

7. Will you relocate? What do you feel would be the most difficult aspect of relocating?

8. Are you willing to travel?

9. Why should I hire you?

Academic Assessment

1. Why did you select your college or university?

2. What changes would you make at your alma mater?

3. What led you to choose your major?

4. What subjects did you like best and least? Why?

5. If you could, how would you plan your academic study differently? Why?

6. Describe your most rewarding college experience.

7. How has your college experience prepared you for this career?

8. Do you think that your grades are a good indication of your ability to succeed with this organization?

9. Do you have plans for continued study?

Knowledge of the Employer

1. If you were hiring a graduate of your school for this position, what qualities would you look for?

2. What do you think it takes to be successful in an organization like ours?

3. In what ways do you think you can make a contribution to our organization?

4. Why did you choose to seek a position with this organization?

The interviewer wants a response to each question but is also gauging your enthusiasm, preparedness, and willingness to communicate. In each response you should provide some information about yourself that can be related to the employer's needs. A common mistake is to give too much information. Answer each question completely, but be careful not to run on too long with extensive details or examples.

Questions About Underdeveloped Skills

Most employers interview people who have met some minimum criteria of education and experience. They interview candidates to see who they are, to learn what kind of personality they exhibit, and to get some sense of how this person might fit into the existing organization. It may be that you are asked about skills the employer hopes to find and that you have not documented. Maybe it's grant-writing experience, knowledge of the European political system, or a knowledge of the film world.

To questions about skills and experiences you don't have, answer honestly and forthrightly and try to offer some additional information about skills you do have. For example, perhaps the employer is disappointed you have no grant-writing experience. An honest answer may be as follows:

> No, unfortunately, I was never in a position to acquire those skills. I do understand something of the complexities of the grant-writing process and feel confident that my attention to detail, careful reading skills, and strong writing would make grants a wonderful challenge in a new job. I think I could get up on the learning curve quickly.

The employer hears an honest admission of lack of experience but is reassured by some specific skill details that do relate to grant writing and a confident manner that suggests enthusiasm and interest in a challenge.

For many students, questions about their possible contribution to an employer's organization can prove challenging. Because your education has probably not included specific training for a job, you need to review your academic record and select capabilities you have developed in your major that an employer can appreciate. For example, perhaps you read well and can analyze and condense what you've read into smaller, more focused pieces. That could be valuable. Or maybe you did some serious research and you know you have valuable investigative skills. Your public speaking might be highly developed and you might use visual aids appropriately and effectively. Or maybe your skill at correspondence, memos, and messages is effective. Whatever it is, you must take it out of the academic context and put it into a new, employer-friendly context so your interviewer can best judge how you could help the organization.

Exhibiting knowledge of the organization will, without a doubt, show the interviewer that you are interested enough in the available position to have done some legwork in preparation for the interview. Remember, it is not necessary to know every detail of the organization's history, but rather to have a general knowledge about why it is in business and how the industry is faring.

Sometime during the interview, generally after the midway point, you'll be asked if you have any questions for the interviewer. Your questions will tell the employer much about your attitude and your desire to understand the organization's expectations so you can compare it to your own strengths. The following are some selected questions you might want to ask:

1. What are the main responsibilities of the position?

2. What are the opportunities and challenges associated with this position?

3. Could you outline some possible career paths beginning with this position?

4. How regularly do performance evaluations occur?

5. What is the communication style of the organization? (meetings, memos, and so forth)

6. What would a typical day in this position be like for me?

7. What kinds of opportunities might exist for me to improve my professional skills within the organization?

8. What have been some of the interesting challenges and opportunities your organization has recently faced?

Most interviews draw to a natural closing point, so be careful not to prolong the discussion. At a signal from the interviewer, wind up your presentation, express your appreciation for the opportunity, and be sure to ask what the next stage in the process will be. When can you expect to hear from them?

Will they be conducting second-tier interviews? If you're interested and haven't heard, would they mind a phone call? Be sure to collect a business card with the name and phone number of your interviewer. On your way out, you might have an opportunity to pick up organizational literature you haven't seen before.

With the right preparation—a thorough self-assessment, professional clothing, and employer information—you'll be able to set and achieve the goals you have established for the interview process.

CHAPTER SIX

NETWORKING OR INTERVIEW FOLLOW-UP

uite often there is a considerable time lag between interviewing for a position and being hired or, in the case of the networker, between your phone call or letter to a possible contact and the opportunity of a meeting. This can be frustrating. "Why aren't they contacting me?" "I thought I'd get another interview, but no one has telephoned." "Am I out of the running?" You don't know what is happening.

CONSIDER THE DIFFERING PERSPECTIVES

Of course, there is another perspective—that of the networker or hiring organization. Organizations are complex, with multiple tasks that need to be accomplished each day. Hiring is but one discrete activity that does not occur as frequently as other job assignments. The hiring process might have to take second place to other, more immediate organizational needs. Although it may be very important to you, and it is certainly ultimately significant to the employer, other issues such as fiscal management, planning and product development, employer vacation periods, or financial constraints may prevent an organization or individual within that organization from acting on your employment or your request for information as quickly as you or they would prefer.

USE YOUR COMMUNICATION SKILLS

Good communication is essential here to resolve any anxieties, and the responsibility is on you, the job or information seeker. Too many job seekers

and networkers offer as an excuse that they don't want to "bother" the organization by writing letters or calling. Let us assure you here and now, once
and for all, that if you are troubling an organization by over-communicating,
someone will indicate that situation to you quite clearly. If not, you can
only assume you are a worthwhile prospect and the employer appreciates
being reminded of your availability and interest in them. Let's look at
follow-up practices in both the job interview process and the networking
situation separately.

FOLLOWING UP ON THE EMPLOYMENT INTERVIEW

A brief thank-you note following an interview is an excellent and polite way
to begin a series of follow-up communications with a potential employer with
whom you have interviewed and want to remain in touch. It should be just
that—a thank you for a good meeting. If you failed to mention some fact
or experience during your interview that you think might add to your candidacy, you may use this note to do that. However, this should be essentially
a note whose overall tone is appreciative and, if appropriate, indicative of a
continuing interest in pursuing any opportunity that may exist with that
organization. It is one of the few pieces of business correspondence that may
be handwritten, but always use plain, good quality, standard-size paper.

If, however, at this point you are no longer interested in the employer,
the thank-you note is an appropriate time to indicate that. You are under no
obligation to identify any reason for not continuing to pursue employment
with that organization, but if you are so inclined to indicate your professional
reasons (pursuing other employers more akin to your interests, looking for
greater income production than this employer can provide, a different geographic location than is available), you certainly may. It should not be written with an eye to negotiation for it will not be interpreted as such.

As part of your interview closing, you should have taken the initiative to
establish lines of communication for continuing information about your candidacy. If you asked permission to telephone, wait a week following your
thank-you note, then telephone your contact simply to inquire how things
are progressing on your employment status. The feedback you receive here
should be taken at face value. If your interviewer simply has no information,
he or she will tell you so and indicate whether you should call again and when.
Don't be discouraged if this should continue over some period of time.

If during this time something occurs that you think improves or changes
your candidacy (some new qualification or experience you may have had),
including any offers from other organizations, by all means telephone or write
to inform the employer about this. In the case of an offer from a competing

but less desirable or equally desirable organization, telephone your contact, explain what has happened, express your real interest in the organization, and inquire whether some determination on your employment might be made before you must respond to this other offer. If the organization is truly interested in you, they may be moved to make a decision about your candidacy. Equally possible is the scenario in which they are not yet ready to make a decision and so advise you to take the offer that has been presented. Again, you have no ethical alternative but to deal with the information presented in a straightforward manner.

When accepting other employment, be sure to contact any employers still actively considering you and inform them of your new job. Thank them graciously for their consideration. There are many other job seekers out there just like you who will benefit from having their candidacy improved when others bow out of the race. Who knows, you might at some future time have occasion to interact professionally with one of the organizations with whom you sought employment. How embarrassing to have someone remember you as the candidate who failed to notify them of taking a job elsewhere!

In all of your follow-up communications, keep good notes of whom you spoke with, when you called, and any instructions that were given about return communications. This will prevent any misunderstandings and provide you with good records of what has transpired.

FOLLOWING UP ON THE NETWORK CONTACT

Far more common than the forgotten follow-up after an interview is the situation where a good network contact is allowed to lapse. Good communications are the essence of a network, and follow-up is not so much a matter of courtesy here as it is a necessity. In networking for job information and contacts, you are the active network link. Without you, and without continual contact from you, there is no network. You and your need for employment are often the only shared elements between members of the network. Because network contacts were made regardless of the availability of any particular employment, it is incumbent upon the job seeker, if not simple common sense, that unless you stay in regular communication with the network, you will not be available for consideration should some job become available in the future.

This brings up the issue of responsibility, which is likewise very clear. The job seeker initiates network contacts and is responsible for maintaining those contacts; therefore, the entire responsibility for the network belongs with him or her. This becomes patently obvious if the network is left unattended. It very shortly falls out of existence because it cannot survive without careful attention by the networker.

A variety of ways are open to you to keep the lines of communication open and to attempt to interest the network in you as a possible employee. You are limited only by your own enthusiasm for members of the network and your creativity. However, you as a networker are well advised to keep good records of whom you have met and contacted in each organization. Be sure to send thank-you notes to anyone who has spent any time with you, be it an E-mail message containing information or advice, a quick tour of a department, or a sit-down informational interview. All of these communications should, in addition to their ostensible reason, add some information about you and your particular combination of strengths and attributes.

You can contact your network at any time to convey continued interest, to comment on some recent article you came across concerning an organization, to add information about your training or changes in your qualifications, to ask advice or seek guidance in your job search, or to request referrals to other possible network opportunities. Sometimes just a simple note to network members reminding them of your job search, indicating that you have been using their advice, and noting that you are still actively pursuing leads and hope to continue to interact with them is enough to keep communications alive.

The Internet has opened up the world of networking. You may be able to find networkers who graduated from your high school or from the college you're attending, who live in a geographic region where you hope to work, or who are employed in a given industry. The Internet makes it easy to reach out to many people, but don't let this perceived ease lull you into complacency. Internet networking demands the same level of preparation as the more traditional forms of networking do.

Because networks have been abused in the past, it's important that your conduct be above reproach. Networks are exploratory options, they are not backdoor access to employers. The network works best for someone who is exploring a new industry or making a transition into a new area of employment and who needs to find information or to alert people to his or her search activity. Always be candid and direct with contacts in expressing the purpose of your E-mail, call, or letter and your interest in their help or information about their organization. In follow-up contacts keep the tone professional and direct. Your honesty will be appreciated, and people will respond as best they can if your qualifications appear to meet their forthcoming needs. The network does not owe you anything, and that tone should be clear to each person you meet.

FEEDBACK FROM FOLLOW-UPS

A network contact may prove to be miscalculated. Perhaps you were referred to someone and it became clear that your goals and his or her particular needs did not make a good match. Or the network contact may simply not be in a position to provide you with the information you are seeking. Or in some unfortunate situations, the contact may become annoyed by being contacted for this purpose. In such a situation, many job seekers simply say "Thank you" and move on.

If the contact is simply not the right connection, but the individual you are speaking with is not annoyed by the call, it might be a better tactic to express regret that the contact was misplaced and then tell the person what you are seeking and ask for his or her advice or possible suggestions as to a next step. The more people who are aware you are seeking employment, the better your chances of connecting, and that is the purpose of a network. Most people in a profession have excellent knowledge of their field and varying amounts of expertise on areas near to or tangent to their own. Use their expertise and seek some guidance before you dissolve the contact. You may be pleasantly surprised.

Occasionally, networkers will express the feeling that they have done as much as they can or provided all the information that is available to them. This may be a cue that they would like to be released from your network. Be alert to such attempts to terminate, graciously thank the individual by letter, and move on in your network development. A network is always changing, adding, and losing members, and you want the network to be composed only of those who are actively interested in supporting you.

A FINAL POINT ON NETWORKING FOR FOREIGN LANGUAGE MAJORS

. . . .

In any of the fields a foreign language major might consider as a potential career path, it's important to remember that networkers and interviewers will be critically evaluating all of your written and oral communications. As a language major, this should be gratifying, but at the same time it should serve to emphasize the importance of the quality of your presentations to people in a position to help you in your job search.

. . . .

CHAPTER SEVEN

JOB OFFER CONSIDERATIONS

*f*or many recent college graduates, the thrill of their first job and, for some, the most substantial regular income they have ever earned seems an excess of good fortune coming at once. To question that first income or to be critical in any way of the conditions of employment at the time of the initial offer seems like looking a gift horse in the mouth. It doesn't seem to occur to many new hires even to attempt to negotiate any aspect of their first job. And, as many employers who deal with entry-level jobs for recent college graduates will readily confirm, the reality is that there simply isn't much movement in salary available to these new college recruits. The entry-level hire generally does not have an employment track record on a professional level to provide any leverage for negotiation. Real negotiations on salary, benefits, retirement provisions, and so forth, come to those with significant employment records at higher income levels.

Of course, the job offer is more than just money. It can be composed of geographic assignment, duties and responsibilities, training, benefits, health and medical insurance, educational assistance, car allowance or company vehicle, and a host of other items. All of this is generally detailed in the formal letter that presents the final job offer. In most cases this is a follow-up to a personal phone call from the employer representative who has been principally responsible for your hiring process.

That initial telephone offer is certainly binding as a verbal agreement, but most firms follow up with a detailed letter outlining the most significant parts of your employment contract. You may certainly choose to respond immediately at the time of the telephone offer (which would be considered a binding oral contract), but you will also be required to formally answer the letter of offer with a letter of acceptance, restating the salient elements of the employer's description of your position, salary, and benefits. This ensures that both parties are clear on the terms and conditions of employment and remuneration and any other outstanding aspects of the job offer.

IS THIS THE JOB YOU WANT?

Most new employees will write this letter of acceptance back, glad to be in the position to accept employment. If you've worked hard to get the offer and the job market is tight, other offers may not be in sight, so you will say, "Yes, I accept!" What is important here is that the job offer you accept be one that does fit your particular needs, values, and interests as you've outlined them in your self-assessment process. Moreover, it should be a job that will not only use your skills and education, but also challenge you to develop new skills and talents.

Jobs are sometimes accepted too hastily, for the wrong reasons, and without proper scrutiny by the applicant. For example, an individual might readily accept a sales job only to find the continual rejection by potential clients unendurable. An office worker might realize within weeks the constraints of a desk job and yearn for more activity. Employment is an important part of our lives. It is, for most of our adult lives, our most continuous productive activity. We want to make good choices based on the right criteria.

If you have a low tolerance for risk, a job based on commission will certainly be very anxiety-provoking. If being near your family is important, issues of relocation could present a decision crisis for you. If you're an adventurous person, a job with frequent travel would provide needed excitement and be very desirable. The importance of income, the need to continue your education, your personal health situation—all of these have an impact on whether the job you are considering will ultimately meet your needs. Unless you've spent some time understanding and thinking about these issues, it will be difficult to evaluate offers you do receive.

More important, if you make a decision that you cannot tolerate and feel you must leave that job, you will then have both unemployment and self-esteem issues to contend with. These will combine to make the next job search tough going, indeed. So make your acceptance a carefully considered decision.

NEGOTIATING YOUR OFFER

It may be that there is some aspect of your job offer that is not particularly attractive to you. Perhaps there is no relocation allotment to help you move your possessions, and this presents some financial hardship for you. It may be that the medical and health insurance is less than you had hoped. Your initial assignment may be different from what you expected, either in its location or in the duties and responsibilities that comprise it. Or it may simply be that the salary is less than you anticipated. Other considerations may be your official starting date of employment, vacation time, evening hours, dates of training programs or schools, and other concerns.

If you are considering not accepting the job because of some item or items in the job offer "package" that do not meet your needs, you should know that most employers emphatically wish that you would bring that issue to their attention. It may be that the employer can alter it to make the offer more agreeable for you. In some cases it cannot be changed. In any event the employer would generally like to have the opportunity to try to remedy a difficulty rather than risk losing a good potential employee over an issue that might have been resolved. After all, they have spent time and funds in securing your services, and they certainly deserve an opportunity to resolve any possible differences.

Honesty is the best approach in discussing any objections or uneasiness you might have over the employer's offer. Having received your formal offer in writing, contact your employer representative and indicate your particular dissatisfaction in a straightforward manner. For example, you might explain that, while very interested in being employed by this organization, the salary (or any other benefit) is less than you have determined you require. State the terms you do need, and listen to the response. You may be asked to put this in writing, or you may be asked to hold off until the firm can decide on a response. If you are dealing with a senior representative of the organization, one who has been involved in hiring for some time, you may get an immediate response or a solid indication of possible outcomes.

Perhaps the issue is one of relocation. Your initial assignment is in the Midwest, and because you had indicated a strong West Coast preference, you are surprised at the actual assignment. You might simply indicate that, while you understand the need for the company to assign you based on its needs, you are disappointed and had hoped to be placed on the West Coast. You could inquire if that were still possible and, if not, would it be reasonable to expect a West Coast relocation in the future.

If your request is presented in a reasonable way, most employers will not see this as jeopardizing your offer. If they can agree to your proposal, they will. If not, they will simply tell you so, and you may choose to continue your candidacy with them or remove yourself from consideration as a possible employee. The choice will be up to you.

Some firms will adjust benefits within their parameters to meet the candidate's need if at all possible. If a candidate requires a relocation cost allowance, he or she may be asked to forgo tuition benefits for the first year to accomplish this adjustment. An increase in life insurance may be adjusted by some other benefit trade-off; perhaps a family dental plan is not needed. In these decisions you are called upon, sometimes under time pressure, to know how you value these issues and how important each is to you.

Many employers find they are more comfortable negotiating for candidates who have unique qualifications or who bring especially needed expertise to the organization. Employers hiring large numbers of entry-level college graduates may be far more reluctant to accommodate any changes in offer conditions. They are well supplied with candidates with similar education and experience, so that if rejected by one candidate, they can draw new candidates from an ample labor pool.

COMPARING OFFERS

The conditions of the economy, the job seekers' academic major and particular geographic job market, and their own needs and demands for certain employment conditions may not provide more than one job offer at a time. Some job seekers may feel that no reasonable offer should go unaccepted for the simple fear there won't be another.

In a tough job market, or if the job you seek is not widely available, or when your job search goes on too long and becomes difficult to sustain financially and emotionally, it may be necessary to accept an offer. The alternative is continued unemployment. Even here, when you feel you don't have a choice, you can at least understand that in accepting this particular offer, there may be limitations and conditions you don't appreciate. At the time of acceptance, there were no other alternatives, but the new employee can begin to use that position to gain the experience and talent to move toward a more attractive position.

Sometimes, however, more than one offer is received at one time, and the candidate has the luxury of choice. If the job seeker knows what he or she wants and has done the necessary self-assessment honestly and thoroughly, it may be clear that one of the offers conforms more closely to those expressed wants and needs.

However, if, as so often happens, the offers are similar in terms of conditions and salary, the question then becomes which organization might provide the necessary climate, opportunities, and advantages for your professional development and growth. This is the time when solid employer research and astute questioning during the interviews really pays off. How much did you learn about the employer through your own research and skillful questioning? When the interviewer asked during the interview "Do you have any questions?" did you ask the kinds of questions that would help resolve a choice between one organization and another? Just as an employer must decide among numerous applicants, so must the applicant learn to assess the potential employer. Both are partners in the job search.

RENEGING ON AN OFFER

An especially disturbing occurrence for employers and career counseling professionals is when a job seeker formally (either verbally or by written contract) accepts employment with one organization and later reneges on the agreement and goes with another employer.

There are all kinds of rationalizations offered for this unethical behavior. None of them satisfies. The sad irony is that what the job seeker is willing to do to the employer—make a promise and then break it—he or she would be outraged to have done to them—have the job offer pulled. It is a very bad way to begin a career. It suggests the individual has not taken the time to do the necessary self-assessment and self-awareness exercises to think and judge critically. The new offer taken may, in fact, be no better or worse than the one refused. Job candidates should be aware that there have been incidents of legal action following job candidates' reneging on an offer. This adds a very sour note to what should be a harmonious beginning of a lifelong adventure.

CHAPTER EIGHT

THE GRADUATE SCHOOL CHOICE

he reasons for continuing one's education in graduate school can be as varied and unique as the individuals electing this course of action. Many continue their studies at an advanced level because they simply find it difficult to end the educational process. They love what they are learning and want to learn more and continue their academic exploration.

....

Maybe you had a practicum experience or internship in your foreign language program that intrigued you about the possibilities of teaching. You saw firsthand the transforming power of a teacher and the classroom, and maybe you felt strongly that you could make a contribution. Or perhaps you've traveled and want more exposure, in an academic sense, to countries where the language you've studied is lived and spoken. Some foreign language majors have enjoyed their academic work but learning the language wasn't enough. They want to learn more about the culture, history, and social and political movements. Graduate school can offer that.

Others go to graduate school for purely practical reasons; they have examined employment prospects in their field of study, and all indications are that a graduate degree is requisite. Certainly, in foreign languages, a graduate degree is required for all full-time teaching positions. There are still many community and technical college systems that will hire full-time faculty with a master's degree, but these schools seldom offer much in foreign language course work.

You may not want to teach, and yet you still want to devote some advance study to your language of choice, perhaps combined with studies of literature, art, music, or any other facet of culture. You might then want to begin by reviewing jobs in the areas mentioned and their advanced degree requirements. Alumni working in college teaching, museum studies, government, business, publishing, or other areas where advanced degree foreign language studies are used can provide wonderful insights to guide your decision making. Ask at your career office for some alumni names and give those people a telephone call or send them an E-mail. Prepare some questions on specific job prospects in their field at each degree level. A thorough examination of the marketplace and talking to employers and professionals will give you a sense of the scope of employment for a bachelor's degree, master's degree, or doctorate.

· ·

CONSIDER YOUR MOTIVES

The answer to the question of "Why graduate school?" is a personal one for each applicant. Nevertheless, it is important to consider your motives carefully. Graduate school involves additional time out of the employment market, a high degree of critical evaluation, significant autonomy as you pursue your studies, and considerable financial expenditure. For some students in doctoral programs, there may be additional life choice issues, such as relationships, marriage, and parenthood, that may present real challenges while in a program of study. You would be well advised to consider the following questions as you think about your decision to continue your studies.

Are You Postponing Some Tough Decisions by Going to School?

Graduate school is not a place to go to avoid life's problems. There is intense competition for graduate school slots and for the fellowships, scholarships, and financial aid available. This competition means extensive interviewing, resume submission, and essay writing that rivals corporate recruitment. Likewise, the graduate school process is a mentored one in which faculty stay aware of and involved in the academic progress of their students and continually challenge the quality of their work. Many graduate students are called upon to participate in teaching and professional writing and research as well.

In other words, this is no place to hide from the spotlight. Graduate students work very hard and much is demanded of them individually. If you elect to go to graduate school to avoid the stresses and strains of the "real world," you will find no safe place in higher academics. Vivid accounts, both fictional and nonfictional, have depicted quite accurately the personal and professional demands of graduate school work.

The selection of graduate studies as a career option should be a positive choice—something you *want* to do. It shouldn't be selected as an escape from other, less attractive or more challenging options, nor should it be selected as the option of last resort (i.e., "I can't do anything else; I'd better just stay in school."). If you're in some doubt about the strength of your reasoning about continuing in school, discuss the issues with a career counselor. Together you can clarify your reasoning, and you'll get some sound feedback on what you're about to undertake.

On the other hand, staying on in graduate school because of a particularly poor employment market and a lack of jobs at entry-level positions has proven to be an effective "stalling" strategy. If you can afford it, pursuing a graduate degree immediately after your undergraduate education gives you a year or two to "wait out" a difficult economic climate while at the same time acquiring a potentially valuable credential.

Have You Done Some "Hands-On" Reality Testing?

There are experiential options available to give some reality to your decision-making process about graduate school. Internships or work in the field can give you a good idea about employment demands, conditions, and atmosphere.

••

Perhaps as a Spanish major, you're considering a graduate program in Spanish. A summer job or internship that puts you in contact with professionals who are working in a field that interests you will help you to further define your graduate school objectives. Even with the experience of only one employment setting, you have a stronger concept of the pace of the job, interaction with colleagues, subject matter, opportunities for personal development, and the amount of paperwork required. Talking to people and asking questions is invaluable as an exercise to help you better understand the objective of your graduate study.

For foreign language majors, the opportunity to do this kind of reality testing is invaluable. It demonstrates far more authoritatively than any other method what your real-world skills are, how they can be put to use, and what aspects of your academic preparation you rely on. It's evident in today's employment market that language skills are valued. But the job candidate has to bring *more* than that. Internships, practica, and co-op experiences speed that process up and prevent the frustrating and expensive process of investigation many graduates begin only after graduation.

....

Do You Need an Advanced Degree to Work in Your Field?

Certainly there are fields such as law, psychiatry, medicine, and college teaching that demand advanced degrees. Is the field of employment you're considering one that also puts a premium on an advanced degree? You may be surprised. Read job ads on the Internet and in a number of major Sunday newspapers for positions you would enjoy. How many of those require an advanced degree?

Retailing, for example, has always put a premium on what people can do, rather than how much education they have had. Successful people in retailing come from all academic preparations. A Ph.D. in your field may bring only more prestige to a job, but it may not bring a more senior position or better pay. In fact, it may disqualify you for some jobs because an employer might believe you will be unhappy to be overqualified for a particular position. Or your motives in applying for the work may be misconstrued, and the employer might think you will only be working at this level until something better comes along. None of this may be true for you, but it comes about because you are working outside of the usual territory for that degree level.

When economic times are especially difficult, we tend to see stories featured about individuals with advanced degrees doing what is considered unsuitable work, such as the Ph.D. in French driving a cab or the Ph.D. in chemistry waiting tables. Actually, this is not particularly surprising when you consider that as your degree level advances, the job market narrows appreciably. At any one time, regardless of economic circumstances, there are only so many jobs for your particular level of expertise. If you cannot find employment for your advanced degree level, chances are you will be considered suspect for many other kinds of employment and may be forced into temporary work far removed from your original intention.

Before making an important decision such as graduate study, learn your options and carefully consider what you want to do with your advanced degree. Ask yourself whether it is reasonable to think you can achieve your goals. Will there be jobs when you graduate? Where will they be? What will they pay? How competitive will the market be at that time, based on current predictions?

If you're uncertain about the degree requirements for the fields you're interested in, you should check a publication such as the U.S. Department of Labor's *Occupational Outlook Handbook* (www.bls.gov). Each entry has a section on training and other qualifications that will indicate clearly what the minimum educational requirement is for employment, what degree is the standard, and what employment may be possible without the required credential.

For example, for physicists and astronomers a doctoral degree in physics or a closely related field is essential. Certainly this is the degree of choice in academic institutions. However, the *Occupational Outlook Handbook* also indicates what kinds of employment may be available to individuals holding a master's or even a bachelor's degree in physics.

Have You Compared Your Expectations of What Graduate School Will Do for You with What It Has Done for Alumni of the Program You're Considering?

Most colleges and universities perform some kind of postgraduate survey of their students to ascertain where they are employed, what additional education they have received, and what levels of salary they are enjoying. Ask to see this information either from the university you are considering applying to or from your own alma mater, especially if it has a similar graduate program. Such surveys often reveal surprises about occupational decisions, salaries, and work satisfaction. This information may affect your decision.

The value of self-assessment (the process of examining and making decisions about your own hierarchy of values and goals) is especially important in this process of analyzing the desirability of possible career paths involving graduate education. Sometimes a job requiring advanced education seems to hold real promise but is disappointing in salary potential or number of opportunities available. Certainly it is better to research this information before embarking on a program of graduate studies. It may not change your mind about your decision, but by becoming better informed about your choice, you become better prepared for your future.

Have You Talked with People in Your Field to Explore What You Might Be Doing After Graduate School?

In pursuing your undergraduate degree, you will have come into contact with many individuals trained in the field you are considering. You might also have the opportunity to attend professional conferences, workshops, seminars, and job fairs where you can expand your network of contacts. Talk to them all! Find out about their individual career paths, discuss your own plans and hopes, get their feedback on the reality of your expectations, and heed their advice about your prospects. Each will have a unique tale to tell, and each will bring a different perspective on the current marketplace for the credentials you are seeking. Talking to enough people will make you an expert on what's out there.

Are You Excited by the Idea of Studying the Particular Field You Have in Mind?

This question may be the most important one of all. If you are going to spend several years in advanced study, perhaps engendering some debt or postponing some lifestyle decisions for an advanced degree, you simply ought to enjoy what you're doing. Examine your work in the discipline so far. Has it been fun? Have you found yourself exploring various paths of thought? Do you read in your area for fun? Do you enjoy talking about it, thinking about it, and sharing it with others? Advanced degrees often are the beginning of a lifetime's involvement with a particular subject. Choose carefully a field that will hold your interest and your enthusiasm.

It is fairly obvious by now that we think you should give some careful thought to your decision and take some action. If nothing else, do the following:

- Talk and question (remember to listen!)

- Reality test

- Soul-search by yourself or with a person you trust

FINDING THE RIGHT PROGRAM FOR YOU: SOME CONSIDERATIONS

There are several important factors in coming to a sound decision about the right graduate program for you. You'll want to begin by locating institutions that offer appropriate programs, examining each of these programs and their requirements, undertaking the application process by reviewing catalogs and obtaining application materials, visiting campuses if possible, arranging for letters of recommendation, writing your application statement, and, finally, following up on your applications.

Locate Institutions with Appropriate Programs

Once you decide on a particular advanced degree, it's important to develop a list of schools offering such a degree program. Perhaps the best source of graduate program information is Peterson's. Their website (www.petersons .com) and their printed *Guides to Graduate Study* allow you to search for information by institution name, location, or academic area. The website also allows you to do a keyword search. Use their website and guides to build your list. In addition, you may want to consult the College Board's *Index of Majors and Graduate Degrees,* which will help you find graduate programs offering the degree you seek. It is indexed by academic major and then categorized by state.

Now, this may be a considerable list. You may want to narrow the choices down further by a number of criteria: tuition, availability of financial aid, public versus private institutions, United States versus international institutions, size of student body, size of faculty, application fee, and geographic location. This is only a partial list; you will have your own important considerations. Perhaps you are an avid scuba diver and you find it unrealistic to think you could pursue graduate study for a number of years without being able to ocean dive from time to time. Good! That's a decision and it's honest. Now, how far from the ocean is too far, and what schools meet your other needs? In any case, and according to your own criteria, begin to build a reasonable list of graduate schools that you are willing to spend time investigating.

Examine the Degree Programs and Their Requirements

Once you've determined the criteria by which you want to develop a list of graduate schools, you can begin to examine the degree program requirements, faculty composition, and institutional research orientation. Again, using resources such as Peterson's website or guides can reveal an amazingly rich level of material by which to judge your possible selections.

In addition to degree programs and degree requirements, entries will include information about application fees, entrance test requirements, tuition, percentage of applicants accepted, numbers of applicants receiving financial aid, gender breakdown of students, numbers of full- and part-time faculty, and often gender breakdown of faculty as well. Numbers graduating in each program and research orientations of departments are also included in some entries. There is information on graduate housing; student services; and library, research, and computer facilities. A contact person, phone number, and address are also standard pieces of information in these listings.

It can be helpful to draw up a chart and enter relevant information about each school you are considering in order to have a ready reference on points of information that are important to you.

Undertake the Application Process

Program Information. Once you've decided on a selection of schools, obtain program information and applications. Nearly every school has a website that contains most of the detailed information you need to narrow your choices. In addition, applications can be printed from the site. If, however, you don't want to print out lots of information, you can request that a copy of the catalog and application materials be sent to you.

When you have your information in hand, give it all a careful reading and make notes of issues you might want to discuss via E-mail, on the telephone, or in a personal interview.

. . . .

If you are interested in graduate work in Spanish and Portuguese, for example, in addition to graduate courses in the languages, are there additional courses in film, rapid reading and translation, Hispanic language and culture, Caribbean identities/societies, Spanish literature and culture's golden age, history of the Spanish language, and others?

. . . .

What is the ratio of faculty to the required number of courses for your degree? How often will you encounter the same faculty member as an instructor?

If, for example, your program offers a practicum or off-campus experience, who arranges this? Does the graduate school select a site and place you there, or is it your responsibility? What are the professional affiliations of the faculty? Does the program merit any outside professional endorsement or accreditation?

Critically evaluate the catalogs of each of the programs you are considering. List any questions you have and ask current or former teachers and colleagues for their impressions as well.

The Application. Preview each application thoroughly to determine what you need to provide in the way of letters of recommendation, transcripts from undergraduate schools or any previous graduate work, and personal essays that may be required. Make a notation for each application of what you need to complete that document.

Additionally, you'll want to determine entrance testing requirements for each institution and immediately arrange to register for appropriate tests. Information can be obtained from associated websites, including www.ets.org (GRE, GMAT, TOEFL, PRAXIS, SLS, Higher Education Assessment), www.lsat.org (LSAT), and www.tpcweb.com/mat (MAT). Your college career office should also be able to provide you with advice and additional information.

Visit the Campus if Possible

If time and finances allow, a visit, interview, and tour can help make your decision easier. You can develop a sense of the student body, meet some of the faculty, and hear up-to-date information on resources and the curriculum. You will have a brief opportunity to "try out" the surroundings to see if they fit your needs. After all, it will be home for a while. If a visit is not possible but you have questions, don't hesitate to call and speak with the dean of the graduate school. Most are more than happy to talk to candidates and want them to have the answers they seek. Graduate school admission is a very personal and individual process.

Arrange for Letters of Recommendation

This is also the time to begin to assemble a group of individuals who will support your candidacy as a graduate student by writing letters of recommendation or completing recommendation forms. Some schools will ask you to provide letters of recommendation to be included with your application or sent directly to the school by the recommender. Other graduate programs will provide a recommendation form that must be completed by the recommender. These graduate school forms vary greatly in the amount of space provided for a written recommendation. So that you can use letters as you need to, ask your recommenders to address their letters "To Whom It May Concern," unless one of your recommenders has a particular connection to one of your graduate schools or knows an official at the school.

Choose recommenders who can speak authoritatively about the criteria important to selection officials at your graduate school. In other words, choose recommenders who can write about your grasp of the literature in your field of study, your ability to write and speak effectively, your class performance, and demonstrated interest in the field outside of class. Other characteristics that graduate schools are interested in assessing include your emotional maturity, leadership ability, breadth of general knowledge, intellectual ability, motivation, perseverance, and ability to engage in independent inquiry.

When requesting recommendations, it's especially helpful to put the request in writing. Explain your graduate school intentions and express some of your thoughts about graduate school and your appreciation for their support. Don't be shy about "prompting" your recommenders with some suggestions of what you would appreciate being included in their comments. Most recommenders will find this direction helpful and will want to produce a statement of support that you can both stand behind. Consequently, if your interaction with one recommender was especially focused on research projects, he or she might be best able to speak of those skills and your critical thinking ability. Another recommender may have good comments to make about your public presentation skills.

Give your recommenders plenty of lead time in which to complete your recommendation, and set a date by which they should respond. If they fail to meet your deadline, be prepared to make a polite call or visit to inquire if they need more information or if there is anything you can do to move the process along.

Whether or not you are providing a graduate school form or asking for an original letter to be mailed, be sure to provide an envelope and postage if the recommender must mail the form or letter directly to the graduate school.

Each recommendation you request should provide a different piece of information about you for the selection committee. It might be pleasant for letters of recommendation to say that you are a fine, upstanding individual, but a selection committee for graduate school will require specific information. Each recommender has had a unique relationship with you, and their letters should reflect that. Think of each letter as helping to build a more complete portrait of you as a potential graduate student.

Write Your Application Statement

....

For a foreign language major, this should be an exciting and challenging assignment and one you should be able

to complete successfully. Certainly, any required essays on a graduate application for foreign languages will weigh heavily in the decision process of the graduate school admissions committee.

....

An excellent source to help in thinking about writing this essay is *How to Write a Winning Personal Statement for Graduate and Professional School,* by Richard J. Stelzer. It has been written from the perspective of what graduate school selection committees are looking for when they read these essays. It provides helpful tips to keep your essay targeted on the kinds of issues and criteria that are important to selection committees and that provide them with the kind of information they can best utilize in making their decision.

Follow Up on Your Applications

After you have finished each application and mailed it along with your transcript requests and letters of recommendation, be sure to follow up on the progress of your file. For example, call the graduate school administrative staff to see whether your transcripts have arrived. If the school required your recommenders to fill out a specific recommendation form that had to be mailed directly to the school, you will want to ensure that they have all arrived in good time for the processing of your application. It is your responsibility to make certain that all required information is received by the institution.

RESEARCHING FINANCIAL AID
SOURCES, SCHOLARSHIPS, AND FELLOWSHIPS

Financial aid information is available from each graduate school. You may be eligible for federal, state, and/or institutional support. There are lengthy forms to complete, and some of these will vary by school, type of school (public versus private), and state. Be sure to note the deadline dates on each form.

There are many excellent resources available to help you explore all of your financial aid options. Visit your college career office or local public library to find out about the range of materials available. Two excellent resources are Peterson's website (www.petersons.com) and its book *Grants for Graduate Students.* Another good reference is the Foundation Center's *Foundation Grants to Individuals.* These types of resources generally contain information that can be accessed by indexes including field of study, specific eligibility requirements, administering agency, and geographic focus.

EVALUATING ACCEPTANCES

If you apply to and are accepted at more than one school, it is time to return to your initial research and self-assessment to evaluate your options and select the program that will best help you achieve the goals you set for pursuing graduate study. You'll want to choose a program that will allow you to complete your studies in a timely and cost-effective way. This may be a good time to get additional feedback from professors and career professionals who are familiar with your interests and plans. Ultimately, the decision is yours, so be sure you get answers to all the questions you can think of.

SOME NOTES ABOUT REJECTION

Each graduate school is searching for applicants who appear to have the qualifications necessary to succeed in its program. Applications are evaluated on a combination of undergraduate grade point average, strength of letters of recommendation, standardized test scores, and personal statements written for the application.

A carelessly completed application is one reason many applicants are denied admission to a graduate program. To avoid this type of needless rejection, be sure to carefully and completely answer all appropriate questions on the application form, focus your personal statement given the instructions provided, and submit your materials well in advance of the deadline. Remember that your test scores and recommendations are considered a part of your application, so they must also be received by the deadline.

If you are rejected by a school that especially interests you, you may want to contact the dean of graduate studies to discuss the strengths and weaknesses of your application. Information provided by the dean will be useful in reapplying to the program later on or applying to other, similar programs.

PART TWO

THE CAREER PATHS

Language is civilization itself.
—THOMAS MANN

CHAPTER NINE

INTRODUCTION TO THE FOREIGN LANGUAGE CAREER PATHS

oreign language study is wonderful preparation for any number of careers. With its emphasis on communication and skills in writing, speaking, reading, and simply making connections between people, knowledge of a foreign language is also an education in your own language. This knowledge will serve the graduate well in any sector of the employment market.

As you examine several career paths possible with a foreign language degree, keep in mind that these are only representative career paths, and typical ones at that. A Spanish major can become an accountant, and someone with a graduate degree in Romance languages can manage an organization. An academic degree is only one small part of what we have to offer an employer; it represents only a fraction of our interests and experience. We bring our life experiences and our paid and unpaid work history as well as our academic degree to the employment market.

But prospective employers can make some assumptions about foreign language graduates: they are skilled communicators, and they are interested in other cultures. In addition, employers could logically assume that students of foreign language are flexible, open to change, and tolerant of diversity. Even without having met you, an employer reading your resume and seeing your degree in a foreign language could easily make these assumptions about you as a person and a potential worker.

ARE LANGUAGE SKILLS PRACTICAL?

The practical applications of knowing another language are obvious. When you travel, your experiences, meetings with native speakers, and cultural understanding do not have to be filtered through the medium of translation. Americans learning a language often say, "But what does this mean in English?" They seem to be suggesting that French or German or Spanish or any other language is simply English encoded in some other system. French is French and not just a code for English. There are countless expressions, moods, idiomatic phrases, proverbs, and jokes in any language that simply cannot be translated. One must appreciate them in the original. To translate them is to receive out-of-focus images of the original.

If you know a foreign language, you do not have to resort to transcribing everything back into English. When traveling, you can avoid the cultural filtering process that results in relating everything new to something already within your cultural context. For many, a *croissant* becomes a "roll" or a "breakfast roll," neither of which English translations even begins to approximate what is suggested by the French. If we use the translation "crescent roll," which does suggest something of the French word, we unfortunately bring to mind an American product that couldn't be further in appearance or taste from the French original.

There are native speakers in every country who do not speak English. Without a foreign language, you cannot easily approach these individuals to hear their stories, their words. Using an intermediary to translate is a very different experience. It is a filtering process of another kind that leaves both parties wondering how their words have been translated and whether the meanings being conveyed are accurate. This certainly gets in the way of honest and direct communication.

Without knowledge of a foreign language, published materials in the foreign language also remain inaccessible. The detail and information they provide may be translated in some superficial way, but the original information in its completeness may be available only to those who know the language.

HOW WILL YOU CHOOSE TO USE YOUR LANGUAGE SKILLS?

Language can be used either as a primary or an auxiliary skill in a career. If a foreign language is a primary skill in your job, you are using the language every day; you could not do your job without your foreign language knowledge. If your language skill use is auxiliary, you are using other skills (e.g., managerial, accounting, writing, computer skills, media technology) along-side your language use, or your foreign language use on the job is intermittent.

After graduation, that first job or decision to attend graduate school will have much to do with whether you desire to place your language skills in a dominant or a peripheral role. If you decide you want to teach German on the college level, you will have to pursue a doctorate in German and will probably want to spend some extended time in German-speaking countries to improve your fluency, idiomatic grasp of the language, and all of the cultural nuances available only to residents. Your language skill will be a primary and defining attribute in your job search.

If, on the other hand, you enjoy your German language skills but also want to try your hand in the business world, you may enter the job market with an organization that does business with companies in Germany. Even if most of the work is conducted in English, there will be ample opportunity to use your German. There will be fax transmissions, telephone calls, and pieces of correspondence in German that will require your expertise.

Or you might find an American firm operating in Germany that has both American and German workers and looks for some appreciation and understanding of both languages in each candidate considered for existing positions. In situations such as this, there will certainly be business visits back and forth in which your knowledge of both cultures could be invaluable. You might begin as an import/export expediter whose job is primarily administrative, but you will use your German language to help with correspondence and some telephone work. Knowledge of German isn't absolutely essential to the job, but it makes you more attractive to your employer.

Occasionally, students with language degrees are surprised and disappointed when business employers hire them on the basis of their language skills but do not necessarily rely on those talents once they are employed. An executive of Eli Lilly, a pharmaceutical manufacturer in Indianapolis, stated the situation as follows:

> Employees with foreign language skills are valued for their understanding of that culture and cultural nuances and their sensitivity to those. If we need translation, either simultaneously verbal or written, we can subcontract that work to specialists, but we need folks within our organization who understand and appreciate other cultures, and that is acquired through language training.

WHERE ELSE CAN YOU WORK?

A random search through the popular website www.careermosaic.com presented several opportunities requiring primary or secondary use of a foreign language. Note the variety, location, emphasis, or lack of emphasis on language skills, breadth of employers (both private and governmental), and salaries, where indicated:

International Business Consultant. All levels for transfer pricing practice, in-depth analysis of client operations, advising clients, domestic/international manufacturing, R&D, marketing, and financial performance. Some travel is required. Bachelor's degree required and foreign language proficiency a plus. Contact:

Customer Service Professional–English Speaking and Bilingual (Spanish). Starting salary of $23,600–$29,400. Primary telephone contact with customers and physicians for health insurance questions. Contact by E-mail or fax at:

Foreign Language Specialist. U.S. Navy. Translating, interpreting, transcribing, and analyzing foreign language communications. Special requirements: Pass proficiency exam in Arabic, Chinese, French, Hebrew, Korean, Persian, Russian, Spanish, or Vietnamese; be a U.S. citizen and eligible for security clearance; and be younger than thirty-four. Contact:

Medical Translator/Library Technician. Translating various medical documents from English to Spanish and vice versa. Bachelor's degree in a health-related field. Management experience and work in premedicine, psychology, health-care admission preferred. Conact:

Editor/Translator. Excellent communication skills, both English/Spanish or English/Portuguese. Knowledge of MS Word and Internet usage. Contact:

Localization/Globalization Software Test–Japanese, Chinese, German, French, and/or Spanish. Executes prewritten manual test scripts and reports anomalies when found. Four years' work-related experience required. Experience in installation of UNIX version, C++, scripting languages, and some JAVA. Contact:

WHERE CAN YOUR DEGREE TAKE YOU?

Although we speak about careers we want to have, and there are career services offices on college campuses, the word *career* is best applied to a history of work. If you have a job in a retail establishment, you wouldn't be likely to call it a career. But if after ten years you are still working at the retail business in a managerial role, you could justifiably call that a career. In our lifetime progression from job to job, position to position, skill to skill, it is sometimes difficult to separate ourselves from our immediate concerns of job and home in order to view our life and our work from an objective, long-term perspective. Most of us find it hard to be objective about ourselves and what we're doing.

The idea of a career is best applied to a view of one's work over many years. Only then can we begin to see the interconnectedness of our work, which eludes us as we live it. If you ever have an opportunity to visit someone who has spent his or her life in a profession related to the use of another language, you might witness that person's surprise at and new understanding of how many seemingly unrelated jobs helped to build his or her mastery of the profession.

In anticipating the transitions your career might make over the years, consider the possibility that the way you use your foreign language skills will change over time as well. The young government employee working for the Defense Intelligence Agency translating documents might one day become head of a large department and spend more time managing people than employing language skills, the very skills that gained the person his or her initial entry into the job. On the other hand, a college librarian with a Japanese degree may find its usefulness increasing as the college receives increasing numbers of Japanese students and the librarian finds it more helpful to communicate with these students in their native language.

WHAT PATHS CAN YOU TAKE TO BEGIN WITH?

In Chapters 10–15, we will examine several career paths, some of which require the use of a foreign language as a primary skill. These paths include the following:

1. Teaching
2. Translating and interpreting
3. Government

4. Educational administration

5. Business

In the cases of teaching and translating/interpreting, the primary focus of your job and career is facility with the language, both spoken and written. Your employment qualifications will center largely around your language skills. The other paths (government, educational administration, and business) comprise positions in which your foreign language can be used as an auxiliary skill. It is not an essential requirement for the position, but it is certainly a welcome and useful adjunct to your other talents. The focus in these jobs is on a skills package including some degree of foreign language familiarity, but that has other qualifications to offer as well.

The career paths that follow are merely suggestions. They are presented to stimulate your thinking about possible directions as you enter the workforce following graduation. Many travelers begin on the same road, and entry-level jobs, even in different organizations, seem remarkably similar. Soon, however, the road divides, and we each begin to acquire different skills and experiences in our life's work. It is the acquisition of the skills packages that often determines our career direction. The paths suggested are simply some of the many possible starting points.

CHAPTER TEN

PATH 1: TEACHING

*P*erhaps the most familiar career path for people who want to use their foreign language education as a primary skill would be teaching. It is certainly the role model for employment that the student of foreign language has seen most often, and it may be that a particular teacher was the inspiration for the choice of major in college.

It is certainly an attractive life to work with a body of information you love and to share that enjoyment with countless students over the years. There is learning for the instructor, as well, which adds its own excitement. Most teachers readily admit they enjoy being students, and good teachers come to the classroom as ready to learn from students as students arrive hoping to learn from their teachers. Good teachers maintain a regular program of professional development, continuing to learn new classroom techniques and to improve their teaching methods.

Whether in grade school, high school, or at the university level, there is a fellowship and camaraderie among teachers. They share anecdotes about techniques that have or have not worked in the classroom. Many can also share an interest in the growth and development of particular students they pass along through the years. Students often come back and visit their formative teachers, which brings its own rewards to the teacher they visit.

For the foreign language teacher, there is another exciting dimension to what they teach. It is no hyperbole to say that the teacher of another language takes students on a magic carpet ride to a culture they usually know very little about. As they study, they begin to understand different ways of thinking, eating, living, believing, socializing, and celebrating. Other people do things differently, and that's OK. Foreign language teachers instill tolerance and an appreciation of the multiculturalism so evident in our lives today.

With a growing interest in the idea of a world community, the international nature of business, the ease and relatively low cost of foreign travel, the increasing number of exchange programs, and a renewed appreciation for classic liberal arts education, including foreign language preparation, the field of teaching foreign language remains an attractive and viable alternative. Although English continues to be seen as the worldwide language of commerce, industry, and science, there is also a resurgence of traditionalism and a renewed awareness that to let a language die is to lose something irreplaceable.

We have seen this close to home in the Canadian province of Quebec, which has insisted on French as the language of culture, politics, commerce, and even tourism. Those who have insisted on retaining their French roots have been proven correct as Quebec remains popular with English-speaking tourists who make every attempt to speak some French and who enjoy the province's insistence that visitors speak its language.

To the traditional career paths of high school, college, and commercial language school venues, we can now add elementary schools in increasing numbers; these institutions continue to see growth in serious foreign language training for young children. Children in the elementary grades have little self-consciousness and are remarkable mimics. If foreign languages are introduced with a sense of fun and exuberance, these youngsters tend to absorb the material like a sponge, setting the stage for a lifelong involvement with other languages, not to mention increasing the opportunities for prospective teachers like yourself.

The predictable result of an early school introduction to foreign language has been an extension of the foreign language curriculum in high schools to accommodate the proficiency of students arriving from the lower grades with four or even five years of a language. For the foreign language major in education, this sophistication is a pleasant surprise. It is serving to attract more and more foreign language teachers to the secondary level, where material is now taught that was once introduced at the college level. As these students graduate from high school and move on to college, we shall see similar growth in college language programs to provide challenges for this new generation of linguists. This is an exciting and encouraging trend.

DEFINITION OF THE CAREER PATH

Teaching at any level—elementary, secondary, college, postgraduate, or in a professional language school—will provide its own unique rewards. Each setting also has its own employment conditions and hiring requirements, which will be discussed in the sections that follow.

What is shared by all, however, is a love of the language being taught and an enthusiasm in sharing this language with others so that they, too, can master it. No foreign language exists isolated from its history, geography, art, politics, and economic setting, and the teacher of a language must enjoy this aspect of teaching as well. This is the arena of human communication. It is what keeps language vital. Students learn far more than a language; they learn about a culture, an ethos, and a way of life. Teachers must be prepared to share all of that with their students, which suggests that they must be students themselves.

Baking French baguettes with students can be a point of departure not only for a discussion of French diet and eating patterns, but also for comparing the pace of life in various cultures. For a younger classroom of budding Francophiles, it might be enough to learn the French words *pain*, *croissant*, *buerre*, and *baguette* and to have fun baking and eating. For an older group, however, there are many other lessons in such an exercise: The French buy their bread every day. They buy it unwrapped and fresh from the oven, and they would never buy day-old bread for table use. These are quite different from mainstream American habits. One could discuss the implications of this behavior for French views on packaging in general, marketing, and time available to buy groceries daily, as well as French values that esteem small private bakers over large conglomerates.

It is far less unusual today than it was just a few years ago for French teachers in American schools to take students to France for a week or ten days. Planned well and designed to instill a true appreciation for everything French, these field trips can crystallize for many young students a love of language and appreciation for a culture different from their own. Some will go on to study French in college, and others will simply become better world citizens for the experience.

Learning a foreign language is sometimes spoken of as almost impossible to do. As a student of foreign language reading this book, you realize this is not so. It is like learning any new skill; it takes time, and, most of all, it takes practice. But to teach a foreign language well does require creativity, for people learn in different ways.

Your teaching-methods class in college will spend considerable time on the different teaching styles. You will identify your strengths as well as aspects of your basic style that may leave some students unsatisfied. You'll learn how to compensate for that. For master's or doctoral degree graduates who may not have the advantage of the formal teaching-methods preparation required in a teacher education program, they will find the same information through conferences and professional associations of teachers of foreign language. Students' learning styles also vary. Some are visual learners. They enjoy board work, note taking, posters, signs, handouts, and drawings. They retain what they see and connect those memories by use of visual cues. The vocabulary of a barge trip down the Seine may be more easily remembered by watching a video than by listening to the teacher discuss or even pantomime the experience.

Some students have a strong response to auditory stimuli and enjoy hearing the language and listening to others speak it. They can easily mimic intonation and verbal phrasing. Auditory learners enjoy role-playing, theatrical pieces, watching films and videos of native speakers, and listening to a teacher who uses the language in class extensively. Language lab practice is also fun for these kinds of learners.

Movement, action, and participation characterize the learning style of kinesthetic learners. They need to be involved in role-playing, skits, and games to master the intricacies of a foreign language. Learning a Spanish dance helps to reinforce the words that go along with a piece of music. For these students, action is the key to learning.

This need to appeal to the kinesthetic, or action-oriented, learners has actually prompted an entire school of language teaching through the world-renowned efforts of a Dartmouth College French professor, John Arthur Rassias. The Rassias method of engaging students in the learning of language is taught in workshops and conferences all over the United States to help instructors appreciate the energy that can be created by a more interactive, dramatic classroom style. More important, Rassias has documented exponential jumps in learning using his method. It reduces fear and the sense of risk and encourages the learner to plunge into the language and swim.

Teachers must respond to all of these types of learning styles for different ages of students, which requires endless creativity and an awareness of how learning takes place in and out of the classroom. Pretending to be on a train in Spain would be great for some fifth graders, whereas an actual ride on a city subway for older students shows how Spanish is used along with English to give directions and emergency instructions. A visit to a French, Italian, Japanese, or German restaurant will provide opportunities for high school students to use their new language skills, whereas making some simplified dishes in home economics would be perfect for middle-school students. Newspapers, TV programs, sporting events, and a host of other daily activities can reinforce and stimulate learning for the interested teacher and student.

Public and private schoolteachers can find a lifetime of career service in the classroom, exposing many thousands of students to their first foreign language experiences. Foreign language teaching might offer opportunities to travel abroad with students as well as to do collaborative work with theater, music, culinary arts, and other school departments. Administratively, the skilled senior teacher can become a department head and be a force for change in curriculum design, quality of instruction, and departmental management. Public schoolteacher contracts provide increasingly competitive salaries and benefit packages that include tuition reimbursement for additional education related to one's profession.

Teachers at the college level are afforded an opportunity to work with older and more committed students who may have already invested several years in studying a particular language. The work is more sophisticated, more challenging, and can go faster in the college curriculum. Often, too, colleges are well equipped with excellent language laboratories and library collections to support their departments so students can do serious exploration on any number of aspects of language and culture.

College student populations studying language tend to be larger, and consequently faculty size is greater than in public schools. Instead of two French faculty members in a high school, there may be four or five in a small public college and ten or more in a major university department. Many colleges have a general education curriculum that emphasizes the foreign language requirement. Demand has increased for foreign language courses, at least at the first-year and second-year level of the language as students meet these degree requirements.

The kind of collegiality fostered by a college foreign language department has its own attractions for some potential teachers. It can certainly result in an atmosphere more focused on the language and the teaching of that language than is possible in the public school environment, where ancillary duties, disciplinary problems, and shorter classes and attention spans can limit even the most dedicated teacher.

Foreign language teachers who opt for careers in professional language schools will enjoy meeting and teaching a never-ending stream of interesting students from all walks of life. Prospective tourists, business people, missionaries, students, and lifelong learners will make up the language courses that are offered for a fee through commercial agencies. Many of these schools have superior reputations and provide total immersion techniques and high-quality materials to help learners master conversational aspects of a foreign language in a limited time. Some of the larger schools offer reading, writing, and cultural courses as well as language classes.

WORKING CONDITIONS

The various teaching career paths share much that is similar in content knowledge and methodology. However, working conditions do vary dramatically among the teaching options we have cited. A basic difference between schools on the elementary and secondary level and college and professional language schools is the voluntary attendance of students at college and elective curriculums.

Public Schools

Public schoolteachers through the high school level have participated in formal education and teacher training courses to obtain their certification. They have trained in teaching methods and classroom management and have prepared themselves to plan course outlines, select textbooks, assign work over the semester or quarter, and use visual aids and equipment effectively. Public schoolteachers frequently discuss the merits of various teaching methods in their attempt to fulfill the school's curriculum mandate and at the same time inspire and instill knowledge in a group of students who often see school or individual classes as an imposition on the rest of their lives.

In public school teaching, attendance and, to some degree, courses are imposed on the students with a resulting constrained effect on interest, motivation, and performance. Public schoolteachers must be skilled classroom managers and sometimes even disciplinarians to accomplish their academic goals. Individuals can be disruptive and seriously compromise entire classroom environments. School incidents of violence can impact all classes, and many schools impose a number of behavior rules that the teacher is expected to enforce.

Classes may be suspended for other school events, assemblies, and in-service programs for teachers. School days are canceled for weather conditions or physical plant problems, all of which can make it difficult for the classroom teacher to accomplish learning goals and outcomes.

In some school systems, textbooks and other materials are chosen by the school district or the department chair, and the teacher is expected to adopt those texts and teach from them. In other situations, the individual instructor may be given this freedom.

Public schoolteachers have a more rigid work day, with prescribed arrival and departure times. Many teachers are asked to take on extracurricular assignments, such as sports or clubs. Much work is taken home in the evening: grading papers, entering marks into the record, writing reports, and planning for future classes. Offices, if they are available, tend to be shared, and space is limited. Support services are limited; teachers often prepare their own exams, copy them, and do much of the administrative work themselves. In less well-endowed public school districts, teachers report buying supplies with their own funds. Meeting with parents, counseling them about their children, and being responsive to them is another distinctive requirement of this level of foreign language teaching.

Private Schools

The role of the teacher in a private school setting is determined by many variables: whether the school is residential or commuter, the cost of tuition, the type of student clientele it attracts, the degree to which the school is tuition-driven or supported by endowments, and any affiliations the school might have.

Private school salaries tend to be lower than in public schools, although salary is often supplemented with housing and board, which may include the teacher's spouse and children. On the other hand, resident teachers often live in apartments in dormitories or houses on campus and are expected to make evening checks and be available on a more irregular schedule than are public schoolteachers.

In the case of resident campuses, the faculty is part of the school family and is fully expected to attend all meals (in fact, places may be assigned at certain tables), performances, sporting events, and so forth, to ensure group cohesion and esprit de corps. If your self-assessment indicated you must have significant amounts of privacy in your life or a sharp demarcation between work and home, private school resident positions would be most unattractive to you and could engender serious stress if accepted.

One great advantage of many private schools is the smaller teacher-to-student ratio and the attention and concentration on individual student development allowed by these numbers. There is more time to explore issues and topics and more time to work with students who need extra help. In fact, most private schools have excellent learning support systems that capitalize on their size and familiarity with every member of the student body.

In addition to teaching duties, most teachers are expected to coach a sport or sponsor a significant activity such as theater, school newspaper, literary magazine, outing clubs, and the like. Not all of this is out-of-class time, as private school academic schedules tend to be less rigid than their public counterparts. There may be short days or school holidays devoted to certain events or activities.

Private schools tend to have a number of special traditions, buildings, and features that may be attractive to potential faculty. There is a respect for tradition and the past. Although now less true than before, these schools still tend to maintain rather firm criteria for behavior, dress, and interpersonal conduct.

Colleges and Universities

College-level teachers are hired for their advanced degrees and their scholarship; many have had no formal teaching methodology course work. Most would have experienced some teaching assignments during their graduate programs, either as teaching assistants or doing part-time adjunct faculty work or contract courses, but some may not have had this opportunity. Their ability to structure a class and fulfill a curriculum is based in large part on the belief that this will be accomplished just as they mastered much of their own advanced study in their subject—through autonomous learning. Nevertheless, many college faculty arrive with less actual classroom experience than high school teachers (who have had required student teaching) and often no experience with technology, visual aids, and textbook purchasing, much less a formal study of teaching methodologies and modalities.

For the college educator at either the undergraduate or graduate level, there is a different audience. Although some undergraduates are required to study a language, they have several languages to choose from. After those minimum requirements are met, most of the student population in upper-level foreign language classes are interested in and dedicated to the pursuit of excellence in that discipline. Classroom management is not an issue, although there is the same need for lesson plans and organization of learning. College instructors have great freedom in choosing texts, course materials, and class concepts, although they must fulfill the stated intent of the course as published in the college catalog. When several instructors are teaching the same numbered course, they may agree in advance to use the same textbook. This helps to ensure that they meet the same outcome criteria and are fair to students who must change class meeting times. It also helps all who must move into new classes for the next year that are based on the previous course.

Because of the college student's smaller class load, students have more time to devote to any one subject and can thus improve more rapidly. The change from high school to college means fewer classes for students overall and fewer per day. The mature student studying a foreign language has more time per week to spend working in the language lab and reviewing course materials. College teachers can and do expect more from students and can demand a higher quality of work.

For the student, there may be foreign language film series, student clubs, newsletters, or coffeehouses in which to practice language skills. At one university, the Spanish department holds a weekly Spanish tea, where refreshments are served and only Spanish is spoken in a delightful, easygoing, conversational setting.

Facilities tend to be excellent, and there is usually adequate support staff to type materials and examinations, do copying, and prepare testing materials. A private office is usually provided, and there may be quite a varied menu of faculty privileges. Computers are provided for writing, research, library access, and data manipulation.

At the college level, teaching is the principal job responsibility, although there is certainly a requirement to serve on committees, both departmental and all-college, for any number of issues, programs, and initiatives. Some hours of faculty advising are generally required to make the faculty member available to students for counseling. With seniority, class schedules and routines in general tend to be to the faculty member's taste. Colleges and universities have strict guidelines for promotion and tenure that may put pressure on the faculty member to write, do research, deliver papers at professional meetings, and become involved in outreach to the community and college service in order to rise in academic rank or even retain the position at that institution. In some departments, the role of department chair is rotated and all faculty are expected to serve a term. In other institutions, the chair is a contested office.

Professional Language Schools

For the teacher associated with a commercial language school, this is essentially a salaried position, full- or part-time depending on the teaching load. Full-time positions tend to involve more classes per day than either public or college teaching, and pay may be based on the number of classes taught. There are not the same associated duties, although lesson planning may still be the teacher's responsibility. In some of these schools, materials, books, and even day-to-day schedules are predetermined as part of an overall system that the school subscribes to.

Because these schools are commercial, support materials tend to be good to excellent. Since students are not in degree programs and pay only for the individual courses, there are no grades. There may be, in fact, a tendency to be relatively uncritical to avoid consumer complaints. Employment may be highly responsive to enrollments, and firm contractual agreements are rare.

TRAINING AND QUALIFICATIONS

For the elementary school language teacher, the minimum educational requirements would be a bachelor of education degree with certification appropriate to the state. Because certification requirements are constantly changing, contact the ERIC Clearinghouse on Languages and Linguistics (www.cal.org) for a comprehensive discussion of state certification requirements. The Academic Employment Network website (www.academploy.com) provides a convenient mechanism for checking certification requirements for most states. Be sure to verify the certification information you find on any website, as it may not be up to date. In addition, the Modern Language Association (www.mla.org) recommends that individuals spend time in the country of interest, develop an awareness of foreign language pedagogy, have a supervised teaching experience, have course work beyond the generic education classes, and that their skills in the use of the foreign language be formally assessed. Consider this advertisement listed in *Current Jobs for Graduates*: *The National Employment Bulletin for the Liberal Arts Profession*:

Japanese Teacher (private school in Kentucky): Teach Japanese to Japanese students (grades 1–12). Must be able to read and write Japanese fluently. Teacher's certificate as well as B.A. degree in education. Required ability to manage classroom accordingly. Forward resume to . . .

Secondary school qualifications would be a bachelor of education (secondary) in the language being taught, for example, a bachelor of science in Spanish education. Actual advertisements read as follows:

Spanish Teacher. High school seeks a teacher of Spanish with Russian, Japanese, or German preferred as a secondary proficiency. Please send credentials to . . .

Secondary German Teacher. Classroom instructor (in Arizona). Submit letter of application, completed district application, current resume, copy of credential, and placement file to . . .

Most four-year colleges would require that job candidates possess a doctorate in the foreign language being taught and might, in addition, look for specialized areas of research, publication, prior teaching, or foreign travel in countries where that language is spoken. Occasionally, a college will hire faculty on a nontenured basis with less than a doctoral degree, but the larger the institution, the less likely that this will be the case.

At the senior levels of graduate work for both master's and doctoral degrees, you will be teaching and working with seasoned scholars who are developing their own unique areas of expertise as they pursue the degree you hold. Classes may be very small at this level, even at a large university, and the work is highly collaborative. Your teaching work at this level may be reduced to allow for pure research and writing in your areas of interest and scholarship. You will be called upon frequently to speak to professional and scholarly groups about that research.

If you are hired without an earned doctorate, there may be a stipulation in the contract at hiring indicating how much time can elapse before the degree must be earned. The difficulty here would be to finish the degree while holding down a full-time job. (For many people, the dissertation is the most challenging and time-consuming aspect of the degree.) This certainly should be considered in your negotiations.

The following advertisements were taken from *The Chronicle of Higher Education* (www.chronicle.com), the single most popular source of advertisements for positions in higher education:

> *[Major metro area] State University tenure-track position in Spanish.* Ability to teach: all levels of language courses, introductory courses in linguistics/phonetics, literature. Load may include advising, language lab supervision, and recruitment/retention. Ph.D. required at time of appointment. Salary commensurate with experience. For further information, please contact the chairperson of the search committee . . .

> *French:* The Department of French and Italian at (major southern) University invites applicants for a one-year appointment as a visiting professor, rank open, preferred specialization in French medieval studies. Candidates must hold the Ph.D. Teaching responsibilities include undergraduate language and literature courses and, possibly, one graduate seminar in French medieval literature. Send letter of application, curriculum vitae, and names and addresses of three references to . . . Applications will be accepted until May 1. University is an equal-opportunity employer and encourages applications from women, minorities, and other traditional underrepresented groups.

Professional language institutes and commercial language schools will vary dramatically in what types of qualifications they demand of applicants. The following advertisement from a school teaching Spanish to non-Spanish speakers simply says the following:

> *Experienced Spanish Instructors:* To teach conversational, business, and intensive courses in Spanish to small, group classes. Resume and letter to . . .

EARNINGS

Public elementary and secondary schoolteachers of foreign language are paid according to the same salary schedules as other teachers in their school district.

Salaries across the nation vary depending on location, which affects the cost of living and level of state and community support for education as reflected in the school budget. Because published reports on teacher salaries are generally three to five years out of date, contact the National Education Association or your state's Department of Education to get the latest figures available. Public school salaries are public information, so a call to the school district you are interested in will give you the median salaries for each level of degree and for different amounts of experience.

Private school salaries are generally lower than those of local public schoolteachers. On average, public schoolteachers earn between 25 to 119 percent more than private schoolteachers earn. Additionally, some of the same locational factors that affect public schoolteachers' salaries also affect those working in private schools.

The most recent data available for college faculty indicate that salaries at four-year public institutions range from $31,889 for an instructor to $58,105 for a full professor. The overall average salary for all ranks of academic standing was $46,399 at public schools and $52,591 at private institutions.

CAREER OUTLOOK

The National Center for Education Statistics (www.nces.ed.gov) cites a number of interesting trends that impact public schoolteachers of foreign language. In the mid-1990s, on average less than 1 percent of teaching positions were vacant, meaning there are more applicants than jobs. So while your elementary or secondary teaching degree is a valuable credential, you are entering a highly competitive market and you will need to be aggressive in your job search. The well-prepared job seeker will also be able to discuss current trends in curriculum choices for foreign languages at the elementary and secondary levels.

Private school foreign language teaching positions are expected to see only the growth demanded by a slightly increasing student pool. Hiring will increase only modestly over the next decade. Fortunately, the private school system has always emphasized foreign language in their usually classic curriculums, and the private school market remains a viable alternative for employment in the future. The choice of languages has more breadth in the private schools than in the public schools, and that may be a factor for some candidates.

As for higher education and prospective teaching in foreign language, the Modern Language Association (www.mla.org) reports that 90 percent of foreign language Ph.D.s were employed as follows: 40 percent in tenure-track positions, 26 percent in nontenure-track full-time positions, 8 percent in nontenure-track part-time positions, 2 percent in postdoctoral fellowships, 1 percent in academic administration, and 9 percent in outside higher education. The remaining 10 percent were reported as not employed.

One important trend worth researching as you consider employment in academe is the increasing use of part-time faculty. In 1970, 22 percent of the professoriate worked part-time. As we begin the twenty-first century, the figure has grown to almost 50 percent. There are many reasons for the shift, but the bottom line for you means that there is a heavy competition for full-time positions in higher education.

Other factors worth researching are current trends in the use of tenure; population trends and the resulting number of students expected to attend college; whether a minimum faculty retirement age is currently required; and the number of individuals currently pursuing an advanced degree in foreign language.

Given your investment of time and financial resources there is much to consider. Both the *Chronicle of Higher Education*'s website (www.chronicle.com) and the American Association of University Professors' website (www.aaup.org) will have the latest information on these topics.

STRATEGY FOR FINDING THE JOBS IN ELEMENTARY AND SECONDARY PUBLIC SCHOOLS

To secure a teaching post in a market for which supply outstrips demand in many localities argues for approaching the job search strategy with an almost military precision. You need to think of working on several fronts at the same time. All of your activity should be geared to securing an interview with school hiring officials. Given solid interview skills as outlined earlier in this book, the more interview opportunities you have, the greater the probability of your being offered a teaching contract.

Consider the question of relocation carefully. If openings are not plentiful in the area where you currently live, seek out information on supply and demand elsewhere and think positively about the advantages of a move. Although there is certainly the risk of the unfamiliar in a move, to have a job that utilizes your education is a wonderful accomplishment. With that under your belt, you can go about putting down roots in a new community, making new friends, and learning the advantages of your new home.

Begin with Your Degree-Granting Institution

Register with Credentials Services. Let's outline the different approaches to the teaching marketplace. Begin with your degree-granting institution. Make certain that before you leave campus you have a good understanding of and are registered with all the available placement services. They may be located not only in the career office but also in the school of education offices. Many schools have credentials files, which contain copies of your teaching resume, your letters of recommendation, and other qualifying documents. As you leave school and begin your job search, the credentials office will mail this packet of materials to anyone of your choosing. There is often a modest fee for this service. Its advantages are convenience, usually quick response time, and a centralized spot for all your records.

Review Campus Job Postings. Your college will also be in receipt of job postings from local and state schools for teaching positions. Find out where these job postings are displayed and review them frequently. Apply for every reasonable position. In most cases, you don't really learn about the details of a position until you have the opportunity for an interview, and there will be ample time to discuss details of a job offering.

Review Newspaper Job Listings

The public schoolteacher candidate is advised to make a regular practice of scanning all newspapers advertising in and around the geographic region being considered for teaching assignments. Newspapers need not be purchased. If a newspaper has a website, job listings can be reviewed on-line. And most libraries subscribe to a selection of local papers. Be sure to check the Sunday listings via either of these locations on a regular basis.

Expand Your Network of Contacts

Contact School Officials. Send a cover letter and resume to schools where you would like to work. State departments of education publish directories of all public schools in the state, including the names of superintendents, principals, and other administrators. Names, addresses, and phone numbers are regularly included in these listings. This information is generally provided on state websites. Many libraries and college career counseling centers will have this same information on file.

Attend Job Fairs. Your college career office or teacher placement center will also have listings of annual teacher job fairs around the country. Take note of any in your area and call or write about registration requirements, fees, and other details. Teacher recruitment fairs often include opportunities to meet principals and superintendents and schedule time for brief interviews that may lead to additional meetings at another time.

STRATEGY FOR FINDING THE JOBS IN PRIVATE SCHOOLS

The U.S. Department of Education's National Center for Education Statistics (http://nces.ed.gov) reported a total of more than 2.9 million teachers in the United States in 1994. Be sure to check this website for the latest statistics. Of this group, almost 13 percent were private schoolteachers. Accessing the private school market is a very different process than seeking a public school situation. In general, there is not a significant amount of crossover between the two systems, and teachers within a private school system tend to stay within that educational environment.

Private schools list positions and send out job notices but seldom advertise in newspapers to ensure a more select pool of candidates and maintain a lower profile than their public school counterparts. As tuition-driven institutions, they do not have the core franchise market of students that public schools automatically obtain and must seek students through reputation and advertising. Consequently, their recruitment and hiring efforts are low key.

Contact Private Schools Directly

Send a cover letter and resume to each private school you would like to work for. You can find information on Peterson's website (www.peterson.com). Choose the "Select a Private School" option and begin exploring. The site also provides information on how to contact each school. Use it as appropriate to find out about jobs they may have available. Also review the sources listed in the directories section that follows.

Attend Job Fairs

Find out about job fairs and attend as many as you can. Job fairs for private schools, both here in the United States and abroad, are held year-round. Many are administered by recruiting firms. These fairs serve as a major entree for many job seekers into the private school system. You register your credentials with a private school placement agency, which then provides access to a private school job fair. There you can meet and interact with a number of hiring officials from a regional or national base. Your college career office can put you in touch with some of these private school recruiting firms or give you a schedule of teaching job fairs around the country.

For Public or Private Employment, Evaluate Placement Agencies

There are many reputable teacher placement agencies around the country, and if your job search becomes particularly challenging, you might consider investigating one of these services. Before you sign a contract, be certain you've taken it home and studied it to understand all the conditions and costs associated with the services being offered. Many of these firms are providing services that duplicate those your college career office or teacher placement center is providing or can arrange to provide for you at another college through reciprocity agreements.

You can find placement agencies on the Web by checking sites like Job-Hunt.Org's Academia/Education section (www.job-hunt.org). No matter how you locate an agency check them out with the local Better Business Bureau, talk to your career office about placement agencies to learn what their experience has been, and find out whether the agency itself will allow you to contact previous clients to discuss their experiences with the agency. All of these efforts will help you to reduce the risk associated with fee-based agencies.

Special Note: Consider Relocating

You will want to know exactly in which states your certification is valid and try to be as mobile as possible in your job search. Studies have shown that new teachers in their first job often do not relocate more than twenty-five miles from their home. Sometimes this decision is financially driven when new-teacher salaries make it difficult to rent an apartment, finance and insure a vehicle, and pay all the associated expenses of living away from home. However, every year teaching districts do without teachers because they are too rural or too remote for consideration by some candidates. Ironically, often these job sites will provide not only the warmest welcome for a needed teacher but also the supportive atmosphere and climate so important to a new recruit in a demanding position. What these locales may lack in services, they may make up for in a lower cost of living and an opportunity to make a difference in young people's lives.

STRATEGY FOR FINDING THE JOBS IN COLLEGES AND UNIVERSITIES

Acquiring a college teaching position nearly always demands that you relocate to an institution other than where you received your degree. Higher education has limited openings at any one time, and part-time work or adjunct faculty status at one institution is no guarantee of earning a full-time spot. Most departments have budget lines dedicated to full-time, potentially tenured faculty. This means that faculty who are hired in those budget lines are expected to become a permanent part of the faculty and earn tenure and promotion when they qualify.

Consequently, although there may be schools you would enjoy teaching at or areas of the country you would prefer, the supply and demand for college professorships usually will require you to relocate.

Go to "The Source"

The Chronicle of Higher Education (www.chronicle.com) is the weekly national publication listing junior college, four-year college, and university teaching positions in foreign language. Many of these advertisements are large display ads that detail in full the requirements and duties of the positions advertised. Your career center, department office, and college library will also have copies you can review each week.

Network with Faculty Colleagues

Another excellent source of college-level positions will be the faculty colleague contacts you make as you pursue your advanced degree. There is a well-established network that becomes active when schools are seeking to fill a position. A personal recommendation from a friend or former teaching associate will be welcomed by faculty at the hiring institution. For this reason, it's important to ensure that your faculty mentors and colleagues are well aware of your teaching and research interests and geographic preferences so they can respond for you and move the process along if an opportunity presents itself.

Attend Professional Meetings

Interviews are often conducted at professional meetings, where recent job openings may be announced or posted in a conspicuous place at the registration table. As a graduate student, many of these conferences are available to you at substantially reduced fees or no fee at all. You should take advantage of them for the professional content and the opportunity to meet representatives of departments at other institutions.

POSSIBLE EMPLOYERS

Teaching has become an intensely competitive field, with supply in many disciplines far outstripping demand. There are a number of considerations to keep in mind as you seek an employer. Your principal goal is to teach your language at the educational level you have trained and prepared for. If that is not possible, the next easiest transition would be to accept a different grade or age level. If that is not available, consider using your teaching credentials in a different way. In the public schools, this could mean teaching in another content area (with provisional certification), substituting, or serving as an aide until something permanent appears in the school district. At the college level, it may mean part-time instructing as an adjunct faculty member until an opening occurs.

In teaching, the possible employers are fortunately very well documented. We have identified resources that can provide the names of potential employers.

Directories

Patterson's Elementary Education and *Patterson's American Education* are annual lists of public and private elementary and secondary schools, school districts and superintendents, postsecondary schools, and others, including nursery schools, YMCA programs, and the like. Use these directories to conduct your proactive job search activities: mailing out cover letters and resumes, networking, and telephone follow-up.

Private schools are identified on Peterson's website (www.petersons.com) or in the *Handbook of Private Schools* (Porter Sargent Publishers). *Independent School* is the journal of the National Association of Independent Schools (www.nais.org). It is published three times a year and contains articles on issues of concern to private schools, and it contains a number of display advertisements.

Some resources that can be used to identify schools if you are considering teaching a foreign language beyond high school include *Peterson's Guide to Two-Year Colleges, Peterson's Guide to Four-Year Colleges, Peterson's Annual Guides to Graduate Study* (www.petersons.com), and the *College Board Index of Majors and Graduate Degrees.*

Career Office Postings

Career offices often carry national job vacancy listings that include teaching positions. Some of these listings include *Current Jobs for Graduates in Education, The Job Hunter, Community Jobs, Current Jobs for Graduates,* and *The Chronicle of Higher Education.*

Professional Associations

Be sure to carefully review the list of professional associations for teachers of foreign languages that follows this section. For several associations there is a line labeled "Job Listings." Any activities that the association undertakes to assist its members in finding employment are shown.

ASCUS Annual

The American Association for Employment in Education (www.ub-careers. buffalo.edu) has a wonderful website that includes information on how to find a job, associations you can turn to for assistance, and salary information. Be sure to find out if your university is a member of this association and whether there is additional information available through your school's membership.

STRATEGY FOR FINDING THE JOBS IN PROFESSIONAL LANGUAGE SCHOOLS

Professional language schools are located in large metropolitan areas where they can be close to their principal market. Their clients include international travelers and businesspeople, students seeking to enhance regular academic work in a language or to take a refresher course for examinations or travel, and individuals seeking self-improvement.

To enlist students, these schools must advertise heavily. Check Sunday editions of metropolitan newspapers, or search the Internet using www.big book.com for the state where you want to work. A sampling showed more than 275 language schools listed for New York, 52 were listed for Washington, DC, 30 in Minnesota, and 540 in California.

POSSIBLE JOB TITLES

There certainly is not a great range in terms of the job titles you will be looking for. *Teacher* is a job title that speaks volumes in itself. But do not be surprised to see advertisements for elementary school language teacher, high school language teacher, language instructor, or linguist. In higher education, instructor, assistant professor, associate professor, and professor of foreign language or professor of French, Spanish, German, and so forth, are the titles to look for.

RELATED OCCUPATIONS

Some related occupations will allow you to directly use your language skills, as teaching does, while others may only allow occasional use of your language expertise. These related occupations include the following:

ESL Teacher	Translator/Interpreter
Import/Export Agent	Hotel Manager
Airline Customer Service Agent	Travel Agent

Teachers share certain personality traits with other types of workers, according to Holland's theory of careers. If you are considering other types of work, be sure to read job descriptions for the following:

Librarian	Undercover Agent
Passenger Service Representative	Claim Agent
Volunteer Services Director	Production Agent

PROFESSIONAL ASSOCIATIONS FOR TEACHERS OF FOREIGN LANGUAGE

As you will see in looking through the following list, there is an association for nearly every language that is taught. Draw on these associations to find out about job listings and enhance your professional skills.

American Association of Teachers of Arabic
c/o Brigham Young University
280 HRCB
Provo, UT 84602
Website: http://humanities.byu.edu
Members/Purpose: To contribute to the enhancement of study, criticism, and research in the field of Arabic language, literature, and linguistics.
Journal/Publication: *Al-Arabiyya; AATA Newsletter.*
Job Listings: Publishes a short list of jobs for Arabic teachers.

American Association of Teachers of Esperanto
5140 San Lorenzo Dr.
Santa Barbara, CA 93111-2521
Members/Purpose: Persons who are teaching or have taught Esperanto and educators interested in Esperanto.
Journal/Publication: *AATE Bulletin.*

American Association of Teachers of French
Mailcode: 4510
Southern Illinois University
Carbondale, IL 62901-4510
Website: http://aatf.utsa.edu
Members/Purpose: Sponsors programs for students such as the French
honor society at the high school level, a national French contest, and
scholarships.
Journal/Publication: *AATF National Bulletin; French Review.*
Job Listings: Publishes placement listings for higher education once a
month.

American Association of Teachers of German
112 Haddontowne Ct., Suite 104
Cherry Hill, NJ 08034
Website: www.aatg.org
Members/Purpose: Teachers of German at all levels; individuals interested
in German language and culture.
Training: Offers in-service teacher training workshops.
Journal/Publication: *AATG Newsletter; Die Unterrichtspraxis; German
Quarterly.*

American Association of Teachers of Italian
Department of Foreign Languages
Arizona State University
Tempe, AZ 85287-0202
Website: www.italianstudies.org/aati
Members/Purpose: Professional society of college and secondary
schoolteachers and others interested in Italian language and culture.
Journal/Publication: *AATI Newsletter.*

American Association of Teachers of Spanish and Portuguese
University of Northern Colorado
Gunther Hall, Room 106
Greeley, CO 80639
Website: www.aatsp.org
Members/Purpose: Teachers of Spanish and Portuguese languages and
literatures and others interested in Hispanic culture.
Journal/Publication: *Hispania.*
Job Listings: Has placement bureau for members.

American Association of Teachers of Turkish

Near Eastern Studies
110 Jones Hall
Princeton University
Princeton, NJ 08544-1008
Members/Purpose: Teachers of the Turkish language; universities,
    including language schools in government services; other institutions.
Journal/Publication: Newsletter.

American Classical League

Miami University
Oxford, OH 45056
Website: www.aclclassics.org
Members/Purpose: Teachers of classical languages in high schools and
    colleges. To promote the teaching of Latin and other classical languages.
Journal/Publication: *Classical Outlook*; newsletter; *Prima*.
Job Listings: Offers placement service (most active in August and
    September).

American Conference for Irish Studies

% Department of History
St. Joseph's College
Patchogue, NY 11772
Website: www.acisweb.com
Members/Purpose: Scholars interested in Irish arts, folklore, history,
    language, literature, and social sciences.
Journal/Publication: *ACIS Newsletter*; *A Guide to Irish Studies in the
United States*.

American Council of Teachers of Russian

1776 Massachusetts Ave. NW, 5th Floor, Suite 700
Washington, DC 20036
Website: www.actr.org
Members/Purpose: Teachers of Russian language, literature, and culture.
Journal/Publication: *ACTR Newsletter*; *Russian Language Journal*.

American Council on the Teaching of Foreign Languages

6 Executive Plaza
Yonkers, NY 10701

Website: www.actfl.org

Members/Purpose: Individuals interested in the teaching of classical and modern foreign languages in schools and colleges throughout America.

Training: Conducts seminars and workshops.

Journal/Publication: *Foreign Language Annals*; newsletter.

Association of Teachers of Japanese

Japanese Program/Hillcrest

Middlebury College

Middlebury, VT 05753

Members/Purpose: Those with a professional interest in the teaching of Japanese as a foreign language and in the allied fields of Japanese linguistics and literature.

Journal/Publication: *ATJ Newsletter*; *Journal of the Association of Teachers of Japanese*.

Job Listings: See *ATJ Newsletter*.

College Language Association

James P. Brawley Dr. at Fair St. SW

Atlanta, GA 30314

Members/Purpose: Teachers of English and modern foreign languages, primarily in historically black colleges and universities.

Journal/Publication: Journal.

Modern Language Association of America

10 Astor Pl.

New York, NY 10003-6981

Website: www.mla.org

Members/Purpose: College and university teachers of English and of modern foreign languages. Seeks to advance all aspects of literary and linguistic study.

Journal/Publication: Directory; *MLA Newsletter*.

Job Listings: Listings for college teaching positions.

National Association for Bilingual Education

1220L St. NW, Suite 605

Washington, DC 20005

Website: www.nabe.org

Members/Purpose: Educators, administrators, paraprofessionals, community and laypeople, and students. Purposes are to recognize, promote, and publicize bilingual education.
Training: Conferences and workshops.
Journal/Publication: Annual conference journal; journal; newsletter.

National Council of State Supervisors of Foreign Languages

State House, Room 229, Foreign Language Education Consultant
Indianapolis, IN 46204
Members/Purpose: Provides support for foreign language programs at the state level and liaison with other agencies and federal and local government.
Journal/Publication: Mailing list.

Northeast Conference on the Teaching of Foreign Languages (NEC)

Dickson College
P.O. Box 1773
Carlisle, PA 17013
Website: http://omega.dickinson.edu
Members/Purpose: Sponsored by groups or institutions with nonprofit educational status that are actively engaged in teaching. Seeks to further the teaching of foreign languages, classical and modern, in the United States.
Journal/Publication: Conference program; newsletter; report.
Job Listings: Newsletter for members contains classified ads.

Teachers of English to Speakers of Other Languages (TESOL)

700 S. Washington St., Suite 200
Alexandria, VA 22314
Website: www.tesol.edu
Members/Purpose: School, college, and adult education teachers who teach English as a foreign language; students and professional people in the field; colleges and schools are institutional members; publishers are commercial members.
Journal/Publication: *TESOL Newsletter*; membership directory.
Job Listings: See *TESOL Newsletter*; offers placement service.

Women's Caucus for the Modern Languages
West Virginia University Department of English
P.O. Box 6296
Morgantown, WV 26506-6296
Website: www.as.wvu.edu
Members/Purpose: Women working or studying in the modern languages, faculty, administrators, and graduate students. Seeks to improve the status of women in the profession.
Training: Disseminates information; organizes sessions and workshops.
Journal/Publication: *Women's Caucus for the Modern Languages–Concerns.*

CHAPTER ELEVEN

PATH 2: TRANSLATING AND INTERPRETING

n using your foreign language skills in translation or interpretation, you are using the language as a primary skill. Positions using foreign languages as a primary skill require a comprehensive grasp of the language and the cultural context of that language. Gertrude Stein taught us to appreciate beauty and not labels when she wrote, "A rose is a rose is a rose." Knowing your literature is one thing, but could you quickly quote something comparable to this famous line in the foreign language you have studied?

To achieve the necessary fluency to work as an interpreter or translator demands extensive study of the language, perhaps periods of time as a resident of a country using that language, and a complete grasp of the cultural context, literature, music, economics, and history of those who speak that language. A simultaneous interpreter of Spanish, for example, represents the apogee of the art of moving instantaneously between two cultures. A quote from Shakespeare in English might be rendered immediately into something appropriate from Cervantes, and vice versa.

Even with the requisite language skills, your work in translating or interpreting might take you into new and unexplored areas. For example, medicine, science, ecology, and anthropology each would represent a specialized vocabulary to be mastered and concepts to be understood. Constant study and acquisition of these knowledge bases is a hallmark of the superior practitioner of translation or interpretation. It is well worth a lifetime's involvement, for the acquisition of knowledge never ends.

DEFINITION OF THE CAREER PATH

Interpreters and translators are needed all over the world where peoples of differing cultures and languages come together, either physically, on the printed page, or through some other medium. Publishers, educational institutions, hospitals, trade organizations, and governments all make use of both positions.

Translators deal with written documents and interpreters with oral expression. Some translators work in only one direction, for example, from Japanese to English, whereas others are comfortable translating in either direction. Interpreters, on the other hand, because they are involved in social situations, are often called on to communicate in both languages. The highly skilled and justifiably famous simultaneous interpreters of the United Nations work very intently in relatively short shifts interpreting in one direction. They rotate several interpreters to maintain concentration and because each interpreter must produce an approved text of his or her work for that shift.

Most interpreters translate from one or two "passive" languages into an "active" one, their mother tongue. The best definition of mother tongue may be that in which nursery rhymes are familiar. Interpreter positions frequently call for a degree in foreign languages, a minimum fluency in three languages (mother tongue included), and successful scores on written and oral examinations.

The Benefits of Living Abroad

Even entry-level positions for translators or interpreters emphasize superior language skills and will seldom compromise on this aspect of the job specification. There may be both written and oral tests of your language skill by other foreign language practitioners. Many interpreters and translators speak highly of the fluency skills they gained by living abroad in a geographic area where their language is spoken exclusively. You should seriously consider this important, but not necessarily academic, part of your job preparation.

If you are in high school, speak with your guidance counselor about the Experiment in International Living and similar programs that will place you with a family in another country while you go to school for a year in a local high school. Many alumni of this program make lifelong friends and return to their placement site often throughout their lives and host their families and friends on visits to the United States. More important, diligent students find it gives them a quantum leap in language skill and cultural understanding.

Your college may have existing exchange programs of its own or may belong to a consortium of schools that share academic year or semester abroad programs. Tuition is usually similar to your regular school tuition, but room, board, and transportation will almost always represent an increased cost. These programs allow you a chance to continue your education and experience living in a foreign country. Many graduates of these programs recommend investigating the options carefully. Some are disappointed to find their foreign schooling is actually an American experience; Americans are grouped together, the program is essentially composed of English speakers, or it is difficult to make contact with native speakers and the culture.

Even if your classes are in English, check out off-campus living arrangements in boarding houses, pensiones, or small hotels that may offer attractive long-term rates. This will allow you to inhabit a neighborhood, meet some locals, and experience life away from your academics. The American Institute for Foreign Study (College Division) publishes a large catalog of programs each year for Austria, China, France, Germany, Italy, Mexico, Spain, Russia, and a number of English-speaking countries as well.

Short-term working experiences in service occupations can be arranged through the long-established Council on International Educational Exchange (CIEE). It places students in jobs in France, Germany, Costa Rica, and some English-speaking countries. It provides assistance with job placement, visas, work permits, and inexpensive overseas airline flights. Each year it publishes *Work Abroad*, a pamphlet outlining its program. This material is available in many college career offices and from the CIEE offices at 205 East 42nd Street, New York, NY 10017.

Work-Study-Travel Abroad: The Whole World Handbook is a volume of information also published by the Council on International Educational Exchange. Distinct from its work abroad programs, it is a guide for anyone looking for the details of working, living, or studying in more than seventy-six different countries. There are excellent sections on Eastern Europe, Africa, Asia, South America, Western Europe, the Caribbean, Mexico and Central America, and India and Nepal.

The prolific career advising team of Ronald Krannich and Caryl Krannich has also published an excellent guide for exploring the possibilities of living abroad. *International Jobs and Careers* is a job search guide that identifies possible employment sectors in the non-U.S. employment market and gives valuable tips and techniques on securing employment. Living abroad is valued not only by those who have the experience themselves, but also by potential employers.

The following advertisement refers to this period of foreign residency:

Foreign Linguists. To work on a potential government contract in support of the National Immigrant Visa Center. Any/all languages desired, but especially Russian, Chinese (Malnland, Hong Kong, Taiwanese), Japanese, Korean, and Thai. Multilinguists and those with previous foreign residency are particularly desirable. U.S. residency not required. Send resume to . . .

The Need for Superior English Skills

Love of and proficiency with the foreign language under consideration are not the only criteria for success. The essence of interpreter/translator positions is effective communication, and that means superior skills in your own language and culture. Because no one language can be easily translated into another, interpreters and translators must do the best they can to convey accurately the essence of the language. For this reason, there is usually ongoing debate in translator/interpreter circles about the words and citations from literature that may or may not have been the most effective choice in a particular situation of rendering one language into another.

Given the breadth of possible choices in effective and meaningful translation or interpretation, it follows that the individual performing this transformation must have at his or her command all the possibilities inherent in the English language as well. Translators and interpreters need mastery of a variety of syntactical structures, comprehensive vocabulary, encyclopedic knowledge of literary and musical allusions, and a solid grasp of the history and sweep of English language and literature as embodied in written and spoken forms. Add to this requirement the daunting fact that often the knowledge of one or more additional languages is necessary for success in the field. In both Eastern and Western Europe, there has been such a tradition of cultural interchange and flow between nations that to limit yourself to one language could restrict your possibilities for employment.

As the economy grows more global and as people everywhere begin to appreciate cultural pluralism, the need for skilled individuals to bring us together and allow us to make meaning of our interactions will continue to grow. Interpreters and translators are bridge builders, connecting cultures, minds, thoughts, beauty, and science between two worlds that might otherwise not be able to connect. It is an exciting, worthwhile career—and a needed one.

WORKING CONDITIONS

Many literary translators are self-employed, or, like their counterparts who do interpreting on a freelance basis, they have another occupation to support them, perhaps a teaching position or work in publishing or editing. Some U.S. corporations employ both translators and interpreters on a full-time basis, but the total number employed full-time in the commercial sector remains in the hundreds. The U.S. government, through its agencies, also employs significant numbers of interpreters and translators. Many government employees are former military personnel who gained their language training or additional significant language skills at the Defense Language Institute in Monterey, California.

The consequences of not finding full-time work as an interpreter or translator are twofold: first, you must be prepared (and qualified!) to be employed in some other capacity. This suggests other skills and talents that you can market to an employer that are perhaps not connected in any way with foreign languages and interpretation or translation.

Second, you must have working conditions that will allow you to continue to do the necessary marketing to seek self-employment for your foreign language skills. This might mean making phone calls, sending out letters or brochures, or even being able to leave work briefly for an interview or meeting. Juggling a full-time job and staying available for translating or interpreting jobs can be difficult. The alternative of not using your foreign language skills, even in a part-time manner, and risking loss of fluency may be equally disagreeable and unacceptable.

Working exclusively as an interpreter or translator in a less than full-time capacity means having a strong tolerance for low job security. Benefits will be nonexistent, except perhaps during periods of extended employment, and there may be weeks or even months during which you are unemployed. Additionally, it is difficult to be actively seeking freelance positions if you are working on another freelance position full-time. The cycle may become work, no work, seeking work, working again.

There are important differences in working conditions between interpreters and translators. Interpreters, by the nature of their work, must work at the venues where their services are required (e.g., the conference table, the international media fair, or the university colloquium). Their work is immediate, very involved with personalities, nuance, and subtlety. They work on their feet, at meals, and on the move. They work exposed to all around them and often under intense pressure.

Translators, on the other hand, can work in libraries, at home, or in quiet offices, crafting their work alone and wrestling with problems and discovering solutions in private. Freelance translators also work on-site at conferences and symposia to prepare written materials, including edited transcripts of speakers, panels, and discussions.

Both types of jobs can involve significant amounts of travel and demand flexibility and the willingness to handle the problems associated with travel. Interpreters especially, and to some degree translators as well, must be prepared to set up housekeeping and workstations anywhere.

Interpreters and translators often specialize in a particular area (science, medicine, literature, for example), but it is obvious that the more broad their interests, vocabularies (in their nonnative tongue), and experiences, the more work opportunities may present themselves. Although you may be working regularly as a translator of medical texts, if you are willing to broaden your horizons, you may find substantial additional translation work in different fields. For example, recently there has been heightened interest in ethnic knitting traditions, and more American knitters are seeking Andean, Norwegian, and Chinese knitting patterns. Children's literature from all over the world has become popular, and the demand for skilled translators in this field is up. Opportunities present themselves to those who seek them.

TRAINING AND QUALIFICATIONS

The following are edited versions of advertisements for translators and interpreters that have appeared in the national press. They are good examples of how training and qualifications might be expressed by the hiring officials:

Translators. Qualified in Spanish/English. Resume to . . .

Translators. Full-time/part-time translator positions for translation from English to all foreign languages. Computer experience a plus. Urgent requirements for Dutch, German, Spanish, French, Italian, Swedish. Resume only . . .

Big City Language Institute has two openings: program coordinator, English as a second language, and project manager for translation and interpreting service. Letters and resumes to directors of appropriate departments . . .

We have emphasized throughout this discussion of translating and interpreting careers that a superior level of skill in your native tongue, in addition to fluency with the written and oral expression of the foreign language, is essential. In the case of simultaneous interpretation, speed and accuracy are critical. Consecutive interpretation, in which the translation occurs following the speaker, places emphasis on the interpreter's memory.

Whatever the role, both positions argue for excellent academic preparation in language, grammar, punctuation, and syntax. Foreign language training should begin as early as possible. A college degree is essential for these types of positions. Take as many language courses as possible, but don't neglect writing and speaking courses in your own language. If you are interested in working in a particular subject area (politics, economics, literature), then take additional courses in that area as well.

In addition to your traditional academic preparation in high school and college and possibly graduate school, there are a number of specialized schools and institutes where you can acquire specific and intensive language skills suitable for interpreting and translating positions. There are many commercial language schools that can provide training, but the Modern Language Association (www.mla.org) recommends that you undertake a program of study offered by an institution of higher education. A commercial language program will gladly teach you how to ask for a ham sandwich in Arabic, but they may not tell why that is inappropriate. If you believe a commercial language school will meet your needs, check the Yellow Pages under "Language Schools" for programs available in your area.

A selected number of colleges and universities provide training at the certificate or master's degree level in interpretation or translation. These schools include George Mason University in Fairfax, Virginia; Monterey Institute of International Studies in California; Rutgers University in New Brunswick, New Jersey; State University of New York at Binghamton; University of Arkansas in Fayetteville; and University of Iowa in Iowa City.

EARNINGS

Earnings for translators and interpreters vary widely. For those employed full-time by U.S. government agencies, pay at the entry level is in the mid-20s; senior-level positions with the government can pay as much as $60,000. Corporate jobs have a slightly higher starting salary and can, with time of service and promotional raises, provide salaries comparable to and higher than government jobs. Corporate positions, however, even long-term ones, may be for the duration of a particular project.

Most translating positions are freelance with no benefits. Rates are billed by the word, the hour, or the job. Hourly rates can fall between $15 and $30, and a highly skilled translator can earn between $60,000 and $150,000 per year. Conference interpreters often work for a flat fee for the conference, up to $500 a day.

On-line translation services charge from one to four cents per word. Some translation specialists associate with a firm that will do advertising, billing, and serve as a central booking office. While contract translators working under these situations may make less than freelancers, they do not have the overhead for advertising and promotion that independent agents do.

The Translator's Handbook (Year 2000 Edition), by Morry Sofer and published by Schreiber, is a superbly practical guide to all aspects of the translation profession. It is considered a book translators rely on. It has chapters on how to find work, how to charge for translation services and other important financial considerations in freelancing, where to locate the best dictionaries, course work and accreditation, and specific information on more than sixty-four languages.

CAREER OUTLOOK

In the United States, job opportunities for full-time translators are limited. Some of the variables that affect demand are the skill level of the translator/ interpreter and the languages of fluency. There is more demand and less supply for Khmer than for French, for example. The largest employer of translators is the Foreign Broadcast Information Service. It hires translators on a contract basis, many through the Joint Publications Research Service. Most of the translators work at home, sending and receiving work electronically.

Europe may provide a better market for translators but not necessarily American translators. U.S.-educated students will have to compete with citizens of European countries with excellent training in English as well as fluency in their native tongue and often several other languages. Additionally, most European Community (EC) members must first hire from their native labor pool before hiring foreigners (U.S. citizens). Asian countries also have well-established English language programs beginning in elementary school, and fluency in English increases each year with these populations.

There are many large placement agencies in Europe that operate similarly to temporary employment agencies in this country. Students may work temporarily without a work visa, but placement agencies in Europe report to us that they seldom are perceived as the contractor for translators or interpreters and usually do not fill these types of positions. Nonstudents must have a work visa to work at all, and to gain such a visa they must be guaranteed employment with a foreign employer.

No matter who the employer is, most demand for interpreters and translators is less than full-time. As a result, individuals hired to perform these functions usually need other skills and attributes to recommend them to a hiring organization. The translating or interpreting role is certainly important but only intermittent.

STRATEGY FOR FINDING THE JOBS

Become a Busy Translator/Interpreter

Creativity is the watchword for finding jobs in translating and interpreting. We have discussed the educational background and language fluency requisite for interpreters and translators. Let's assume the ability to move effortlessly between languages is one of your skills. How do you get started on a career in translating or interpreting? Where are the jobs and who will hire you without experience? If it's hard to get hired without some experience, how do you get that experience?

Whether you are seeking permanent staff employment in a civilian or government situation or are willing to risk the exigencies of a freelance career, you'll need to begin acquiring experience as soon as possible, even while you're in school. Call and write your local hospitals, schools, and Chambers of Commerce. Let them know you are available to translate or interpret for visitors or guests who have difficulty with English. In some communities, orchestras, choral groups, and even school children visiting foreign countries on educational or cultural programs might appreciate the voluntary services of an interpreter or translator. Some of these organizations may be able and willing to cover your transportation expenses. As you acquire some of these experiences, ask for letters of reference to begin to build a portfolio to support a more substantial job search.

Being reactive and watching for job advertisements in newspapers is another resource you certainly should use. After all, you know there is a job opening when you see an ad, you know what qualifications and experience are being requested, and you're told exactly how to apply. Log on to www.about.com and under their "Careers" section you can locate jobs listed by individual states or you can check out the classified sections of newspapers around the country.

In addition to Web-surfing the classifieds, don't forget to check out some of the bigger websites devoted to jobs for recent college graduates, such as www.careermosiac.com and www.monster.com.

Become a Translator/Interpreter Who Networks

Networking is another key strategy for finding jobs in interpreting and translating. Let people know you are seeking work and ask to be recommended by those you have worked with on projects. When attending conferences, meet and talk with as many of your colleagues as possible. Be sure to have some simple business cards made up with your name, language proficiency, address, and telephone number to pass out as a reminder. The International Labor Organization (ILO), a large user of interpreters, has a staff of resident interpreters to draw on, yet it uses freelance interpreters 80 percent of the time. Often, one freelancer is asked to recommend others to the employer.

Joining professional groups such as the American Translators Association (www.atanet.org) opens up additional opportunities, including that of becoming credentialed. These organizations not only provide the opportunity to network with colleagues at national, international, and regional meetings, but also publish newsletters and annuals that contain important editorial material and display ads from employers, programs, schools, and organizations offering products. Student membership is modest.

Become a High-Tech Translator/Interpreter

Don't expect to get called back on jobs if you're tapping out your work on an old electric typewriter. Professionals and bureaus use sophisticated software and produce a finished product in a format that bespeaks competence, professionalism, and quality, ensuring repeat business.

Keep excellent records of your contacts, get back in touch with people promptly, and treat everyone as a potential client. Consult with clients thoroughly to understand their needs, format specifications, and all associated details before tackling a job, and then meet all deadlines.

Have distinctive stationery and billing forms made up. Even your answering machine message is an indication of your professionalism and seriousness of purpose. Clients easily generalize from these outward image associations to conjectures of the quality of your work.

Become a Consistently Better Interpreter/Translator

Reading books, practicing your skills using tapes and videos, and attending films, conferences, and training sessions all improve your fluency and general information level. Take advantage of any and all opportunities to get better at what you do. Your jobs may range from conferences on polymer chemistry to apiary techniques. You cannot afford to be ignorant of vocabularies or concepts.

POSSIBLE EMPLOYERS

There is a range of employers who hire workers to use foreign language skills as either a primary or an auxiliary job function. These employers include commercial language schools, publishers, hospitals, federal government agencies, state and local governments, foreign firms operating in the United States, American firms operating in foreign countries, U.S. manufacturing firms exporting to other countries or importing from other nations, translation agencies, and other employers.

Commercial Language Schools

Commercial language schools often offer translating and interpreting services; check the Yellow Pages on your webserver under "language school" to find potential employers in a specific city. The authors found 101 listings for Manhattan, New York. These listings contain phone numbers, addresses, Web map and direction links, and, frequently, an E-mail account.

Publishers

Literary translators work for publishers under either an authorial or a work-for-hire agreement. Approximately 1,500 translated books are published each year in the United States; this number has not changed significantly in the past ten years and is not expected to grow dramatically.

In 2000, the ten publicly held book publishers were Random House (http://randomhouse.com), Simon & Schuster, Inc. (www.simonsays.com), Penguin Putnam, Inc. (www.penguinputnam.com), Time Warner Bookmark (www.twbookmark.com), HarperCollins (www.harpercollins.com), Avon Books (www.avonbooks.com), Nolo Press (www.nolo.com), John Wiley & Sons (http://wiley.com), Houghton Mifflin (www.hmco.com), and W.W. Norton (www.wwnorton.com).

Moody's directories, other corporate directories, and the Yellow Pages for metropolitan areas can be used to identify additional publishers that you may be interested in contacting.

Hospitals

Nearly every hospital that serves a sizeable population of non-English speakers has interpreters on its staff. In a recent phone conversation with a personnel administrator at a large hospital in the Boston area, we were told that hospitals consider interpreters to be a critical component in generating new income for the facility. Some large hospitals employ ten to fifteen interpreters, depending on the number of languages used in the community and the number of people using those languages. Again, the Yellow Pages are an excellent resource for identifying hospitals in a given geographic region. A website that can help you locate any hospital or medical facility in the country may be found at www.hospitaldirectories.com.

Federal Government

Various federal government agencies hire individuals with in-depth knowledge of various cultures, geographic regions, and languages. These agencies include the Defense Intelligence Agency (www.dia.mil/), Voice of America (www.voa.gov/), U.S. Information Agency (www.usia.gov/), Drug Enforcement Administration (www.usdoj.gov), National Endowment for the Humanities (www.neh.fed.us/), Library of Congress (www.loc.gov/), National Security Agency (www.nsa.gov/), and Federal Bureau of Investigation (www.fbi.com).

The federal government, even with budget cutbacks and extended hiring freezes, is still a very large employer. Future budget cutbacks will affect the number of entry-level government positions available, but there continues to be a need for federal employees.

State and Local Government

Interpreters, translators, and others with language fluencies work in many capacities for state and local governments. Just a few of the possibilities are described here. Contact the personnel office of your state of residence and talk with an employment specialist about other possibilities. You can locate all state personnel offices through the website at www.piperinfo.com.

States fund social service agencies that serve new immigrants and non-English-speaking people. These agencies hire interpreters and more specifically trained workers, such as social workers, who are fluent in at least two languages. Check with the appropriate state personnel office for more information on the types of positions available and regions of the state where those workers are employed.

Some economic development offices, or arms of those agencies (international trade centers or offices), interact with officials representing both U.S. and foreign firms. There is often a need for translators and interpreters to assist in importing and exporting goods and services, and many of these state offices compile lists of individuals and firms who provide translation services. Contact your state economic development office for more information on how you can be included on its list. State courts also need to make use of the services of freelance translators and interpreters in the courtroom.

Foreign Firms Operating in the United States

The *Directory of Foreign Firms Operating in the U.S.* lists companies by home country, alphabetically by company name, and alphabetically by American affiliate. This volume is an invaluable resource for identifying organizations in which foreign language skills could play an important role in your being hired.

American Firms Operating in Foreign Countries

A three-volume directory titled *Directory of American Firms Operating in Foreign Countries* lists companies alphabetically by company name and by the foreign country in which they do business. As with the *Directory of Foreign Firms Operating in the U.S.,* this is an excellent resource for identifying companies that present opportunities for using a foreign language, either as a primary or an auxiliary job requirement.

Exporting/Importing

Several resources can be used to direct the job seeker to organizations involved in exporting and importing. These organizations need the skills of people fluent in foreign languages. State or regional business journals and magazines contain lists of firms in this type of business as well as marketing companies offering services to exporters and importers. Directories of exporters and importers can be found in many college and larger public libraries. Resources such as the *2000 Directory of United States Importers and Exporters* (2 vol), published by the Journal of Commerce, can be especially useful. In addition, economic development agencies often will provide lists of these types of firms.

Translation Agencies

Translation agencies like Berlitz Translation Services (located in every major city) and others hire workers on a freelance basis. These companies can work with up to 200 freelancers a year. Ninety percent of these people translate from some other language into English. Translation agencies usually hire experienced workers, and when they need to bring on additional translators, they ask for names from the people they are currently working with. Most of these agencies can be found in New York, Washington, Chicago, Dallas, and San Francisco. Use the Yellow Pages and Web Yellow Pages to locate organizations in your area; they may be listed under "Translation Agencies" or "Translators and Interpreters."

Other Employers

Many other types of employers hire translators and interpreters. They include airlines, law firms specializing in patents or immigration, shipping companies, travel agencies, banks, TV networks, radio stations, museums, advertising agencies, and foundations such as the Red Cross or the Ford Foundation. Consult with library professionals you are working with to find appropriate resources that will allow you to develop a list of companies or agencies to contact.

POSSIBLE JOB TITLES

Interpreters and translators are usually called just that. There are some specializations within these fields, and other job titles you may see include linguist, language specialist, precis reporter, literary translator, conference interpreter, and judicial interpreter/translator.

When you are interested in using your language skills to interpret or translate as a secondary job function, any number of job titles can apply. A federal visa applications office might hire a secretary who speaks French fluently, an administrative assistant who can translate Spanish, and a director who is fluent in German. These are just three of the hundreds of possible examples of job titles to consider. Use the information contained in this chapter to help you brainstorm a list of possible job titles.

RELATED OCCUPATIONS

The skills required to be successful in translating and interpreting are also needed in other kinds of jobs, including news editing, news directing, reporting, technical writing, newscasting, and creative writing. According to the *Dictionary of Holland Occupational Codes*, the personality traits associated with people working as translators are similar to those of people working as microbiologists and bursars. Interpreters are like lawyers, brewing directors, producers, artist's managers, and recreation supervisors (to name just a few) in terms of personality traits. In looking at related occupations or occupations that draw on your strengths, abilities, and values, use what you discovered about yourself in the self-assessment portion of this book to consider all the possibilities.

PROFESSIONAL ASSOCIATIONS FOR INTERPRETERS AND TRANSLATORS

There are myriad professional associations that individuals interested in interpreting or translating can join. Membership in these organizations can provide many benefits: a better understanding of what working in the profession is really like and current challenges facing the profession; notification of opportunities for additional training and professional development; inclusion in a directory that potential employers might use for hiring purposes; and access to actual job listings or referrals. If you would like to find out more about any of these organizations, contact information has been provided.

The American Association of Language Specialists
1000 Connecticut Ave. NW, Suite 9
Washington, DC 20036
Website: www.taals.net
Members/Purpose: Professional association of interpreters, translators, revisers, precis writers, and terminologists at the international conference or international organization level.
Journal/Publication: Yearbook.

American Literary Translators Association
Box 830688 (MC35)
University of Texas, Dallas
Richardson, TX 75083-0688
Website: www.utdallas.edu
Members/Purpose: Literary translators who translate from any language into English and institutions that wish to support efforts to improve the quality of literary translation; to expand the market and expedite contact between translators and publishers.
Journal/Publication: Newsletter; *Translation Review.*
Job Listings: Developing computerized index of translators, authors, publishers, and grants; newsletter contains occasional job listings.

American Society of Interpreters
P.O. Box 9603
Washington, DC 20016
Members/Purpose: Professional interpreters interested in fostering a high code of ethics among interpreters.

Training: Keeps members informed of new developments in the profession.
Journal/Publication: Newsletter; *Interpretation Service Handbook.*
Job Listings: Offers member referrals to meeting organizers; recommends experienced chief interpreters and specialized organizations to prospective meeting organizers.

American Translators Association

225 Reinekers Ln., Suite 590
Alexandria, VA 22314
Website: www.atanet.org
Members/Purpose: Professional society of translators and interpreters. Promotes recognition of translation as a profession and improvement of standards and quality of translation. Administers an accreditation exam.
Journal/Publication: *ATA Chronicle; Translation Services Directory* (must pass ATA accreditation exam to be listed).
Job Listings: See *ATA Chronicle.*

Buddhist Text Translation Society

Sagely City of Ten Thousand Buddhas
Talmage, CA 95481
Members/Purpose: Includes some lay scholars (although many members are Buddhist monks and nuns) with a minimum of three years of intensive study in Buddhist scriptures, practices, and scriptural languages. Purpose of the group is to translate the Chinese Buddhist canon into other languages, primarily English. Generally, translators work on a volunteer basis.
Journal/Publication: *Proper Dharma Seal; Vajra Bodhi Sea.*

Chinese-English Translation Assistance Group

3910 Knowles
P.O. Box 400
Kensington, MD 20895-0400
Members/Purpose: Includes Chinese language and computer specialists from academe, government, and business in this participatory cooperative organization designed to improve computer-stored and computer-printed Chinese-English dictionaries. This group develops on-line tools for translators.
Journal/Publication: Bulletin.

International Association of Conference Interpreters

10, avenue de Secheron
CH-1202 Geneva, Switzerland

Website: www.aiic.net

Members/Purpose: Professional conference interpreters from sixty-seven countries who assess the levels of linguistic competence of members. Ensures the maintenance of high ethical standards throughout the profession. Recommends criteria designed to improve standards of training in interpreters' schools. Maintains liaison with the UN, European Community, and international employers.

Journal/Publication: Bulletin; yearbook; code of ethics.

International Association of Conference Translators

15, route des Morillons

CH-1218 Grand-Saconnex, Switzerland

Members/Purpose: Conference translators, editors, precis writers, and revisers from twenty countries who work to maintain professional standards, handle problems, and represent interests of the membership.

Journal/Publication: Bulletin; directory.

International Federation of Translators

Heiveldstraat 245

B-9040 Sint-Amandsberg, Belgium

Website: www.fit-ift.org

Members/Purpose: Societies of translators and interpreters in forty-nine countries who work to keep members informed of current developments and practical and theoretical questions in the field of translation.

Training: Organizes roundtables and conferences.

Journal/Publication: *Babel*; *Nouvelles de la FIT*; *Proceedings of Triennial Convention.*

Israel Translators' Association

P.O. Box 9082

91090 Jerusalem, Israel

Members/Purpose: Translators and others interested in translation. Promotes and protects members' interests.

Training: Sponsors lectures, discussions, and workshops on editing, linguistics, and translation.

Journal/Publication: *Directory of Israeli Translators*; *Targima.*

Job Listings: Offers placement service.

Modern Language Association of America

Ten Astor Pl., 5th Floor

New York, NY 10003

Website: www.mla.org

Members/Purpose: College and university teachers of English and of modern foreign languages. Seeks to advance all aspects of literary and linguistic study.

Journal/Publication: *MLA International Bibliography*.

Job Listing: MLA Job Information contains job listings for college and university-level positions.

National Association of Judicial Interpreters and Translators

551 Fifth Ave., Suite 3025

New York, NY 10176

Website: www.najit.org

Members/Purpose: Interpreters working on a staff or per diem basis in municipal, state, or federal courts; translators specializing in legal translations.

Training: Conducts workshops on consecutive/simultaneous court interpreting; seminars and semiannual symposia on professional ethics and practice.

Journal/Publication: Annual membership directory; *Citations*; monograph series on interpreting issues; monographs and other professional aids; *Dictionary: Key Verbs for Court Interpreters, Glossary of Terms Used in Federal Court*.

Job Listings: Provides directory of members to lawyers seeking to hire interpreters or translators.

Society of Federal Linguists

P.O. Box 7765

Washington, DC 20044

Website: www.federal-linguists.org

Members/Purpose: Translators, interpreters, and others employed by the U.S. government who use foreign language in their work; nongovernment individuals working at language jobs, e.g., teachers, abstracters, editors, cataloguers, and librarians.

Journal/Publications: Newsletter; membership directory.

CHAPTER TWELVE

USING LANGUAGE AS AN AUXILIARY SKILL

hapters 13–15 will cover career paths in government, educational administration, and business, industry, and commerce. These three chapters discuss options available to the foreign languages graduate who chooses not to be hired primarily for his or her foreign language abilities. There are any number of reasons why you, as the graduate, seek such employment and why an employer seeking workers may consider education in a foreign language important to the career but not of prime importance.

One reason would be that your language skills are not sufficiently developed to stake your career on them. Perhaps you graduated with a degree in Russian language and literature. You had never studied Russian before college, and although you were a good student in college and have been to Russia once or twice, you simply are not fluent or confident enough in your command of Russian to seek a position that would depend on this talent.

Still, you love the Russian language and have enjoyed your exposure to the Russian culture. You hope to stay involved with that through your work, perhaps even finding a professional opportunity to visit Russia again. Your intentions might even include continuing to study the language. On the other hand, you have many other skills, talents, and interests that allow you to present yourself to an employer as someone other than a linguist. You might have substantial computer expertise, administrative ability, writing talent, or public presentation skills. Perhaps your quantitative abilities are strong and you like working out problems with facts and numbers. Any number of opportunities are open to you that make use of these nonlanguage talents and your foreign language preparation.

On the employer's side, there may be reluctance to feature language skills as a requirement for employment and thus hire a new individual who may have only that talent. Most American organizations cannot afford to hire someone to work full-time solely on foreign language projects. In fact, when foreign language talent is a need, many business firms simply subcontract that work to local translators or interpreters for the time they need it. If they go abroad, they will hire someone for the length of time required. No matter how expensive this kind of short-term service may be, it is far less expensive than employing someone year-round with a salary and benefits package. Some organizations have local employees abroad who are skilled in both their native tongue and English. An employer with European or Slavic subsidiaries might appreciate your language background and have every intention of using it occasionally, but the employer will require other qualifications in addition.

One persistent myth about putting your foreign language training to work for an American-based organization is that you will go to work immediately for some branch or subsidiary office based in the country whose language you speak. Nothing could be further from the truth. The reality is, in most cases, you cannot expect to be assigned overseas until you have mastered the corporate culture and climate of the employer. Foreign staffs are smaller and more exposed to the public and the press than are their domestic counterparts. It is essential that each employee sent overseas be thoroughly grounded in an understanding of and appreciation for the employing organization and its mission before representing it on foreign soil. You need to learn the ropes and pay your dues in the United States before securing a transfer, and this may take several years.

Sometimes this means putting your use of the language on hold while you acquire other skills for the organization. You may be learning the product line for a consumer goods firm, acquiring detailed information about the manufacturing process in an industrial setting, or studying immigration and naturalization protocols as part of a position in collegiate student affairs. During your period of training in any job, you'll be learning about the competitive marketplace, accounting, computer systems, research, and any number of other business skills. Your employer may be well aware of your language background, so don't neglect it. When the call comes from your supervisor asking you to consider a foreign trip or assignment, he or she will expect your language skills to still be top-notch. Keep your skills fresh with an occasional evening course or self-directed learning program. Use any opportunities that present themselves at work to indicate your background and interests in that particular area of the world.

Another possible reason for not putting your language degree up front as a prime qualification for employment may have to do with how you see yourself. Perhaps in reviewing the exercises in the self-assessment chapter that opened this book, you realized there was much more to your aspirations and dreams about life after college than just using your academic major. Most of us choose our majors rather early in our college years in order to complete the requirements for graduation. But during those extremely productive and formative years of college life, you were hardly static. You change, grow, and become a different person. You have innumerable new experiences, so the person who graduates is often very different from the person who entered college. And yet your major may remain the same while you, as an individual, have come very far from the thinking and intentions that originally drew you to that degree.

You may have different ideas now about what you want to do with your life. College has exposed you to other valuable skills. Maybe you realize you have good negotiation skills and you'd like to try those out in a career. College may have uncovered some creative abilities in art, theater, music, or dance that you were unaware of when you entered and now would like to continue to explore. Yet your degree and major remain constant. Nevertheless, you may want to try something new: sales, banking, theater administration, social work, or sports management. Not only is that reasonable, but you may also be surprised to find that your degree will not be undervalued.

CHAPTER THIRTEEN

PATH 3: GOVERNMENT

"Government is a trust, and the officers of the government are trustees; and both the trust and the trustees are created for the benefit of the people."
—Henry Clay

THE FEDERAL GOVERNMENT

It does not take much exploration of how to use a degree in foreign languages to recognize the employment possibilities in the U.S. government. The federal government, even with much-talked-about reductions in force, employed more than 2.7 million civilians at the beginning of the year 2000. Almost all (97.7 percent) were working in the executive branch, 1.1 percent were employed in the legislative branch, and 1.2 percent worked in the judicial branch of government. Government workers can be found in tens of thousands of agencies, boards, bureaus, commissions, and departments. The kinds of people hired reflect the nature of the work done in a particular unit. Agencies hiring the largest numbers of college graduates range from Veterans Affairs to Education, from Treasury to Energy. Federal jobs are much more likely to be white-collar, professional, or administrative positions than is true in the economy overall.

GOVERNMENT AGENCIES NEED WELL-EDUCATED WORKERS

Another consideration in seeking government employment is the nature of government agency work and the desired qualifications of candidates for that work. Specialized education and training, which includes training in foreign languages, is required for many of these positions. Initially, it can be a challenge to determine specific qualifications that the government is seeking. It will take some follow-up on your part to find out which jobs require the skills you possess. The following job advertisement, which appeared recently on the Internet, highlights the general nature of some job listings:

> *Benefit Authorizer.* Major duties: Make final determinations to adjust, resume, reinstate, suspend, withhold, and/or terminate benefits and compute the benefit payment rates in accordance with provisions of the Social Security Act considering such factors as type of benefit, age, family maximum, changes in family composition, prior or simultaneous entitlement to other types of benefits, and periods of nonentitlement. To qualify for consideration, you must be a college graduate and be proficient in both English and Spanish. Applicants must submit a copy of their college transcript or a list of college courses that includes hours and grades. You may apply by submitting a resume or an "Optional Application for Federal Employment" (OF-612) for this vacancy announcement.

Government Agencies Need Foreign Language Majors

Many government agencies and departments need foreign language expertise, if not as a primary skill, then as an important auxiliary talent. Although the job listed above is for a benefit authorizer, and it requires a college degree, one important criterion for selection is that applicants are able to demonstrate Spanish and English language proficiency. This chapter will look at a number of both of these possibilities with the caveat that agency needs change frequently, especially in today's global village. A government agency that previously had little need for employees with foreign language skills may now have a requirement for these very skills.

Be Ready to Go Through a Screening Process

The government screening process takes skill, care, and lots of questioning to complete satisfactorily. That certainly may help to weed out those who are easily discouraged, who have difficulty doing research, and who find forms and documents an impossible challenge. The government employment process probably does play a part in self-selecting good candidates.

Know the Federal Pay Systems

Federal workers are paid according to one of two major pay systems: the *Statutory Pay Systems* or the *Other Major Pay Systems*. There are three statutory pay systems that include the General Schedule, Foreign Service, or Veterans Health Administration system. Other major pay systems include the Federal Wage System, the Executive Schedule, an Administratively Determined system, and the Senior Executive Service pay system. The three systems most pertinent to this discussion are the General Schedule, Foreign Service, and Administratively Determined systems. You can find a complete discussion of these systems in a report made available on the Office of Personnel Management's website (www.opm.gov) titled, "Federal Civilian Workforce Statistics: Employment and Trends."

Those paid according to the General Schedule (GS) are largely white-collar, professional, administrative, scientific, and technical employees. Entry-level positions for most college graduates begin at the GS-5 or GS-7 level. A schedule has been established for within-grade advancement, and once you become a government employee your eligibility for positions at a higher grade is enhanced. Foreign Service pay plans and schedules have been established for officers (pay plan FO) and personnel (FP). Within this pay system, the lower the class number, the higher the pay. Tables for both the GS and Foreign Service plans are shown in the earnings section of this chapter. Administratively Determined pay systems are fixed by authorized heads of agencies. These positions are typically even more competitive than General Schedule positions and may require rigorous background checks that often take a year to complete. Entry-level salaries are correspondingly higher.

Understand the Obstacles to Employment

Especially in the case of federal positions, one major obstacle prevents many from actively pursuing this option: the forms/procedures that candidates must complete. A sample of recent job listings showed the following requirements:

- Each applicant must submit a separate completed application for federal employment (SF-171), optional application for federal employment (OF-612), or a resume for each grade level you wish consideration for, listing your work duties and accomplishments relating to the job for which you are applying.

- Candidates are to submit (1) an application (e.g., SF-171, OF-612, resume, etc.) which is signed and dated; (2) an OF-306, Declaration for Employment (if submitting OF-612 or resume); (3) a DD-214 if claiming a five-point veterans' preference, SF-15 if claiming a ten-point veterans' preference, Certificate of Release, etc.; (4) transcripts, memberships, etc. (if appropriate); and (5) an SF-50 (if applying as a transfer or reinstatement eligible).

- Candidates selected for these positions must sign agreements outlining the conditions of employment prior to the appointment.

- You will be required to complete a Declaration for Federal Employment (OF-306) to determine your suitability for federal employment and to authorize a background investigation. You will also be required to sign and certify the accuracy of all the information in your application.

- If selected, male applicants born after 12/31/59 must confirm their selective service registration status.

- Public law requires all new appointees to present proof of identity and employment eligibility.

- A background security investigation will be required for all new hires.

- This position requires completion of a one-year probationary period.

- Successful completion of a thorough medical examination, a polygraph interview, and an extensive background investigation.

If language skills are a job requirement, you will see a statement in the job listing similar to the one shown below:

- Applicants for this position must be bilingual in English and Spanish. Candidates must able to communicate in English and Spanish with individuals for the purpose of obtaining information and conveying an understanding of complex requirements of federal programs. The ability of potential candidates to communicate in English and Spanish will be determined in an interview conducted in English and Spanish. Candidates who do not have the ability to communicate in English

and Spanish sufficient for successful performance in the job will not
be eligible for the position.

Don't let these kinds of requirements put you off! The federal government and civil service jobs in general can provide solid employment prospects.
Government jobs can provide excellent income, superior working conditions,
and, to many who are employed in this sector, an ambiance no different from
any major employer. If government employment is not on your list to explore,
consider adding it.

The federal government has not, however, been immune from the downsizing and layoffs that have occurred throughout the economy. Those seeking federal or state government jobs with some guarantee of permanency are
misinformed. In 1990, federal civilian employment for the executive branch
agencies totaled 2.25 million. That figure dropped to 1.8 million by the year
2000.

FEDERAL DEPARTMENTS AND AGENCIES

The federal government continues to hire new college graduates to fill
full-time, permanent positions as well as temporary and part-time positions.
Every government agency fills these positions, and an increasing number of
them require fluency in a foreign language. Some of the larger federal agencies and departments that hire workers with language skills are described
below.

State Department

The State Department (www.state.gov), founded in 1789, is the lead federal
institution for the conduct of American diplomacy. The department hires foreign service officers, foreign service specialists, and civil service employees.
Applicants interested in a foreign service career must select a "Functional Area
of Specialization," or "cone," when applying to take the required written
examination. The foreign service cones are administrative, consular, economic, political, and public diplomacy. Fluency in certain foreign languages
may qualify candidates for language incentive pay while serving at posts where
these languages are spoken. The department's website provides the details
you'll want to know as you explore this option.

Central Intelligence Agency

This agency services the United States as an invaluable source of information on trends and current events abroad. It is the agency that coordinates

our nation's intelligence activities by collecting, disseminating, and evaluating foreign intelligence that affects our national security. Most CIA positions are located in the Washington, D.C., area and salaries are administratively determined. Because of the sensitive nature of this department, applicants undergo a rigorous process of screening, including medical, psychiatric, and background investigations and a polygraph interview. Interested applicants should visit the CIA's website (www.cia.gov) to learn more about working for the CIA and to review current job openings.

Office of International Information Programs

The Office of International Information Programs (IIP) (www.usinfo.gov) is the principal international strategic communications service for the foreign affairs community. The office is part of the State Department. IIP designs, develops, and implements a variety of information initiatives and strategic communications programs, including Internet and print publications, traveling and electronically transmitted speaker programs, and information resource services. These reach—and are created strictly for—key international audiences, such as the media, government officials, opinion leaders, and the general public in more than 140 countries around the world. Visit the website to learn more about the office and then visit the State Department's website to learn more about current jobs and hiring procedures.

The Voice of America

For more than fifty years, the Voice of America (VOA) (www.voa.gov) has provided news, features, and music to its international audience. Competing with nearly 125 similar broadcast services worldwide, VOA is one of the top international broadcasters in today's vast global media market. Each week eighty-six million listeners around the world tune in to VOA programs that are broadcast in fifty-two languages, including English, via direct medium wave (AM) and shortwave broadcasts. Millions more listen to VOA programs placed on local AM and FM stations around the world, giving VOA a vast and unequaled global reach. VOA also offers TV programming and information via the Internet. For current employment information, visit the VOA's website and review advertisements for international radio and TV broadcasting positions.

Immigration and Naturalization

Under the Department of Justice, the Immigration and Naturalization Service (INS) (www.ins.usdoj.gov) is both a law-enforcement and service-oriented agency with a wide range of responsibilities over the admittance, processing, and possible exclusion of aliens with respect to citizenship in the United States. Some of the major occupations in the agency are border patrol agent, inspections officer, investigations agent, detention and deportation officer, information technology specialist, and a number of administrative jobs. Many positions require the ability to speak or learn Spanish and other languages. Visit the INS website for more information, then follow the instructions given to view current job postings.

Department of Defense

The Department of Defense (DOD) (www.dod.gov) provides the military forces needed to deter war and protect the United States. The major departments of this unit are the Army, Navy, Air Force, Marine Corps, National Imagery and Mapping Agency, National Reconnaissance Office, and National Security Agency. With hundreds of thousands of civilian employees, there is a broad range of employment possibilities and the need for a variety of preparations, including a foreign languages background. Visit the following website to connect with the various departments of this agency: http://140.47.5.4/pers/html/websites.html.

Peace Corps

Founded in 1961 by President John F. Kennedy, the Peace Corps (www .peacecorps.gov) is an international development agency of the federal government. It places volunteers in countries throughout the developing world in a variety of projects. Currently, more than 7,000 Peace Corps volunteers are serving in seventy-seven countries, working to bring clean water to communities, teach children, help start new small businesses, and stop the spread of AIDS. Since its founding, more than 155,000 Americans have joined the Peace Corps, serving in 134 nations. The appreciation of another culture through foreign language training is valued by the Peace Corps. Its website shows current openings and guides you through applying on-line.

National Endowment for the Humanities

In 1963, Congress enacted the National Endowment for the Humanities (NEH) Act to promote progress and scholarship in the humanities and arts in the United States. This grant-making agency supports research, education, and public programs in the humanities. In order to accomplish its goals, the agency hires some workers with either a bachelor of arts or master of arts degree in languages or linguistics for program specialist positions. Visit the Office of Personnel Management's (www.opm.usjobs.gov) website, select NEH as the agency, then view current job listings.

Department of Justice

The Department of Justice (www.usdoj.gov), which includes the Federal Bureau of Investigation and the Drug Enforcement Administration, hires individuals with language fluencies. This department employs thousands of people throughout the world who are responsible for carrying out law enforcement functions and providing legal services to the government. To review a listing of departments and vacancies, visit the Department of Justice's website.

DEFINITION OF THE CAREER PATH

Entry-level career opportunities in the federal government are widely advertised, and detailed job specifications are available for all but the most classified occupations. Although the application process may initially appear to be challenging, the screening and interview processes are fair and impartial and diversity is encouraged. Entry-level positions are classified according to government pay grades, and promotions and advancement opportunities are clearly indicated. Unlike many civilian occupations, the career path in most government jobs can be well defined. During your interview process you should be prepared to discuss the career path possibilities with representatives of the agency or department you are applying to.

WORKING CONDITIONS

It is difficult and not particularly responsible to generalize about federal government employment. Certainly, we have indicated in this section that the application process, even learning about job openings, is an indication of the size and complexity of the employer. But once hired, can it be so different from any other job? Yes and no. The federal government shares many of the advantages and disadvantages of a very large employer. There is bureaucracy, red tape, some enforced mobility, and some loss of personalization. There are also excellent salaries, benefits, career advancement, training, and mobility. The advantages are largely in the regularity and stability of government employment.

Many federal employees will tell you that the working conditions are no different from the private sector. In fact, most government jobs have more regular hours and make less out-of-hours demands on their staff than does the private sector. Working hours are fairly standardized. Additionally, the working environment may not be as luxurious as the private counterpart. Spending in government positions is complex and purchases come through numerous channels, so working environments tend to be fairly standard to spartan in decor and quality.

Salaries

Salaries are competitive with the private sector except for some specialized positions that may not do as well in the federal pay scales as they would in the private sector. Otherwise, regular pay raises, advancement, and promotion are largely apolitical, and benefits and pension plans are competitive.

Stability

Government jobs are less likely to be immediately responsive to fluctuations in the economy. While there have been some eliminations of government departments over time, the general picture is one of security. Individual jobs, too, must be highly compromised to be replaced. The appeal and grievance procedures are detailed, and abrupt individual job loss is rare, except for malfeasance or gross misconduct.

Drawbacks to Government Employment

Critics could easily take advantages and portray them as disadvantages. For example, the stability and regularity of government salaries are seen by some as a distinct disadvantage. If the economy does well or an individual excels dramatically in his or her job, the private sector can reward performance with increases in salary. That is not possible in a federal job. Let's look at some other frequent complaints.

Bureaucracy. So much paperwork, so many rules, and so many individuals who have made careers from mastering these complex forms and procedures can be frustrating to those who want to cut through red tape and get a job done. Many would say that the bureaucracy discourages risk-taking, innovation, and creativity.

Politics. The government is responsive to the political party in office, without a doubt. This response, however, is rather diffuse and slow. New administrations can bring about large-scale changes in government management, but many day-to-day decisions are compromised by political considerations. Critics charge it's not what's best that is accomplished, but whose political interest holds sway.

Public Esteem. Federal employees and the jobs they do are not generally held in high regard in the United States. Because their efforts do not have the visibility of the private sector, which uses mass media to single out star performers and successful organizations, they are not perceived as interesting or as active in their field. The relationship of the federal budget (including federal salaries) to income taxes is always a subject of public debate, and some people see federal employees as an additional burden on the tax rate.

TRAINING AND QUALIFICATIONS

If you take time to visit the Office of Personnel Management's website (www.usajobs.opm.gov) and look through the entry-level professional job listings, you'll find that many specify the qualifying education as "any four-year degree." For example, when investigating civil service jobs in U.S. State Department, the website says that any B.A. or B.S. degree is useful for their job opportunities. The job announcement shown below does not specify an exact set of credentials but rather shows the kind of background required of applicants.

International Radio Broadcaster, D.C. Knowledge of Kurdish people and American foreign policy required; for more information and application materials contact: Bureau of Broadcasting, Personnel, Washington, D.C.

EARNINGS

Many college graduates are disappointed when they review the entry-level salaries that are paid to many of the federal employees. The value of the benefits received, the relative stability of employment, and the defined system that provides for advancement when performance merits it, are attractive enough to keep federal employment very competitive. Two tables of information are shown, and they will begin to give you a sense of the amount you can earn when working for the U.S. government.

Although the most current GS pay scale can be found on the Internet, at the time this book went to press the following pay information was available:

	Step 1	Step 2	Step 3	Step 4	Step 5
GS-5	$19,969	$20,635	$21,301	$21,967	$22,633
GS-6	22,258	23,000	23,742	24,282	25,226
GS-7	24,734	25,558	26,382	27,206	28,030
GS-8	27,393	28,306	29,219	30,132	31,045
GS-9	30,257	31,266	32,275	33,284	34,293

Starting-level salaries for the Foreign Service pay system are shown below:

	Class 5	Class 6	Class 7	Class 8	Class 9
Step 1	$31,266	$27,951	$24,987	$22,338	$19,969
Step 2	32,204	28,790	25,737	23,008	20,568
Step 3	33,170	29,653	26,509	23,698	21,185
Step 4	34,165	30,543	27,304	24,409	21,821
Step 5	35,190	31,459	28,123	25,142	22,475

CAREER OUTLOOK

Federal hiring may not be as immediately reactive to economic conditions as is private industry, but federal hiring does follow, at some interval of time, shifting national concerns and priorities. Federal government employment is projected to decrease about 5 percent, or by 136,000 jobs, through the year 2008. Given the priorities of the administration in power, some departments and agencies will grow while others will shrink. Even so, this is a competitive employer whose labor force by all standards is better educated, is more technically astute, and has higher language and math skills than the workforce as a whole. Positions are competitive, and, in spite of the number of positions available to any four-year graduate, there is definitely a bias toward individuals with scientific, computer, and other quantitative skills.

Foreign language majors considering government positions that do not rely on language skills could maximize their attractiveness as job candidates by acquiring some additional technical skills while in college. If your quantitative ability has been something you've enjoyed using in the past, take advantage of some related mathematics courses, for example, statistics, linear programming, and perhaps some research design courses, if available. A few of these would make an impressive addition to your degree.

But perhaps mathematics has not been a strong point. Try computers. Take more than the basic introduction course. Enroll in some systems design courses or some MIS courses. Talk to a computer science advisor about what two or three courses would work well together for you as a nonmajor.

These are simply two possible options. You might very well select business management, the natural sciences, political science, or economics instead of math or computer science. A number of possibilities are available on your campus. See what your degree program will accommodate and then make the most of it.

STATE AND LOCAL GOVERNMENTS

State and local governments also need foreign language talent. A large city with a shipping port and foreign docking potential may desire someone with foreign language experience to help develop trade and market its docking and stevedore services. A state economic development office seeking industry to locate within its boundaries might develop a task force for the promotion of industrial sites to foreign manufacturers. The individual who brings a knowledge of a foreign language to these kinds of teams provides an invaluable service.

The need for workers with foreign language skills has become much more pronounced at all levels of civil service employment, including states, cities, towns, and municipalities. Police officers in even midsized cities may find growing communities of people speaking Spanish, Thai, Laotian, or Chinese. Doctors, nurses, social workers, and many officials find knowledge of another language to be a plus in their work and in their enjoyment of their jobs.

State Government

Many state jobs mimic the federal level to a remarkable degree. Depending on the size of the state and the bureaucracy established, the system may be as complex and multitiered as the federal government. However, unlike the federal government, there is apt to be a central personnel office (usually in the capital) and branch personnel offices that list all state openings and can provide specifications sheets for each of these positions. These "spec sheets" list required qualifications or combinations of experience and education necessary to apply, salary schedules, and whether or not a test is part of the application process. Examine the following job ad, which shows various combinations of education and experience that are acceptable for those interested in applying:

Workers' Compensation Claims Supervisor. The [state] Department of Labor has permanent, full-time position. Successful candidate will perform responsible administrative, supervisory, and technical duties as they relate to workers' compensation law. Minimum qualifications: Bachelor's degree in related field. Also two to three years experience in business management, insurance operations, or related field. Experience in processing insurance claims, supervising, or any equivalent combination of education and experience. Contact . . .

Visit a state personnel office, in person or via the Internet, and learn how to file a formal application, read the current job postings, and then stay abreast of additional postings. In some states, you can file one application and indicate the kinds of jobs you want to be considered for, and your application will become part of those applicant pools for a period of time.

If you know where you want to work in state government, visit that location, meet the people associated with the office, and express your interest. Bring a resume or arrange for a formal interview. However, a word of caution is due here. This is best done ahead of any formal job posting. To make such a visit after a job is announced would be disadvantageous for you and deemed inappropriate by personnel in the state office.

The state personnel office can be of great assistance in explaining the various state agencies and directing you to more information about the mission of each of them. Remember, their job is to secure the best-qualified applicants for the state, so they're interested in raising your level of awareness and appreciation of state government.

Local Government

Nowhere will your curiosity, perseverance, and research skills serve you better than in your exploration in search of a job in local government. Unlike the federal and state systems, local governments conform to no overall system; each is different, and informal aspects of a job search (talking directly to local officials) may be far more important here than the formal application process.

There are county governments, towns, cities, villages, unincorporated villages, boroughs, locations (New Hampshire), and plantations (Maine). There are school districts and special districts for water, fire services, sewage, and a number of other missions.

The composition, names of offices, and structure of these various governing organizations is idiosyncratic. The various structures have evolved over time, and the only similarities tend to be in the areas of local government involvement. Education, health care, highway maintenance, police, fire, parks and recreation, and sewage and water quality are among the frequently encountered areas of local government concern.

There is no one strategy for approaching this diversity of local government organizations. Some small towns' hiring practices are very informal, and a resume and letter and request for a formal interview might actually work against you. Other government organizations have job postings, application processes, and pay scale systems that rival their federal and state counterparts.

You must assess each local government structure individually and decide on your best approach. Once again, sharing with people what you are looking for, asking lots of questions, and using local reference sources (such as the local library and its staff) will educate you on the kinds of jobs available, what it might take to fill them, and what kind of application process is used.

STRATEGY FOR FINDING THE JOBS

The end result—obtaining one of the many excellent government jobs for individuals with foreign language degrees—more than justifies the means. Admittedly, the process includes a challenging and sometimes frustratingly detailed and complex set of applications and job posting and hiring rules. It can become a job in itself just to master the various systems. Try to remember that the government—federal, state, or local—is made up of people just like you. They are interested in your application. So, if the going gets tough, and it probably will, ask for help.

Personalize Your Search

Successful government job seekers have indicated that one way to break through the bureaucracy is to personalize your efforts. Begin by calling the agencies or departments you are seeking employment with and speak to a representative. Tell him or her what you're doing and ask for assistance and guidance. This will put a voice and a name to the employer, and he or she will certainly have valuable advice about the job specifications and other details of the job that interest you. Of course, you'll want to be careful not to ask for any special consideration or treatment for your candidacy, simply information on the position and the application procedure.

Uncover All the Job Listings

The government job market is unlike any other. Consequently, your job search strategies here will be different as well. Your first task will be to ascertain that you are seeing as many of the available job postings as you can, because no one location, website, listing, or hotline carries complete coverage of government, especially federal, job openings. If you are a persistent job seeker, plan to check each of the relevant sources described here. Become familiar with each and determine how often new jobs are listed so that you can create a postings review schedule for yourself.

Federal Jobs

A good place to start looking for actual job listings is on the U.S. Government's Office of Personnel Management website (www.usajobs.opm.gov). This site explains the federal employment process, and lets you look at current job openings, get general information on federal agencies, and submit an on-line application.

Several federal agencies were highlighted earlier in the chapter, and their specific website addresses were listed. Remember, not all federal position vacancies are listed on the OPM's site. So if you don't see any job listings for a specific agency where you would like to work, be sure to locate its website and review job vacancies listed there.

Carefully Complete Your Application

Information you include on any government application form is carefully evaluated, so you will want to do the best job you can. Because some of the forms ask for a lot of detailed information and employing a certain strategy will improve your chances of being considered, we direct you to the following resources.

If you would like to be sure that your federal forms address the knowledge, skills, and abilities needed, be sure to read the information provided by the agency or department on its website. Each job advertisement contains details that are important for completing all necessary materials.

Follow Up as You Would with Any Other Employer

Following up on your federal, state, or local government application is just as important as it is in the private sector. You can verify that your materials were received, show the hiring official that you are committed to your job search, and remind him or her that you are qualified and available for employment. If you haven't yet visited the office or agency you would like to work for, and you are able to do so, now is the time to put a face with one of the many applications that these offices receive. Show them who you are and tell them how you can help accomplish their mission given your training, skills, and abilities.

A common impression is that applicants for jobs in the government sector undergo a more formalized screening process. Because of the highly structured classification of employees in these sectors, most applicants believe that once you submit your application, there is little you can do but wait out the process.

Government employers are no different from any others. When faced with a hiring decision, they want to employ the best person for the job and one that will make a nice fit with the existing organization. While potential employee application processes and hiring conditions are certainly more codified than in the private sector, that does not mean you cannot put a face to your application or a voice to your name with a visit or a phone call. If you are near enough to visit a potential employment site, by all means do so. Introduce yourself and indicate that you are seeking employment or that you have an application under consideration. You may get a tour and an opportunity to meet some staff. Be sensitive to any concerns of others that the hiring process is being disturbed. If so, simply withdraw graciously.

If a telephone call is all that is feasible, maybe someone will speak with you about the mission of the particular office you are applying to and talk about current projects and initiatives, if that is possible. Your interest will be appreciated.

POSSIBLE JOB TITLES

The range of possible government job titles would constitute a volume on its own, so we offer just a few teasers. Using information provided throughout this book, add titles as you do your own customized research.

Federal

Foreign Service Officer
Foreign Service Specialist
Passport Examiner
Career Trainee
Junior Officer Trainee
Writer/Editor
International Visitor Exchange Specialist
Academic Exchange Specialist
News Assistant

International Radio Broadcaster
Border Patrol Agent
Immigration Inspector
Special Agent
Personnel Manager
Program Specialist

State
Administrative Assistant
Program Coordinator
Assistant Director
Assistant Manager
Program Monitor
Analyst
Program Aide
Program Assistant
Inspector
Investigator
Supervisor

City/County/Local
Administrative Analyst
Administrative Assistant
Program Analyst
Planner
Investigator
Inspector
Office Manager
Counselor
Program Planner

PROFESSIONAL ASSOCIATIONS FOR GOVERNMENT WORKERS

No matter which occupation you may choose to enter, at least one association will be in existence to serve your professional needs. Some of these associations will be able to assist you now by providing possible leads for networking or actual job listings. Look for groups that have membership directories or some type of job listing service. For the most part you will have to join an association to take full advantage of related services, but if you know that is the field you want to enter, consider it an investment in your future. If you're not sure what type of government work you will seek, review the following list of government-related associations to get an idea for what's out there.

American Federation of State, County, and Municipal Employees
1625 L St. NW
Washington, DC 20036
Website: www.afscme.org
Members/Purpose: AFL-CIO.
Journal/Publication: *AFSCME Leader; Public Employee Newsletter; Women's Newsletter.*

American Foreign Service Association
2101 E St. NW
Washington, DC 20037
Website: www.afsa.org
Members/Purpose: Associate membership is open to individuals and international organizations and corporations interested in foreign affairs, international trade, and economic policy.
Training: Conducts international conferences and symposia.
Journal/Publication: *Foreign Service Journal; Directory of Retired Members.*

Association of Management Analysts in State and Local Government
University of Pennsylvania
Fels Center of Government
3814 Walnut St.
Philadelphia, PA 19104
Members/Purpose: Management analysts from business and state and local government, professors, and heads of university public service institutes and state training institutes.
Journal/Publication: Conference papers; directory of members and conference attendees; *MASLIG Messenger;* workshop manual.

Civil Service Employees Association
P.O. Box 125, Capitol Station
143 Washington Ave.
Albany, NY 12210
Members/Purpose: AFL-CIO. Members are state and local government employees from all public employee classifications.
Training: Conducts training and education programs.
Journal/Publication: Newsletter; *Public Sector.*

Federal Managers Association
1641 Prince St.
Alexandria, VA 22314-2818
Website: www.fedmanagers.org
Journal/Publication: Membership directory.

Government Finance Officers Association of U.S. and Canada
180 North Michigan Ave., Suite 800
Chicago, IL 60601
Members/Purpose: Finance officers from city, county, state, provincial, and federal governments, schools, and other special districts; retirement systems, colleges, universities, public accounting firms, financial institutions, and others in the United States and Canada interested in government finance.
Journal/Publication: Bulletin; *GAAFR Review*; newsletter; membership directory; *Public Investor*; *Government Finance Review*.
Job Listings: See newsletter.

International City Management Association
777 North Capitol St. NE, Suite 500
Washington, DC 20002
Website: www.icma.org
Members/Purpose: International professional and educational organization for appointed administrators and assistant administrators serving cities, counties, districts, and regions.
Training: Operates ICMA Training Institute.
Journal/Publication: *Municipal Year Book*; newsletter; *Public Management*.
Job Listings: Has biweekly national job bulletin that can be purchased for $12.

International Military Club Executive Association
1800 Diagonal Rd., Suite 285
Alexandria, VA 22314
Members/Purpose: Naval, Army, Air Force, Marine, and Coast Guard personnel who manage military clubs, golf courses, and bowling centers.
Training: Conducts seminars on club management training.
Journal/Publications: *Military Clubs and Recreation*; *Pro-Gram Newsletter*; *Who's Who in Military Club Management*.
Job Listings: Encourages recruitment activities.

National Association of Government Communicators
526 King St., Suite 423
Alexandria, VA 22314
Website: www.nagc.com

Members/Purpose: Government employees, retired persons, nongovernment affiliates, and students. Seeks to advance communications as an essential professional resource at every level of national, state, and local government.
Journal/Publications: *GC Magazine.*
Job Listings: Maintains placement service.

National Association of Government Employees
159 Burgin Pkwy.
Quincy, MA 02169
Website: www.nage.org
Members/Purpose: Union of civilian federal government employees with locals and members in military agencies, Internal Revenue Service, Postal Services, Veterans Administration, General Services Administration, Federal Aviation Administration, and other federal agencies, as well as state and local agencies.
Training: Offers seminars.
Journal/Publication: *Fednews.*

National Association of Government Inspectors and Quality Assurance Personnel
P.O. Box 484
Beaufort, NC 28516
Journal/Publication: Newsletter.

National Association of Governmental Labor Officials
444 North Capital St. NW, Suite 401
Washington, DC 20001
Website: www.naglo.org
Members/Purpose: Elected and appointed heads of state labor departments. Seeks to assist labor officials in performing their duties and to improve employment conditions for American workers.
Journal/Publication: Membership directory; *ANGLE News.*

National Organization of Black County Officials
440 First St. NW, Suite 500
Washington, DC 20001
Website: www.nobco.org
Members/Purpose: Black county officials organized to provide program planning and management assistance to selected counties in the United States. Acts as a technical information exchange to develop resolutions to problems on the local and national levels.
Training: Conducts seminars.
Journal/Publication: *County Compass.*

Society of Government Meeting Planners
219 East Main St.
Mechanicsburg, PA 17055
Website: www.sgmp.org
Members/Purpose: Individuals involved in planning government meetings
on a full- or part-time basis; suppliers of services to government planners.
Provides education in basic and advanced areas of meeting planning and
facilitates professional contact with other government planners and
suppliers knowledgeable in government contracting.
Journal/Publication: Membership directory; newsletter.

Women Executives in State Government
1225 New York Ave. NW, Suite 350
Washington, DC 20005
Website: www.wesg.org
Members/Purpose: Women executives employed in elected or appointed
state government positions. Works to enhance members' skills in
management, public policy development, government and business
relations, and leadership.
Journal/Publication: Annual report; newsletter; membership directory.
Job Listings: Operates job search assistance and referral service.

Women in Municipal Government
1301 Pennsylvania Ave. NW
Washington, DC 20004
Members/Purpose: Women who are elected and appointed city officials
including mayors, council members, and commissioners.
Journal/Publication: *WIMG Update*; membership directory.

CHAPTER FOURTEEN

PATH 4: EDUCATIONAL ADMINISTRATION

ne of the most delightful and exciting aspects of studying a foreign language is meeting and communicating with people from different cultures and regions of the world. In fact, that very well may have been your reason for selecting foreign language as a course of study in college. For some students, the language itself was the enticement. You enjoyed getting inside another cultural context and being able to communicate. For others, the study of another language was a new and exciting way to connect with people.

Your foreign language instructors in high school and college may have been born and raised in another country, or they may have spent extended periods in residence abroad, and you found that exciting and stimulating. Maybe you met foreign exchange students from other countries who spoke the language you studied. Or you may have had an opportunity to visit another country and practice your language skills on the spot. No matter what your range of experience, you were drawn to learn more about other peoples and how to communicate with them on their terms.

Edwin O. Reischauer, professor of history at Harvard and former ambassador to Japan, made a forceful statement about the need for true connections in our shrinking world. People who are trained in and sensitive to the differences among peoples and who are interested in and trained in bridging cultures, ideas, and people are the people creating the connections. In *Toward the 21st Century: Education for a Changing World*, Reischauer states the following:

While the world is becoming a single great global community, it retains attitudes and habits more appropriate to a different technological age. . . . Before long, humanity will face many grave difficulties that can only be solved on a global scale. Education, however, as it is presently conducted in this country, is not moving rapidly enough in the right direction to produce the knowledge about the outside world and the attitudes toward other peoples that may be essential for human survival within a generation or two.

There are many ways to create or facilitate these connections. Teaching may not be what you want to do, or perhaps your educational progress in the language is not sufficient qualification for a teaching career. Traveling and living outside the United States may or may not be an option for you. Nevertheless, you love your language studies and the understanding it has brought you. You want to stay involved with the language, the culture, and, most of all, the people who share your interests. The field of educational administration is a career path worth exploring.

DEFINITION OF THE CAREER PATH

To those wondering just what kinds of careers there may be in administering educational programs, how many programs there are, and what level of diversity exists, take a stroll through your nearest good-sized library or go exploring on the Internet; it will prove instructive. A number of magazines and journals are devoted to education exchange programs, both for study and employment. More and more Americans are discovering internships, foreign travel through established programs and groups, and study abroad programs for summers, vacations, and school terms. All have a pronounced positive impact on education and career development. Each of these programs requires administrative staff who care about the introduction of American youth into another culture or foreign youth into American culture so that it is a positive experience for participants on both sides of the exchange.

The following educational administration environments differ in work settings, salary levels, nature of the work, and advancement tracks:

- American-sponsored private schools abroad

- Foreign study exchange programs

- American college programs abroad

- International student programs

- Corporate programs for foreign transfers

- International not-for-profit organizations

What these environments share is a belief in the value of experiencing other cultures. Each is cited because language training other than English is not the principal hiring qualification. Each environment will make different demands on the foreign language graduate in terms of needed and desired qualifications. The job advertisements shown below will begin to give you a good sense of these different demands.

Assistant Director of International House and Programs, State University. Duties: Assists in directing the International House Programs and services to international students; provides leadership for the program members; secures qualified students, both American and International, and supervises their activities; solicits and manages funds for the programs and coordinates activities with the International House Foundation and its supporters; assists all International House students on J-1 visas and provides assistance to the general international student population in F-1 visas. Provides cultural orientation for international students; provides academic advisement and orientation to the university community; speaks and corresponds with outside exchange agencies, university faculty, organizations that support the International House, members of professional organizations, and others; reads and assists with the implementations of U.S. State Department and others. Reads and assists with the U.S. Department and other appropriate INS regulations, student scholarship applications and forms, NAFSA documents. Drafts reports including annual report of goals and activities, annual budget, five-year plans, and required federal reports. Qualifications: Bachelor's degree in related field, with master's preferred. Must meet qualifications set by U.S. Department for issuing student visas. Must possess a valid driver's license. International living experience and practical foreign language fluency are preferred qualifications. Send application (available on our website at www.xxx.edu), letter of interest, resume or vita, and the names, addresses, and phone numbers of at least three references to: State University, Personnel Services . . .

A U.S.-based nonprofit development organization that advances the pace of progress in emerging democracies and developing countries seeks candidates for a *Project Assistant, Europe and Eurasia Division, Washington, D.C.* Duties include providing administrative support to projects, maintaining files and responding to information requests, acting as liaison between Washington and field offices, and supporting proposal development activities. Bachelor's degree required. Russian or European language and computer skills preferred. Good verbal and written skills are a must. Send resume, cover letter, and history to: P.O. Box . . . , Washington, D.C.

Placement Services Coordinator, Au Pair in America. Responsible for matching host families with a given region of the United Sates with au pairs coming from thirty-eight different countries. Position requirements: Customer service and sales experience required. Ability to work effectively on the telephone and handle multiple priorities is vital. Excellent verbal, listening, and problem-solving skills are important. Must have good data-entry and writing skills. Experience with Microsoft Word, Lotus Notes, database systems, E-mail, and Internet helpful. Minimum bachelor's degree required.

State University, Coordinator of International Admissions; $3,290 to $3,960 per month. Office of Admissions is seeking a qualified individual to coordinate, develop, and implement standards and guidelines; review of international and domestic transcripts, financial statements, and related immigration documents according to CSU, university, and federal guidelines; counsel and advise prospective and admitted students regarding nonroutine, borderline, and complex situations. Qualifications: Graduation from a four-year college or university in a related field. At least one year of progressively responsible professional student services work experience. Requires application, resume, and supplemental questionnaire. Call to request application package for Job #00 SA 030. Please visit our website at www.xxx.edu for additional information regarding position. AA/EOE/ADA.

American-Sponsored Private Schools Abroad

An extensive network of private elementary and secondary American-sponsored schools abroad duplicates almost every aspect of traditional

American schools. Each school needs skilled and sensitive administrators to work in non-U.S. settings. Whether it be the Middle East, Europe, or the South Pacific, these schools need administrators, coaches, teachers, and guidance counselors to ensure the American-sponsored school provides an enhanced cultural awareness. It cannot serve as a cultural island in its foreign setting. Because of the homogeneity of the student and staff backgrounds, it would be all too easy for these communities to become replicas of traditional American culture and values with little interchange or exchange with the communities in which they are located. Administrators with a love of foreign language and culture will provide the leadership needed to bring these schools in contact with the communities they share.

Cultural exchanges are frequently made when American schools celebrate holidays and invite local schoolchildren or residents to participate by viewing a Christmas pageant, a reenactment of the first Thanksgiving, or a mock presidential election. But it can also be accomplished by sharing school facilities with local residents when needed for civic events such as fairs or dances, or by opening up concerts or lectures to the public. Each of these bridge-building activities further entrenches the school in the community as a recognized and valued resource and not a foreign appendage.

Foreign Study Exchange Programs

The college division of the American Institute for Foreign Study (www.aifs .org) is a good example of a national organization that provides comprehensive information on hundreds of college foreign study exchange programs. Umbrella organizations such as this need staff members who understand the important transition that study abroad programs represent for an American student. Many exchange program staff members bring their own individual foreign study experiences into constant use on the job and share techniques with prospective students and parents for increasing the likelihood of a student's foreign study being a rewarding and successful experience.

Because many foreign study exchange administrators have participated in these educational experiences themselves, they understand and appreciate the many practical issues of living abroad that need to be solved before students can get on with the experience of learning. They may suggest places to live where participants can experience a real neighborhood setting or family atmosphere that will allow the student an opportunity to improve speaking skills and idiomatic vocabulary. These administrators can also direct students to vacation or weekend trips to destinations of cultural, historical, or artistic interest that might have been overlooked. They will provide advice on transportation, clothing, living expenses, and many other topics that they have tried and perfected.

Jobs such as these may not rely on or even require fluency in a foreign language, but that doesn't mean language skills are unimportant. Many people who want to stay close to a foreign language in their work are often skilled in the use of that language. They simply may not want their job to revolve around reactive work such as interpreting: Someone says something and you respond, or something is written and you write a translation. If you are more interested in autonomy, self-direction, and proactivity in your work environment, you will find it in foreign study exchange program administration. You can use your language skills on the telephone, in interactions with people, and in writing letters, but not as the single most important aspect of what you do.

Working as a foreign study program administrator in the United States will allow you to use your foreign language degree and experiences to help new generations of students successfully enjoy studying overseas. American staff with foreign language backgrounds work with academic program staff abroad to ensure, on the part of the host institution, successful transitions to a new environment. The gifted individual who has the foreign language training of the host country, an appreciation for and knowledge of the culture, and yet a shared cultural past with the American students becomes the best of guides into a new and exciting world.

American College Programs Abroad

It has become almost a standard expectation of many high school seniors that the colleges they are considering will have some program for exchange study or resident study abroad in one or more countries. Many universities have established branches of their U.S. colleges in one or sometimes many countries. Even smaller schools can participate with other similar institutions in consortium programs that share curriculums and overseas facilities.

Administrators for these programs need to be more than paperwork experts. They need to know all about the destinations of the students they are advising. They may be asked to advise on the language skill level needed for success, the level of culture shock that might be encountered, or the challenges for the student in a new country. In addition, these administrators are an authoritative voice for all that will be exciting and wonderful for the students interested in this experience.

International Student Programs

Here in the United States, all large and many midsized colleges and universities have staff specializing in international students' concerns. Staff are drawn from candidates who have an interest in international students, are pursuing a career in student affairs, and who have had foreign travel or residential experience, either academic, personal, or through a program such as the Peace Corps. Staff members in these positions help foreign students integrate into campus life by providing counseling, tutorial assistance, directories of on- and off-campus services, placement assistance for part-time employment or spousal employment, and social activities. An important part of their job is creating events to express and share the cultural plurality their students bring to the campus community. They often coordinate groups of local residents who will serve as hosts and friends of foreign students while they attend the American institution.

Corporate Programs for Foreign Transfers

Just as student affairs professionals help to integrate foreign students into the life of the university and surrounding community, corporate liaison specialists do similar work for Americans working abroad.

Many international corporations maintain large staffs in foreign cities including Paris, Brussels, Tokyo, Beijing, or Moscow. Families who follow a working member to these cities rely on foreign liaison staff to teach them the ins and outs of a new culture. It includes familiarizing family members with transportation issues, introducing children to schools, assisting in procuring housing, and providing information about recreational activities and shopping. While liaison personnel may be considered invaluable for locating a source of American peanut butter, they also know what's good on a sushi bar, a satay stand, or a pirogi tray.

These positions are often called "education officer," and the individuals filling these roles will produce informative "fact sheets" and informational brochures and papers on all aspects of the host country's culture. They will produce workshops and provide background materials for corporate planning efforts. Their efforts determine, in large measure, how happy and comfortable employees are in their new surroundings and how the corporate presence adapts to life in a new country. In addition to their liaison duties, these individuals may have other assignments within the human resources area.

International Not-for-Profit Organizations

Not-for-profit organizations that operate abroad also provide job opportunities well suited to foreign language majors who do not want to use language skills as their primary capability but still want to work with another culture. Home offices in the United States and site offices abroad service many volunteer workers. For example, WorldTeach (www.worldteach.org), a nonprofit nongovernmental organization based at Harvard University, provides volunteer opportunities to those who are interested in teaching in developing countries. This organization recently advertised for home-office staffers who are interested in using a foreign language proficiency. The nonprofit sector is an exciting and growing field of employment that gives its workers lots of opportunities and challenges and the risks and rewards that come with extending yourself and trying to do great things with limited resources. In this area of employment, individuals are encouraged to stretch and grow as they help to fulfill the mission and goals of the organization that employs them.

There are nonprofits organized around religious beliefs, political ideologies, human values, and educational aims in science, medicine, language, birth control, disease prevention, agriculture, and natural resources preservation. Bikes Not Bombs recycles bicycles to promote nonpolluting and equitable transportation. The Boston Mobilization for Survival organizes grassroots support for peace and justice issues. The Network in Solidarity with the People of Guatemala is a group of local committees supporting grassroots initiatives for economic and social justice in Guatemala. The International Medical Corps is a nonsectarian, nonpolitical medical organization that provides medical assistance and health-care training in developing countries.

Although all of these organizations do important work, because pay scales on the average tend to be below their commercial counterparts and resources and supplies are less abundant, it is critically important that employees care deeply about the work they do as individuals and believe in the overall mission and goals of the organization.

WORKING CONDITIONS

The six career paths outlined in this chapter share an appreciation for diversity, a curiosity about other cultures, and an interest in seeing diversity shared with others. Most of these positions also involve transitions and learning about change. Effective transitions require planning and an understanding of how people best accept change and how good learning can be effected in a changing environment. These are also service jobs, and, like other careers in the helping professions, it can be difficult to define a "typical day" in any of them. When one is serving as a leader, teacher, helper, or guide, the need for change can come at different times. People in these positions must be comfortable with and flexible about their availability and accessibility.

It isn't just students who experience the transitions, either. Many administrators who have spent time shuttling between U.S. and foreign centers of operation will speak of their frustration in not having a home base and failing to fully develop relationships in either place because of this constant mobility. Others relish the constant change of scenery and their own ability to easily adapt to new locations, people, diet, and routine. Other work situations may have you feeling like travel agents who never get to take trips for themselves—always advising people on destinations but never having the opportunity yourself. It's important in any job, and particularly in one that may involve residence in a foreign country, or even employment by a non-U.S. organization, to understand the nature of the job to be filled.

We can say these six different career paths share demands of accessibility, flexibility, planning, helping, curiosity, and understanding. Each demands a unique approach to lifestyle, territoriality, need for personal space, and one's definition of "home."

American-Sponsored Private Schools Abroad

American-sponsored private schools abroad work very diligently not only to create communities for themselves, but also to create a community among all associated American schools around the world. In reading a publication such as *The International Educator* (www.tieonline.com), you become aware of the conferences, seminars, transfer assignments, field trips, and exchange programs that bring teachers and administrators of these schools into continual contact with one another. Many of these people obviously love international living and spend a few years at one school and move on to another interesting challenge. Solid work skills in budgetary matters, computer technology, and curriculum planning certainly are necessary, but the ability to make a home in many different places and to make friends and connections easily is also needed. The myth of private schools as having lower educational standards for their faculty and staff is quickly disabused as you read profiles of these professional educators. Educational standards are superb, and these private institutions seek out professional staff who will enhance their reputations.

Foreign Study Exchange Programs

Foreign study exchange programs are administrative devices used to assemble large numbers of similar programs under one unit for ease in marketing, administration, and fiscal control. Despite their apparent size as organizations, the staffs are in fact quite lean. Each individual tends to wear more than one organizational "hat": record keeping, budgetary control, database development, marketing, and sales are some of the traditional tasks associated with working for these organizations. Staff are frequently called on to go on the road and speak at schools and to organizations about exchange program offerings. While most are U.S. based, there may be opportunities to visit member institutions abroad or to lead tour groups to the host country.

American College Programs Abroad

American colleges maintaining campuses abroad and foreign schools offering special programs for American students often employ Americans to help staff these programs. Working conditions in these situations would be comparable to that of the staff of any college. Heavy involvement with students, considerable paperwork, and a fairly relaxed pace—except for traditionally busy times of the academic year—all characterize these positions. Certainly, living and working abroad would offer travel opportunities, language improvement, and the chance to meet and interact with foreign nationals on a daily basis.

Language skills would be put to a daily test in resolving student passport, visa, and work permit issues; negotiating living spaces for students; and helping with any contracts or lease arrangements. These skills would also be used in preparing guides to shopping, post offices, and transportation as well as teaching orientation workshops for new arrivals.

International Student Programs

Student affairs staff in this country who focus on international students are involved in much program planning and event production as well as a significant amount of counseling. They work with other departments of student affairs (health, career, physical education, college union, dining services) to integrate their international students into campus life while at the same time educating American students about their fellow students from other countries. Residential campus life positions include arranging and overseeing evening events and attending committee meetings to accomplish the student affairs mission.

Corporate Programs for Foreign Transfers

American corporate positions vary little whether they are located here or in Paris. Most corporations pride themselves on being able to prepare employees to take on their new setting and on accommodating employees' traditional American needs. Consequently, individuals working in human resources and hoping to serve as cultural liaisons will find the working conditions characteristic of any large corporation: fairly fast paced, exciting, competitive, well supplied with resources, and demanding of both qualitative and quantitative output measures for evaluation.

International Not-for-Profit Organizations

You will find most not-for-profit organizations characterized by a shared ideology that moves members toward a common goal. Because many of these organizations were built on an idea of change or political viewpoint, structure and organizational elements may be less than traditional. Organizations such as Food for the Hungry (www.fh.org), an evangelical Christian international relief organization; Save the Children (www.savethechildren.org); Christian Foundation for Children and Aging (www.cfcausa.org), a Catholic Ecumenical Worldwide Charitable Foundation; or World Vision (www.world vision.org), a large Christian humanitarian organization all have philosophies that underpin their efforts in the field. The flexibility may be freeing or it may be confining, depending on your personality.

Since many of these organizations operate on funding that is precarious, working conditions often mean physical settings that are less than ideal, lack of supplies, and the need to spend more time on development of funds than on the implementation of initiatives. But working for a nonprofit may allow you to use your language skills.

TRAINING AND QUALIFICATIONS

The discussion on career paths has made it clear that in each of these educational administration roles, the focus is not entirely on your language skill. Each employment environment will require different additional skills. If specific skills are not demanded, salary is apt to be quite low. Many of these kinds of positions are perceived as very attractive, and supply far outweighs demand. Employers are aware of this and can be quite demanding of qualifications for positions that do not pay particularly well. Spend some time reviewing job postings in all areas of interest to become familiar with job requirements, pay scales for entry-level positions, and the associated lists of duties and responsibilities.

American-Sponsored Private Schools Abroad

Those interested in American schools abroad will find that most require U.S. certification and prefer teaching couples to single employees to help ensure an easy transition to being a minority in a foreign country. In addition, you may need coaching skills, curriculum planning, or other specialized administrative skills to win a spot in these kinds of organizations.

The following advertisement for an experienced director of an international study consortium for U.S. undergraduates seeking opportunities to study abroad is a good example of requirements. Entry-level positions would demand similar backgrounds, though fewer years of experience:

Director, International Education Institute. A master's degree or equivalent training and in-depth knowledge of the U.S. educational system. At least seven years of administrative and supervisory experience in international education or a closely related field with some background in teaching or working abroad is required, as are strong analytical, budgeting, and interpersonal skills and the ability to organize a high volume of work effectively. Excellent writing and communications ability and demonstrated skill in preparing proposals, reports, and program materials are also desired.

Foreign Study Exchange Programs

Working for a foreign study exchange program means understanding and having a background in both American and European schooling systems, good budgetary experience, and program leadership experience. Public presentation skills and some marketing and information publication design experience would also prove valuable. These organizations are in the business of recruiting students for a number of different programs. Because these programs may have high price tags, staff need to present a highly polished, professional image, master a wealth of detail, and be comfortable speaking in front of both small and large groups.

American College Programs Abroad

American colleges with programs abroad will often hire administrators here in the United States to work abroad administering programs on-site. A period of time on the American campus is critical to learn curricula, policies, and procedures and to ensure that the candidate can master the skills of the position. Student-advising experience with curriculums, some counseling, record keeping, and academic administrative experience will be looked at favorably as would your own participation in such a program and any periods of work, study, or travel abroad.

International Student Programs

The student affairs specialist may want to pursue further education in counseling or student affairs administration and take any steps possible while still in college to participate in the kinds of groups and activities they hope to associate with as a professional. Any kind of event planning, budget responsibility, or leadership role and/or training would be helpful. These advisory positions require the use of counseling skills; knowledge acquired through either formal education or on-the-job training in volunteer positions will be looked on favorably. Production of information materials is a big part of these jobs, and experience in writing, editing, and publishing pamphlets is also helpful. As with all these types of positions, public presentation skills are crucial.

Corporate Programs for Foreign Transfers

Corporate liaison officers are often groomed for this position internally, and many already have established expertise in some aspect of human resources management. Areas of expertise might include, for example, benefits administration, outplacement, or retirement and life transitions counseling and referral. The liaisons' interest in and knowledge of the cultural environment they want to work in will also be important to the organization employing them. For example, if you have some Russian language background and have begun a career in human resources management, it would be important to alert your employer to your interest in a Russian posting when available. Once there, use your relocation to your best advantage, developing a good knowledge of the environs, shopping, theater, medical facilities, currency exchange, and perhaps produce a few "fact sheets" for use by your coworkers. If continued relocations of staff prove the need for a permanent corporate liaison official, you would then be well placed to apply.

International Not-for-Profit Organizations

The not-for-profit sector has become increasingly demanding of specialized talents among its workers and volunteers. Strong candidates may have skills in finance or accounting, agriculture or medicine, teaching or construction. Often, workers may need training in Teaching English as a Second Language (TESL). It is a mistake to believe that because these organizations are not-for-profit, their administration is less than excellent. In fact, to attract contributions, either personal or corporate, these organizations need to be highly organized and professional and display just the same competencies as their for-profit counterparts.

Another myth of the not-for-profit industry is that salaries are low. Low salaries exist, certainly, but there also are very competitive salaries now as not-for-profits realize that to gain and hold quality candidates they must pay comparable wages.

In Any Setting . . .

If you have elected to de-emphasize your language fluency or to use your language as a secondary skill, then you must emphasize other talents that would make you employable. Even so, if you desire to stay in contact with the language you studied in college and have the opportunity to speak it, then when selecting educational administration positions, you would be well advised to carefully consider the career environments discussed in this chapter. Select the one most closely suited to what you have to offer or would be willing to add to your training and qualifications and then begin to take the steps necessary to match your experience more closely to job requirements for these positions.

EARNINGS

The six paths we have been discussing all involve the administration of programs that are international in scope and that will keep foreign languages majors in touch with their language of study to some degree. They all emphasize valuing diversity, exploring unfamiliar cultures, and bringing enthusiasm and reassurance to others who may be less familiar with other cultures and consequently less accepting of them.

Your choice of a career path is an amalgam of many other, smaller decisions and reflects your own value system. The business major who chooses corporate marketing certainly will realize a higher income than a marketing major who elects to use his or her skills in promoting AIDS awareness through public service videos for a nonprofit firm. Each has different values regarding income and work orientation.

For the foreign language major, too, different values make for different choices among these career paths based on length of workday, income level, relationships with coworkers, mobility, and stability. As we review some dimensions of each path, with a focus on earnings, consider carefully what you value, what you need, and what will make you happy. The earnings outlined for each path are generalizations only, gathered from the field in numerous conversations with working professionals. Most of these employers are in the private sector, with the exception of state colleges and universities, and salaries are published only in the aggregate for a class of employees by title and years of experience. Compensation packages for positions abroad are completely individual, involving options such as flights home, housing, payment in U.S. dollars or the local currency, tuition assistance for dependents, movement of household goods, and countless site-specific perquisites that make comparisons meaningless.

American-Sponsored Private Schools Abroad

Negotiating salary packages is a crucial part of interviewing for an American private school position overseas. Packages can include spousal employment, tax incentives, and other add-ons that make comparisons between foreign postings very difficult. Websites such as *The International Educator* (www.tieonline.com), the official publication of the Overseas Schools Assistance Corporation, and *NewsLinks*, the publication of International Schools Services (www.iss.edu), have excellent information on salary and benefit negotiations. These reports will compare foreign teaching and administrative positions to their U.S. counterparts and try to make fair comparisons, even with all the nonsalary benefits. Entry-level salaries for administrators often start at $25,000.

Foreign Study Exchange Programs

A foreign studies exchange program administrator could fill any number of roles: marketing, sales, recruitment, credentials processing, or direct mail managing. Salaries would be competitive with other academic service enterprises. What may be disappointing about this type of position is your distance from the foreign community, unless you are afforded the opportunity to travel to member schools or lead groups of students on educational tours. These are consortium administration positions that are essential to bringing together and marketing large numbers of foreign study programs, but these positions might leave you feeling far away from the action and the use of your foreign language skills. The range here is quite broad, depending on the scope and size of the employer, with entry-level salaries from $24,000 to $31,000.

American College Programs Abroad

A job as an administrator for an American college at its non-U.S. campus will probably mean a salary based on a similar position in the United States, with adjustments made for the country in which you would be living. Whereas you might earn approximately $24,000 a year as an admissions representative for an American university in London, you might also be given a housing allowance or some cost-of-living adjustment for living in one of the more expensive cities in Europe. These positions begin at a level equivalent to $24,000 to $29,000 and up, depending on your experience.

International Student Programs

A student affairs specialist with a bachelor's degree working with international students would begin in the mid-to-high $20,000 range at most academic institutions and would have regular salary increases, opportunities for promotion, and, in most cases, a superior benefits package. Likewise, he or she might be able to take advantage of benefits offered by the academic employer to pursue an advanced degree at no or low cost to themselves. Here are two advertisements, one offering almost $30,000 but requiring three years' experience. The other position demands more degree work, but the salary offered is lower. Both are certainly within the expected range, but the differences are instructive.

Student Affairs Specialist for International Students: Director of Student Activities, Community College, with responsibility for the Inter-American Center. B.A./B.S. degree with three years administrative experience, $29,916.

International Student Coordinator. Minnesota, four-year college, $27,500; master's degree and three years experience.

Corporate Programs for Foreign Transfers

A corporate liaison for an international firm would make a competitive corporate salary based on education and experience, with adjustments for foreign living. These could include moving allowances, car maintenance costs, provision for children's schooling, housing allowance, cost-of-living allowance, and any number of salary adjustments based on the country. Promotions and increases would be similar to any competitive corporation, as would the effects of a competitive marketplace and the global economy on job stability.

There are two salary figures of importance here. An entry-level human resource officer (generalist) position for a major corporation would begin at a salary of approximately $30,000. With the experience and seniority required to be competitive for an international posting involving corporate-liaison work for transferred employees, the salary would range from $48,000 to $68,000, depending on the associated benefits offered by the corporation to staff living abroad.

International Not-for-Profit Organizations

In many cases, fair or not, this type of not-for-profit employer assumes a "psychic income" based on working for the cause involved or in a foreign location. There may be no salary but, instead, a small stipend with housing provided. When there is a regular salary, it should come as no surprise that these are generally lower than comparable jobs in commerce and industry. More money is paid for unique skills, and many larger, established not-for-profit employers in the United States have competitive salary scales. Along with this has come an attendant bureaucratic complexity similar to any large organization and an increased competitiveness for jobs.

Review the salary information we have given you for American-sponsored private schools abroad, foreign study exchange programs, American college programs abroad, and international student programs, and know that if you decide to work for an international not-for-profit organization your salary will probably be lower than the other ranges we've shown. Some of the position titles generally open to entry-level workers include home office manager, program manager, counselor, and outreach worker. Talk directly with a representative of an organization you are interested in to find out more about the entry-level salaries it offers.

CAREER OUTLOOK

You don't need to be a career specialist to notice the robust outlook for jobs in educational administration abroad. Talk to parents, neighbors, and classmates, and you will hear of family, friends, and friends of friends who are studying or living abroad or who have worked abroad for a period of time. Notice the exchange students attending high school and colleges in this country and remember that they have their counterparts from your schools who are away in other countries learning equally valuable lessons about someone else's culture. The increasing ease of entering foreign countries and heightened interest in the exchange of ideas have all made study, travel, and living abroad almost commonplace. Many schoolchildren, even at the elementary level, now have opportunities to begin their exploration of other lands at an age that whets their appetite for continued exploration later in life.

Through all these changes runs the theme of global interdependence for economic survival, peace, and control and eradication of disease, poverty, and hunger. The stewardship of the health of what we now perceive to be an increasingly fragile planet is also becoming more important. These global concerns have an impact on international programs because they alter the climate of exchange in a positive way and increase the willingness of countries to allow the movement of students and private citizens back and forth. We now realize that our similarities far outweigh our differences. The human exchange that results helps meet the needs of the planet's inhabitants.

The practical side of all of this is an increasing number of jobs for talented individuals with a background in a foreign language who want to use it to some extent in the administration of education programs. As with any growing sector of employment, popularity and growth bring change. The expected change here will be increasingly demanding criteria for employment as programs and the people who are to staff them become correspondingly sophisticated. That may mean employer demands for greater language skills, more extended travel and living abroad experience, and stronger skills packages in business, accounting, management, or administration to offer the employer other than foreign language as an auxiliary skill.

The current market for overseas study programs includes young people in increasing numbers whose parents have also experienced an educational program outside the United States. This adds to the level of expectation and demand for quality. Employers react by raising their eligibility standards for new hires in an effort to meet demands for better housing, more substantial course offerings, increased ease of transferring credits between institutions, and competitive fees for their programs. The lines of prospective job candidates get longer, but the number chosen does not rise in the same proportion.

The outlook is bright, the demands clear. Whether your focus is academic, nonprofit, or corporate, make sure that your language and cultural knowledge base is strong. Make every attempt to have some foreign travel and living abroad experience. A period of study in some formal curriculum program abroad is also highly advantageous. Most important, don't neglect developing a skills package. This may be fund-raising, benefits administration, program design and implementation, counseling and advising, or strong experience in organizing volunteers. You'll need some of each of these experiences and skills to enter and stay competitive in the field of educational administration for programs outside the United States.

STRATEGY FOR FINDING THE JOBS

The good news in the educational administration career path for foreign languages graduates is the wide advertisement of these positions. All the possible employers we discuss in the career paths maintain high visibility to attract students, investors, and contributors. Many publish an array of attractive and informative literature detailing who they are and what their specific goals and objectives include. Your research in this area will go very quickly because of the high profile of all of these employers.

Learn All You Can

Acquire and read the literature you discover. Educational institutions have individual programs, a unique emphasis on student success or academic achievement, and various specific selling points they use to attract students. Not-for-profits are founded to support important ideas or positions on issues, and you'll want to understand those. Corporations have products or services with individual features and selling points. It's important to learn about these and judge which setting may be most comfortable for you as a potential employee. We offer you here some excellent beginning resources to use in your search for employers. Left to your own devices, a visit to your college career office or exploring on the Internet will reveal many more.

Use Two Tactics

Locating the specific jobs can be approached on two fronts simultaneously. First, make sure you have access to the publications that advertise jobs in this area. We've listed some of these, such as *The International Educator* (www.tieonline.com), *Transitions Abroad* (www.transabroad.com), *Community Jobs*, and *The Chronicle of Higher Education* (www.chronicle.com). Keep a roster of who advertises the jobs you're seeking and put yourself on a regular schedule to check those advertisements and be ready to send a resume and cover letter and any requested recommendations in response. This tactic is no different from other job searches. But these few publications do not cover the entire marketplace. Merely responding to their ads would not expose you to all the available jobs in educational administration that could be filled by a foreign language major.

Second, you'll need to take a more aggressive approach and initiate contact with some employers. Perhaps in your initial identification of employers, there were several institutional positions described that you haven't seen advertised. You may be hoping to administer the junior year abroad program on the French campus of an American college or perhaps you're seeking employment with a firm that packages study/travel/learn abroad programs for students. Maybe you'd like to put your administrative skills to use in a program providing medical doctors and materials to the African continent. You know these jobs exist, but they don't seem to appear in help wanted ads. To locate these employers, watch for advertisements of the programs being offered and then contact them to find out about employment possibilities.

Be Proactive, Not Reactive

You will need to reach out to these organizations, first by written correspondence, then by telephone, and, finally, in person. Prepare a letter indicating your interest in the organization, your belief in how you could make a contribution, and some specifics on what form that contribution would take. How you express those thoughts will depend on both the thoroughness of your self-assessment and your appreciation for the mission and objectives of the organization, not to mention your persuasive ability. E-mail or send your letter.

Follow up your letter with a phone call to the individual you addressed in your letter. Try to arrange a mutually convenient time and place to sit down together and discuss your qualifications and the needs of the employer in greater detail. If distances are too great for a personal meeting, arrange a convenient time for a longer-than-usual phone conversation and prepare some good questions for your interview.

It's unlikely that one meeting will result in an offer of employment. If you develop some mutual interest, you might be invited to return for another meeting or be asked to pursue the relationship in another way, such as providing a writing sample or meeting a referral.

When an employer meets someone in this way who has obviously done his or her homework and made a concerted effort to understand the operation, it is difficult to dismiss the person, even if it is not a propitious time to hire. There may be an offer of part-time work leading to a full-time position. Or the employer might give you specific information about when an opening is expected to occur and encourage you to apply at that time, if you are still available. Occasionally, an employer will overhire in anticipation of a projected loss, rather than let a potentially valuable employee slip by.

Use What You Learn

No matter what kind of response you get, each of these experiences—letters, telephone calls, and visits—will only serve to sharpen your presentation skills, improve your ability to discuss aspects of your particular package of attributes, and help to increase your awareness about these employers' vocabulary, concerns, and issues. All of this information will help further focus your ideas about where you can best fit in and what kind of job will make the best use of your talents.

Although you were probably aware of many of these occupational possibilities in college, they aren't necessarily environments you know much about. As you talk to professionals in any of these areas, take brief notes to remind yourself of the issues and concerns that surface in your conversations. Read all you can find on international students here, Americans abroad, and exchange programs in general to begin to develop a stronger sense of the working life in the career paths.

If you use the information you receive from your reading and contacts, you'll find that your conversations with potential employers become more informed. They'll see you as bright, aware, and on-target with their issues and therefore consider your candidacy seriously.

POSSIBLE EMPLOYERS

These career paths are essentially made up of similar jobs in administration that are educational in setting or purpose and are situated either here or outside the United States. Your search for possible employers can be highly creative. Because the possible employers in the educational administration paths range from private study abroad consortia to traditional public and private schools and colleges as well as the nonprofit sector, you will be locating employers through a variety of sources.

You'll find many American four-year college and university positions listed in *The Chronicle of Higher Education*. Not-for-profit positions might be found listed in the Sunday want ads of a major metropolitan newspaper or in a specialized job listing. Corporate liaison positions will be trickier to locate. These positions will be advertised as human resources positions, and the foreign liaison work may be in addition to other duties and responsibilities. Call consulates and embassies and read periodicals in which possible employers might advertise (such as *Transitions Abroad*). *Peterson's Guide to Four-Year Colleges* (www.petersons.com) would be an excellent source of American college programs abroad. And don't fail to use the career center at your alma mater or to investigate the possibility that some alumni from your college might be doing the very job you are looking for. They'll want to help you and often can provide "insider" advice. Finding the types of employers discussed in this chapter will require you to become an employer detective. Here are some clues to start your search.

American-Sponsored Private Schools Abroad

A word about employment agencies: We have noted before that most of what an employment agency does can be done just as easily and far more inexpensively by a determined and creative individual. That is not the case, however, in the area of private school administration abroad. This employment sector is most often entered through the medium of a teacher/administrator placement agency that gains entrance for its clients to job fairs. There are many reputable firms in the marketplace, they are not difficult to find, and, for the administrator seeking work in a private school abroad, they may be necessary. Many advertise in the newspapers and journals that service this educational setting, such as *Independent School* or *The International Educator* (www.tieonline.com). The most reputable are willing to provide client references whom you can contact to hear firsthand about their placement experience.

Entering the private school administrator market will challenge your perseverance, but once gainfully employed in the private overseas school network, you will notice a continual, and even expected, rotation of teachers and administrators among the various countries. Reading some of the publications that document these moves, such as *TIE* and *International School Services*, you will notice careers that have ranged all over the globe.

Foreign Study Exchange Programs

Saint Michael's College (http://waldo.smcvt.edu) has created a great website that was designed for students interested in studying abroad, but there is also a lot of useful information for you, the job seeker.

There are three organizations to contact if you are interested in working in foreign study exchange program administration. Contact information for these agencies follows:

American Institute for Foreign Study (College Division)
River Plaza, 9 West Broad St.
Stamford, CT 06902-3788
Website: www.aifs.com

People to People International Headquarters
501 E. Armour Blvd.
Kansas City, MO 64109
Website: www.ptpi.org

College Consortium for International Studies
2000 P St. NW, Suite 503
Washington, DC 20036
Website: www.ccisabroad.org

American College Programs Abroad

In addition to the following representative list of possible employers, the job seeker for positions representing American colleges abroad will find it diffi-cult to assemble a comprehensive list of schools having foreign programs. Some are full-year programs, some are just for a term, and others are only for the summer. There are schools and colleges that maintain complete branch campuses and others that house their program under the auspices of a resident college in another country. There are also consortia of American colleges supplying students to the same program.

Peterson's Guide to Four-Year Colleges (www.petersons.com) can be used to identify colleges and universities to contact. Check with schools in a given geographic area to find out whether they have foreign programs.

Brethren Colleges Abroad
605 E. College Ave.
North Manchester, IN 46962-1226
Website: www.bcanet.org

Monterey Institute of International Studies
425 Van Buren St.
Monterey, CA 93940
Website: www.miis.edu

Schiller International University
453 Edgewater Dr.
Dunedin, FL 34698
Website: www.schiller.edu

School for International Training
Kipling Road, P.O. Box 676
Brattleboro, VT 05302-0676
Website: www.sit.edu

International Student Programs

Most of these positions will be listed with a variety of titles in *The Chronicle of Higher Education* (www.chronicle.com). The job seeker will find even small colleges responding to whatever cultural diversity may present itself in their student enrollment. The growth for this particular field promises to be excellent, and more schools feel a responsibility to support cultural pluralism on their campuses and to ease the transition of students from other countries.

Corporate Programs for Foreign Transfers

Individuals seeking employment as liaisons for corporate relocation abroad should keep several points in mind. First, although your ultimate aim is to work abroad, you may have to begin by learning your job and the organizational norms here in this country. Many corporations reserve foreign postings for individuals who have paid their dues by working in the United States. More important, staffs are leaner abroad, and given the distance from the home office and the importance placed on them as representatives of their country, individuals posted abroad need to have earned the company's trust through an established service record.

Second, corporate liaison positions are seldom hired off the street through a general job advertisement unless a firm is hiring a foreign national in the area of operation. These positions tend to be hired from existing staff either here or abroad who have displayed a particular interest and knowledge base in serving as a bridge between the two cultures. Finally, your starting point for hiring should probably be some aspect of human resources or personnel work, such as benefits administration, because these positions are often supplemented by other duties and responsibilities.

Some resources listing employers having this kind of position follow:

Directory of American Firms Operating in Foreign Countries (New York: Uniworld Business Publications).

World Chamber of Commerce Directory (www.chamberofcommerce.com) (Loveland, CO: annual).

Foreign Consular Offices in the United States (Washington, D.C.: Department of State, annual). Lists addresses and phone numbers of consular officials who can advise you on American firms doing business in their countries.

International Not-for-Profit Organizations

Two good Internet sites to explore are International Career Employment Weekly (www.internationaljobs.org) and Monday Developments (www.inter action.org). They have excellent information about working for this kind of organization and allow you to review a sampling of job advertisements. Additionally, ACCESS: Networking in the Public Interest offers a number of job service products. Contact information is provided in the "Help in Locating These Employers" section.

POSSIBLE JOB TITLES

As you examine the following list of possible job titles, you'll see that many of them are director or coordinator positions. Be sure to also consider assistant or associate director positions or assistant coordinator jobs that you see advertised.

Coordinator of International Students
Junior Year Abroad Coordinator
Program Assistant
Director of Summer Programs Abroad
Program Representative
Director of Administration
Assistant Dean, International Services
Director, International Students and Scholars Office
Director, International Office
Director, Division of International Programs Abroad
International Education Director

Director of Study Abroad Programs
Director of Programs Abroad
Program Coordinator
Director, Academic Programs
Foreign Student Advisor
Visiting Student Counselor

RELATED OCCUPATIONS

Just a few of the many related occupations that you could consider include:

Admissions Officer
Student Development Specialist
Human Resources Officer
Counselor
Associate Dean of Students
Coordinator of Student Internships

HELP IN LOCATING THESE EMPLOYERS

A group of organizations that can provide either detailed information on working in educational administration or actual job listings follow:

ACCESS: Networking in the Public Interest
50 Beacon St.
Boston, MA 02108

The Chronicle of Higher Education
P.O. Box 1955
Marion, OH 43306-2055
Website: www.chronicle.com

International Employment Gazette
1525 Wade Hampton Blvd.
Greenville, SC 29609

Council on International Educational Exchange
205 E. 42nd St.
New York, NY 10017
Website: www.ciee.org

The International Educator (TIE)
P.O. Box 513
Cummaquid, MA 02637
Website: www.tieonline.com

The Times Educational Supplement
Times Newspapers Ltd.
Website: www.tes.co.uk

Priory House
St. John's Ln.
London EC1 M4BX
England

Association of American Schools in South America
14750 N.W. 77th Ct., Suite 210
Miami, FL 33016
Website: www.aassa.com

European Council of International Schools
2113 Lavant St.
Petersfield, Hampshire GU32 3EL
England
Website: www.ecis.org

International Educators Cooperative
12 Alcott Rd.
Falmouth, MA 02536

International School Services
Educational Staffing
P.O. Box 5910
Princeton, NJ 08543

Ohio State University
Educational Career Services
110 Arps Hall
1945 N. High St.
Columbus, OH 43210-1172
Website: www.osu.edu

Placement Office
Faculty of Education
Queen's University
Kingston, Ontario K7L 3N6
Canada
Website: http://educ.queensu.ca

Search Associates
P.O. Box 100
Mountaintop, PA 18707

University of Northern Iowa
Overseas Placement Service for Educators
Cedar Falls, IA 50614-0390
Website: www.uni.edu

*Transitions Abroad: The Guide to Learning,
Living and Working Overseas*
Transitions Abroad Publishing, Inc.
18 Hulst Rd.
P.O. Box 1300
Amherst, MA 01004
Website: www.transabroad.com

Schools Abroad of Interest to Americans
Porter Sargent Publishers
11 Beacon St.
Boston, MA 02108

PROFESSIONAL ASSOCIATIONS FOR EDUCATIONAL ADMINISTRATORS

Use the services of the people who staff the professional associations for the fields in which you are interested. Educational administration may seem very attractive to you, and there probably are several career paths that interest you, but you might find it bewildering to know where to actually begin. Begin with the people whose job it is to ensure the professional standards of their organizations, to promote the kind of work they do, and to interest others in it. Call or write them, and you will be amazed at the help they are willing to provide and the materials available.

U.S.-China Education Foundation
Route 5, Box 187
Old Kennedy Mill Rd.
Thomasville, NC 27360-9006
Members/Purpose: To promote the learning of Chinese languages and English language by the Chinese.

Training: Maintains a library; building a research center; conducts short-term study/travel programs.
Journal/Publication: *USCEF Update.*
Job Listings: Provides a placement service.

Institute of International Education
809 United Nations Plaza
New York, NY 10017
Website: www.iie.org
Members/Purpose: To develop better understanding between the people of the United States and peoples of other countries through educational exchange programs of students, teachers, artists, leaders, and specialists.
Training: Sponsors regional and national seminars.
Journal/Publication: *Academic Year Abroad*; *English Language and Orientation Programs in the U.S.*; *Institute of International Education.*
Job Listings: Foreign student locator service, a referral service that matches the needs of corporations with the qualifications of U.S.-trained foreign students.

Council on Standards for International Educational Travel
212 S. Henry St.
Alexandria, VA 22314
Website: www.csiet.org
Members/Purpose: To prepare information for use by educators on international educational travel and exchange programs.
Journal/Publication: *Advisor List of International Educational Travel and Exchange Programs.*

Academic Travel Abroad
3210 Grace St. NW, 1st Floor
Washington, DC 20007
Members/Purpose: To foster intercultural relations and educational cooperation between institutions of higher learning in the United States and countries throughout the world.

National Registration Center for Study Abroad
P.O. Box 1393
Milwaukee, WI 53201
Website: www.nrcsa.com
Members/Purpose: Provides information about member institutions' programs in sixteen countries; establishes and promotes standards of treatment for visitors from abroad, including the appointment of bilingual housing officers and counselors to deal with culture shock.
Journal/Publication: *New Horizons*; newsletter.

Council for International Exchange of Scholars
3007 Tilden St. NW, 5L
Washington, DC 20008-3009
Website: www.iie.org
Members/Purpose: Administration of mutual educational exchange program under the Fulbright-Hays Act (Fulbright Scholars).
Journal/Publication: *Directory of American Fulbright Scholars.*

CHAPTER FIFTEEN

PATH 5: BUSINESS, INDUSTRY, AND COMMERCE

An international pharmaceutical company, the National Bank of Westminster, England, Kentucky Fried Chicken, L.L. Bean, and E.F. Hutton: a seemingly disparate list, yet all these firms have something in common. They operate both in the United States and internationally. They conduct business with employees of many nationalities, in different political and economic environments, and in different time zones. The homogenizing effects of the computer screen, the telephone, and the fax machine cannot erase differences in culture. The umbrella of the same employer does not make every employee the same the world over. Differences remain that need to be understood, appreciated, and managed for success.

In a shrinking world economy, these organizations and the thousands of others that are added every year to the roster of multinational organizations need employees who can make a significant contribution to the mission of the firm in a specific department and also represent the company outside of the United States with the respect and sensitivity that should be the hallmark of every company doing business in another cultural context. For example, the Japanese major who now does financial analysis for a firm in Tokyo knows that the Japanese character for the number four is pronounced the same as the word for death (*shi*). Consequently, some Japanese would not be enthusiastic about opening a new branch office on the fourth day of the month and yet may be reluctant to express that cultural bias to a foreigner for fear of seeming provincial or old-fashioned. In several countries, such as India, the use of the right and left hand are rigidly proscribed, and to contravene these cultural norms is to commit a gaffe.

Examine the following job advertisement that describes foreign language skills as secondary:

Shipboard Hotel Positions/Officer Status: Gain international experience, worldwide travel. Require B.A./B.S. hotel/hospitality experience, cash handling/administrative experience, excellent customer service skills, professional demeanor, prefer computer skills and foreign language fluency. Resume/letter to . . .

DEFINITION OF THE CAREER PATH

What might be important in seeking your first position in which foreign language talent is not the primary consideration is that the employer does offer some opportunity for using that skill. If, for example, you speak Russian and want to continue to be involved in that language and culture, beginning work in sales for a pharmaceutical company that has operations in Russia would be a good move. Your entry-level position would be as a pharmaceutical representative speaking to doctors about the clinical indications and situations best served by your line of prescription drugs. You'll receive sales training, develop product knowledge, and learn how to manage your own territory, schedule appointments, arrange out-of-town travel, and coordinate meetings with your district manager. Periodic sales conferences, refresher training, and home office meetings will allow you to meet with other company executives who have contact with Asian operations and with whom you can discuss your interest. As you develop in your position and build a track record of success, you'll have an opportunity to apply for positions with your company's offices in Russia.

With increasing frequency, American businesses have been successfully launching branches in Russia. Fast-food operations such as Pizza Hut and McDonald's have captured the most media attention because they seem to represent ideological or cultural juxtapositions that Americans find interesting to read about or watch on the news. But these restaurant operations are just visible symptoms of a much larger effort by consumer goods retailers and manufacturers to find a market in the Russian Republic. When they do initiate plans to enter a new market such as Russia, one of the first things they do is to canvass their own employees to see who has Russian language, culture, or travel experience and what they might be able to offer in the planning process.

Many American software firms have found the Russian market particularly welcoming, because working with data and machine processes reduces some of the strains of communicating across cultural boundaries. Nevertheless, the American technician or consultant with a background in Russian language and culture would be a valuable member of a team sent overseas to either sell a product, install it, or advise on its implementation. Computer science may be a language all its own, but in this case a little Russian on one side and some English on the other would work wonders.

Many foreign languages majors working for firms with extensive dealings abroad never leave their desks in this country but instead "travel" all over the world every day via phone, fax, and electronic mail to provide valuable service to clients and customers. Consider this job advertisement placed by a nonprofit international development and disaster relief agency:

> *Miami-based regional coordinator for Southern Africa*: Needed to coordinate, administer, and communicate the agency's regional programs. Requires demonstrated involvement with grassroots development, relevant academic training or equivalent work experience, administrative abilities, and knowledge of Southern Africa.

The drop shipping of cargo (the movement of cargo contents from owner to owner on paper, even though the product itself may not physically leave the dock) often involves international communication. Financial brokerage houses often do extensive business in currency buying and selling that involves international use of the telephone and fax machine.

Occasionally, a firm will reserve foreign service, especially in cities or countries deemed particularly desirable, as a reward for more senior staff. Regardless of your language or educational background, whether you've served with distinction, or whether you are interested in a period of foreign residency, some firms select staff to manage their foreign operations purely by seniority, assuming that these experienced individuals have the talent that is needed abroad. When you are interviewing with an organization that has international operations, even if your initial assignment is domestic, be certain to inquire how personnel for foreign posts are selected and whether such a post will ever be available to you as you grow in your career. Most firms will be quite candid with you during the interview about your chances of serving in a foreign branch office.

In the hospitality industry, a period of exposure to foreign life is considered essential to learning the traditions of fine dining, wines, and hotel management. A foreign assignment is often part of the younger career employee's training as he or she moves up the corporate ladder, perhaps on the way to becoming a chef, a hotel manager, or director of function sales for a larger hotel where the niceties of refined service are an essential part of the knowledge required to create a grand event or occasion.

An individual might start with Holiday Inn in Cleveland as a functions sales manager, selling hotel services for weddings, sweet sixteen parties, summer corporate pool parties, and countless business functions, meetings, luncheons, and the like. These positions can be very creative: booking entertainment, providing decorations, assisting in food and beverage decisions, and helping to create the right ambiance and mood for an event.

Successful progress in this area would lead to a management position and might qualify you to spend time at a Holiday Inn abroad where you could be exposed to a more sophisticated menu, wine service, and guest amenities than are currently available in the United States. This kind of exposure to an older tradition of hotel keeping helps to develop a level of service that will distinguish your work when you return to the United States.

American restaurant chains, pharmaceutical manufacturers, gun manufacturers, and even catalog operations such as L.L. Bean are expanding all across the globe. Staff in home-office positions frequently encounter regular mail, electronic mail, telephone calls, and visits from representatives of these far-flung enterprises who will appreciate dealing with individuals who have not only some language skill in their tongue, but also sensitivity to their cultural context. This can be especially important in the Middle East, where behavioral norms and religious observances dictate work and social life to a far greater degree than is seen in the United States, and where Americans' likelihood of committing a social gaffe is greater without a cultural intermediary.

Advertising, banking, airlines, automobiles, architecture, and health services all present wonderful opportunities for work in other lands and using other languages here in the United States. Even so, some additional cautions need to be delivered. In an era of instant communications, there is less need than ever before for extensive foreign staff. Video telephones, excellent air travel schedules, and automobile availability mean that frequent shorter visits, rather than extended stays in other countries, are more the norm.

Furthermore, as English continues to become the unofficial world language, residents of foreign countries whose English is excellent are often seen by U.S. firms as better choices for staff than Americans. Their salaries are frequently lower, they can be paid in the local currency, there is no hardship in their location, and they are fully conversant with the culture, language, and bureaucracy of the society. What's more, their English is often superb. Strong political and social pressure is often on the U.S. firm to hire local citizens. If there is resistance to the intrusion of a nonnative firm, it can be modified by the employment of resident workers. In increasing numbers of companies, through this combination of excellent transportation systems and telephone and fax communications, there is simply less need for a U.S.-staffed foreign branch or division of a firm. Much can be accomplished from the home office with occasional visits.

WORKING CONDITIONS

We have suggested many possibilities for employment that do not revolve around your language fluency. This means that you will be using a unique combination of other skills and talents to attract an employer, not your language degree alone. As a foreign language major who has decided not to pursue language skill as the primary mechanism of employability, you are what the employer would term a *generalist*.

We can make some predictions about your possible working conditions. Usually only larger organizations can afford to consider generalist candidates. Although a larger firm suggests a competitive salary and benefits package, it should also suggest many candidates vying for few places, so competition will be stiff. Because you do not have a specialized skill, there will probably be an initial training program, either a formal school for several weeks or an informal continuing program of training done during the week at scheduled times away from your regular duties. These training programs are designed not only to integrate you into the culture of your employer but also to help begin the process by which you build specific skills and knowledge the employer can draw on. In other words, without having majored in business, hotel and restaurant management, computer technology, or any other technical major, your principal task once you land a job will be to begin to develop some solid skills and experience in a specific area of business knowledge to remain attractive to your present and future employers.

You will not use your skills in a foreign language as your principal selling point in entering the job market. You will be hired partly for that skill and education but probably also because of your energy, enthusiasm, and potential to be molded to fit the needs of the organization. To grow within that organization or to move out of that organization, you will need to begin immediately to acquire more specific skills that will allow you to succeed on more concrete accomplishments than your original entry.

This initial training period bears little resemblance to the schooling you just completed. It is very demanding, your progress will be closely monitored, and you will be interacting with a number of company representatives who will, in most cases, meet to discuss your merits as an employee and to schedule assignments that make the best use of the attributes they perceive you to be demonstrating. It is a training period but a closely evaluated one.

TRAINING AND QUALIFICATIONS

The training period that will make up the early period of your employment will not only ensure your value to your current employer but also will build a foundation that will help to secure your continued worth in the workplace. Take full advantage of this entry training and of every possible training experience afforded you in your employment.

This training might be in an area such as financial analysis that captures your attention, and you might find you have an affinity for looking at quantitative data in a critical way. You will learn the various ways data can be interpreted for results and how to express those results to help management make effective decisions.

You might find you enjoy the area of human resources management and would like to learn more about the work classification system, drawing up job specifications, and determining duties and responsibilities and their associated pay levels. Or your interest might lie in benefits administration or cross training and staff development.

One area college seldom provides much exposure to, even in the business major, is product management. This is the movement of a product from the raw material stage to the finished product, with countless opportunities for cost savings, efficiency modifications, and quality enhancement. It is an area of specialization all its own and attracts many talented people.

The principal reason for encouraging you to develop some particular skills is that in any job move after this first one, potential employers will be more critical of your past experience. As a new hiree right out of college, most employers will give the nod to a four-year degree without expecting any specialized skills or knowledge. Your degree serves as a guarantee that you can learn what you need to know to become an effective employee. In this first hiring situation, some of your potential is taken on faith. It will not be this way again, so you must take advantage of your situation by becoming a skilled and knowledgeable employee.

Developing Specialized Skills

Let's say you are hired after college as a sales representative for a college textbook publisher. You learn your product line and do a good job of selling that product. You work independently out of your home with occasional supervisory visits and you make an excellent income. After five years, you tire of the routine of visiting college after college, and you decide to make a change. What skills other than college textbook selling have you acquired on the job in five years?

Interpersonal skills have been perfected and polished, certainly. But what about specific skills? A move to a different kind of job will be difficult, even more difficult than getting the first job out of college, because you now have five years of experience with one organization under your belt. But as far as qualifications go, what have you got to offer a new type of employer?

Now, what if during that five years, you asked your employer whether you could solicit some potentially publishable manuscripts from college faculty? Your request might be agreed to and some suggestions made about which fields might be most promising, perhaps the natural sciences. You solicit some materials or proposals for books, read them, make some suggestions and editorial comments, and forward them to your superiors for consideration. Perhaps one of these is published and you gain some recognition for skill and taste in selecting potential new authors and texts. This recognition could easily lead to a transfer to the home office editorial department or new-product planning division, increasing your specialized skills and building valuable experiences for your resume.

Maybe, in your first job, you have an opportunity to develop some plans and see them through to completion. Perhaps you can join a team whose main task is analysis and gain some particular familiarity with that work. You may be able to join a group doing marketing plans or fiscal planning or restructuring of staff. Additional computer training may be available, as well as opportunities to attend graduate courses in the evening related to your work. Take advantage of all these opportunities, because they will help improve your next job presentation.

Not only will this initiative in seeking training improve your daily performance and help you to enjoy your job more, but it also will bring you the attention and possible promotions in status that are the rewards of exceptional effort. And if, like so many new employees, you decide after a year or two to refine your job prospects and seek other employment, your resume will then display an entire new spectrum of skills that will make you attractive to another firm as a potential employee.

Additional Skills: Communication, Analysis, and Research

As a generalist with an excellent liberal arts education, you bring to the workforce excellent oral and written communication skills. Much of your work in business organizations will revolve around communication: face-to-face, on paper, and electronic. Writing and using manuals, procedures, bulletin boards, memoranda, and electronic networks and participating in meetings, meetings, meetings will draw on your ability to communicate clearly, effectively, and powerfully. The following advertisement highlights the need for these skills:

Medical Staff Services Coordinator. Health-care services company seeks qualified individual to work in Physician Services Department. Individual will coordinate credentialing, licensing, and privileging of physicians, including day-to-day communications with various hospitals, interaction with billing and insurance companies, and verification of training and practice history. One to two years' health-care experience and/or B.A./B.S. degree in health care or business administration preferred. PC experience essential. Seek highly organized, detail-oriented individual with excellent verbal and written communication skills. Must be able to work efficiently under tight deadlines and build effective relationships with regulatory boards and agencies. Competitive salary, excellent benefits, professional work environment. Send resume and salary requirements to . . .

Critical thinking is essential, too. Looking at problems and devising solutions will occupy much of your time. Expressing your ideas, interpreting situations, and determining patterns will challenge your ability to think creatively and systematically.

Perhaps you work for a public utility, and in analyzing your market research you notice an area with both a large percentage of Hispanic customers and a low number of requests for home service of gas appliances. Some investigation leads you to discover a lack of Spanish-speaking repair technicians and a reluctance on the part of the Hispanic market to allow a repair person who speaks no Spanish into their homes. Introducing some Spanish-speaking repair technicians into this district is certain to be beneficial to both the customers and the utility.

Your research skills will allow you to compile and analyze relevant information and to present your findings so others can appreciate and use what you have discovered. You will be able to seek out helpful resources, formulate the relevant questions, and develop ways to supply and clarify the answers. Look at the next advertisement to see how an employer relays these needs:

Research Associate. Provides primary research and data collection in nationalities problems and ethnic conflict in Russia. Works closely with executive director to produce policy briefings, memoranda, and reports on issues for internal and external audiences. Minimum requirements: master's in Russian Studies or related subject required, knowledge of nationalities issues in Russia, and good grasp of current international affairs essential. Fluency in Russian required, ability to work in-depth and develop own research standards required. Some travel to Russia may be required. Knowledge of Word and familiarity with school and its systems preferred. Send cover letter and resume to . . .

As a foreign language student, reading and memorization played a large part in your study habits. These are equally valuable skills to mention during an interview. The ability to amass and retain large amounts of detailed data will come in handy in the business world, as will your well-disciplined reading habits. There is always more than enough professional reading material to keep abreast of in business. Let your potential employer know that you are a reader and a learner.

EARNINGS

In this career path a variety of industries, employers, and job titles are discussed. To do justice to the corresponding variety of salaries possible would merit a volume of its own. Fortunately, if you have access to the Web (and don't forget your local library, which frequently will provide free Internet access to patrons for predetermined blocks of time), you can easily "survey the salary surveys"! Here are a few good starting places in your search for an estimated starting salary:

U.S. News and World Report Estimated Starting Salaries (www.usnews.com) is specifically designed for new college graduates and will feature thirty and forty academic majors and their starting salaries for the most recent year for which the survey has data (frequently that translates into two or three years previous to the current year). The *U.S. News and World Report* survey also indicates if the salaries have risen or fallen in the past year.

Another good site for wages and trends within employment areas is America's Career InfoNet, which can be found at www.acinet.org. This site takes a bit of getting used to, but once you learn how it operates you can compare starting salaries in different geographic areas of the United States.

A very comprehensive salary website can be found on www.monster.com. This site is basically a list of "links" that bring you to many different salary and wage surveys listed. It includes familiar links such as *U.S. News and World Report*, discussed on the previous page, and specialized surveys for technical employment.

The *U.S. News and World Report* website also lists "Hot Job Tracks for the 21st Century." Concierge, tissue engineer, and school CEO are just three up-and-coming jobs profiled in more than twenty-one different areas. Each area also profiles a "cold track" job. A "cold track" job is one with a glut of candidates or an endangered career path.

CAREER OUTLOOK

The career outlook for foreign languages majors in business, industry, and commerce is excellent but highly competitive, with job growth better than average for managerial/executive, technical/engineering, media/advertising, travel/tourism, and banking/finance positions. The reasons are twofold. First, the employment candidate we have been discussing in this chapter is being hired for something in addition to his or her language skills: sales skill, financial acumen, managerial potential, or administrative abilities. Second, the involvement of businesses, even smaller firms, in international markets is growing rapidly. The projected strength of the European Community, increasing American investment in the Far East, and dramatic changes in the Russian economic structure all suggest possible new markets in the global economy.

Employers now and in the future will demand increasingly talented employees, and the individual who offers the unusual combination of foreign language talent and another useful skill will be seen as valuable. Today's most effective organizations involve their personnel in training and development. They cross-train employees to learn about each other's duties and responsibilities. The staffing flexibility that results means the organization can respond more quickly to market demands, both challenges and opportunities. The worker best poised for this situation is one with a well-rounded skills package.

Many foreign language majors employed in international business report that not until they went to work did they appreciate their education. They realized their degree taught them far more than language skills. They learned about history, economics, politics, traditions, and personalities. In the work environment, this kind of information and the cultural nuances a foreign language major understands are seen as highly specialized and important knowledge.

The career outlook is clearly positive, but job seekers should be equally clear about what is required to participate in that future. You need a strong foreign language education, regardless of whether you intend to use it as a primary or an auxiliary skill. In the worlds of business, industry, and commerce you will need to have developed other skills to attract employers. Use your elective credits and your summers and vacations to build these skills packages. Most important, continue to learn all you can about the peoples, lands, and cultures that employ the language you have studied. You will then be able to seize any opportunity that might present itself in a volatile and multinational business environment.

STRATEGY FOR FINDING THE JOBS

Now that you have or will get a foreign language degree, you might be thinking, "Isn't the focus in international business on the business aspect of skills and not on the *international*?" Absolutely not! You have a job search advantage in this field that no other undergraduate degree, even business, can duplicate. As the world economy becomes increasingly global, even small and midsized firms are impacted in some way by international developments. You come to this job market with the undeniable proof that you've been thinking internationally for years: you have a degree in a foreign language.

Be Ready to Explain the Relevance of Your Degree

Now use this degree to your best advantage. The worlds of business, industry, and commerce have realized that no matter how much English dominates commercial transactions, it is critical to be able to reach out with the sensitivity and cultural awareness developed from studying the trading partner's language. There's no question that people like you are needed. You simply need to be ready to explain those strengths to an employer.

Find Out About Each Organization

The most appreciative audience for your credentials will be organizations currently doing business overseas or contemplating doing so. Without a business background, you will find that two strategies are critical. First, you need to know something about organizations you will approach for employment. You might not be a trained accountant, marketer, or financial analyst, but you do have the intelligence and education to appreciate how an organization is structured, what its mission is, and what challenges and opportunities it currently faces.

Take the necessary steps to review some information on the organization. An annual report might not be as helpful in creating conversation in the interview as a recent newspaper or magazine article about the industry in general. Many organizations print brochures on opportunities for employment, their operating philosophy, their missions and goals, and any number of other topics. This material might be general, but it will convey the image and expectations of the organization. You can find this material in libraries, career offices, or simply by telephoning the organization and asking someone to send it to you.

Most employers are willing, and even expect, to do considerable on-the-job-training once people are hired. To take the risk of hiring, they need to be assured that you have the flexibility, interest, and enthusiasm to learn all that's necessary. Your degree helps to reduce that risk. It proves you've already undergone some rigorous training in mastering your major. Your willingness to learn about the organization will go a long way in reassuring potential employers about your curiosity and interest in learning more.

The second strategy that you will need to employ if you lack a business background is outlined in the next section.

Relate Your Skills and Abilities to the Business Employer's Needs

You need to help the employer understand how you see yourself contributing to the organization. As they read your resume, you don't want them to think, "Does this person want to be posted overseas?" or "This person is an interpreter; how will I use him or her?" Let the employer know up front that, although you do have language training and you hope to put it to good use for the organization someday, your first goal is to learn the ropes and to build an expertise for yourself that the organization can utilize.

Once a mutual understanding of both your abilities and the organization's needs has been reached, be ready to speak specifically and concretely about the skills and attributes you have identified through your self-assessment and the experiences documented on your resume. Build a strong skills package statement for yourself, to which the employer will respond, "Yes, I need that!"

Highlight Some Specific Skills

In your contacts with employers, especially during interviews, learn how to focus attention on what you do well. You're a foreign language major, not a business major, so focus interview attention on your unique and valuable skills and knowledge base. Rather than discussing accounting procedures, you might talk about the effects of the European Community on national pride. Take stock of your special abilities and keep the interview focused on what you know and do well. This might include reading, writing, and speaking skills; problem analysis; and critical thinking. You might also have some specialized awareness of social customs or political systems or have done an in-depth study on some aspect of a culture. Business is part of the social fabric of a society, and any new business, especially one from another country, will try very hard to integrate itself into the new culture. You can play a vital role in that integration process.

Stay Current

As you read and research the companies you are contacting, try to relate what you learn about their current status, problems, and recent successes to what you have to offer in your skills package. Once you have established a track record and created a definable niche in the organization, then, if the need arises, you can begin exploring how to use your foreign language skills more directly with that employer.

POSSIBLE EMPLOYERS

You'll be pleasantly surprised at the range of firms that hire foreign language degree holders. Consider the following types of companies: environmental firms; sports organizations; advertising departments and agencies; banks, savings and loans, and credit unions; public relations departments and firms; software, hardware, and telecommunications manufacturers; hotels and motels; airlines, railroads, and cruise lines; hospitals and other health-care facilities; magazines, newspapers, radio stations, cable networks, and TV stations; professional associations; and manufacturing firms. Decide where you'd like to begin your search and use the resources listed to help you locate that particular type of employer.

Environmental Firms

Profile. You have a Spanish degree and a lifelong interest in the environment. You want to seek employment with an American-based international manufacturer of pollution control equipment now entering the Mexican market as a result of NAFTA. You hope to be part of a team preparing formal sales presentations for Mexican industries. Where do you start looking for employers?

Help in Locating These Employers. One way to begin identifying potential employers is to find the Standard Industrial Classification (SIC) code for this type of company. The *U.S. Industrial Outlook* (www.ita.doc.gov.) either lists these codes or provides a telephone number you can call for more information. There are many different types of pollution control equipment manufacturers; some of the SIC codes that are used include 3564, 3589, 8417, 8418, and 8421. Use these codes to identify company names in resources such as *America's Corporate Families* (www.d-net.com) or *Moody's Industrial Manuals* (www.moodys.com). Add to your list of potential employers by checking the Yellow Pages for company listings under "Environmental & Ecological Services." The *Environmental Industries Marketplace,* published by Gale Group, is designed to help anyone, including job seekers, gain access to the $100 billion environmental market.

Sports Organizations

Profile. Most of us have many interests and avocations other than just our college major. You may have been a Japanese major in college but also have a lifelong interest in skiing. Japan does not have as well-developed a skiing tradition as the United States, but it is growing rapidly. American ski products have widespread acceptance among the Japanese but require an American sales force and distribution network in Japan to compete. Your degree and skiing awareness combined make you a promising candidate for such a situation.

Help in Locating These Employers. *Sports MarketPlace* is an excellent resource for you if you're interested in combining your foreign languages degree with your sports-related knowledge or skills. It will help you to identify thousands of organizations, such as trade and professional associations, multi-sport publications, TV/radio broadcasters and programmers, corporate sports sponsors, athletic management services, market data services, trade shows, and suppliers and sales agents. Each entry includes background information as well as contact information such as address and telephone number.

Advertising Departments and Agencies

Profile. French yogurt, automobiles, films, and wine. German technology, Chinese fabrics, ceramic tile from Portugal, or knitwear from the Scandinavian countries. Foreign producers have a constant need to find new markets for products. American advertisers know their markets better than anyone. They know how to communicate with potential markets and they know what types of appeals are most effective. Who better to be on an advertising team that services this type of ad agency customer than someone with a background in the language and culture of the product of origin?

Help in Locating These Employers. If you would like to identify the larger agencies that would typically handle this type of account, you can use several resources: VGM's *Careers in Advertising*, Career Advisor Series' *Advertising Career Directory*, and Gale Group's *Business Rankings Annual*. Any of these books will identify employers you could consider approaching.

Banks, Savings and Loans, and Credit Unions

Profile. Joint ventures, new stock market centers, continuing investment easements in other countries, and increasing foreign investments here at home have dramatically changed the face of banking. Even the smallest hometown bank is fully conversant with foreign exchange rates, and many can provide currencies from around the world with only a few days' notice. The banker's market cannot afford to be local any longer. Individuals with a foreign language degree and some appreciation of international relations and economics will find banking an exciting, cosmopolitan, and welcoming work environment.

Help in Locating These Employers. Several types of resources are available if you would like to learn more about this industry. Be sure to check VGM's *Opportunities in Banking Careers*, Peterson's *Job Opportunities in Business*, *Banking Job Finder*, and *Hoover's Handbook of American Business*.

Public Relations Departments and Firms

Profile. Every challenge presented to a public relations department or firm requires drawing deeply on the talents, resources, and expertise of its professional staff to make the best presentation of the client or product. Imagine the difficulties of representing the fur industry, cigarette manufacturers, or any other controversial product, service, or individual. Public relations work requires being constantly aware of and sensitive to how images, words, and associations will be interpreted or understood by the public. Foreign language majors are trained in sensitivity to language through the study of another language and have learned to deal with vocabulary in a precise way—a valued skill in public relations.

Help in Locating These Employers. If you're ready to use your skills in a public relations setting, be sure to review Gale's *Public Relations Career Directory*, VGM's *Opportunities in Public Relations Careers*, O'Dwyer's *Directory of Public Relations Firms*, and see the Public Relations Specialists section in the *Professional Careers Sourcebook*.

Software, Hardware, and Telecommunications Manufacturers

Profile. The products in this category have worldwide markets, and most software is easily reconfigured for foreign users. This is an exciting, volatile, and exponentially growing field in which the foreign language major can not only play a role but also help to define the future. People are needed in this industry who will listen to clients' ideas in Hong Kong or Malaysia and take them back to designers and software writers to create new products and new applications for the technology. If you have a technological interest and are intrigued by communications and data processing, don't be surprised that this industry is equally interested in you.

Help in Locating These Employers. Some specialized resources to consider using when identifying software, hardware, and telecommunications manufacturers include Gale's *Computing and Software Design Career Directory*, VGM's *Careers in Computers* and *Opportunities in Telecommunications Careers*, and *Ward's Business Directory of U.S. Private and Public Companies*.

Hotels, Motels, and Hospitality

Profile. French hotels in China, American hotels in Russia, and growing numbers of tourists all over the world requiring desk service, menus, and safety instructions. Each situation provides ample opportunities for the foreign language major interested in travel and tourism with an emphasis on hospitality. The hotel industry has always put a premium on hard-working individuals who will concentrate on guest comfort. If you would enjoy learning about becoming a professional hotelier or other professional with numerous chances to display your foreign language appreciation and understanding, read up on the hospitality industry.

Help in Locating These Employers. Two books that can provide useful information on working in the hospitality industry are *Opportunities in Hotel and Motel Management Careers* and *Travel and Hospitality Career Directory*.

Airlines, Railroads, and Cruise Lines

Profile. This sector of the economy is the link between people who speak different languages. Leaving one location, you are transported literally and figuratively into new geography, not just of the land but of manners, culture, customs, and economy. These employers actively seek foreign language majors and fully appreciate what they add to the industry. Travel, the opportunity to meet new people, and a sense of adventure are hallmarks of these industries.

Help in Locating These Employers. Quite a number of helpful resources can be found in libraries. These include *Travel and Hospitality Career Directory, How to Get a Job with a Cruise Line, Jobs for People Who Love Travel, Flying High in Travel, Exploring Careers in the Travel Industry,* and *Moody's Transportation Manual.*

Hospitals and Other Health-Care Facilities

Profile. Hospital and health-care administration that is sensitive to the needs of non-English-speaking consumers is currently in demand. Many facilities are located in areas dominated by Laotian, Cambodian, Hispanic, European, Japanese, Chinese, and Korean populations. These health-care facilities must educate, inform, and administer health care and all its associated tasks. The well-educated foreign language major will make a significant contribution to this effort.

Help in Locating These Employers. *Opportunities in Health and Medical Careers, Healthcare Career Directory,* and *Encyclopedia of Medical Organizations and Agencies* are some of the titles available to help you identify hospitals and other health-care facilities.

Magazines, Newspapers, Radio Stations, Cable Networks, and TV Stations

Profile. Just as communications was the essence of your college major, it is the heart of the industries in this group. As we recognize our increasing diversity, we see cultural plurality mirrored in our communications media. A Spanish-language program on Sunday morning television, a Franco-American radio program, cable news direct from all points of the globe, and a host of ethnic magazines and newspapers responding to the different heritages of their readers. Where do you fit in these industries? Perhaps you sell time on radio and TV programs, report on cultural events for a newspaper, or work in the production of a TV news broadcast. Language, communication, and cultural sensitivity and outreach are your talents; this industry will put them all to work.

Help in Locating These Employers. There certainly is no lack of relevant reference materials when it comes to careers in publishing, radio/TV, and communications. Look at *Careers in Communications, Publishers Directory, Opportunities in Television and Video Careers, Telecommunications Directory, Radio and Television Career Directory, Gale Directory of Publications and Broadcast Media,* and *Opportunities in Telecommunications Careers* for direction in locating potential employers.

Professional Associations

Profile. A resource we frequently urge readers to use in their job search is professional associations. They provide information on the professions, training and development, opportunities to meet colleagues, and a never-ending flow of excellent, pertinent literature. However, they are also employers, so we list them in this section as well. Individual staffs are usually small, but the number of organizations is huge. There are enough opportunities that foreign language majors cannot and should not overlook seriously considering professional associations for employment.

With your degree, the association may be academic, commercial, historical, educational, or partisan. Whatever the specific purpose of the group, your vested interest by virtue of your degree will guarantee your resume gets a careful reading. Consider professional associations carefully.

Help in Locating These Employers. Two publications that identify these associations are the *Encyclopedia of Associations* and *National Trade and Professional Associations of the United States*. Both of these have several indexes to help you locate associations by geographic region, name, or focus.

Manufacturing Firms

Profile. The most frequently overlooked area of employment for many foreign language degree holders is manufacturing. The reality is that manufacturing mimics in every manifestation every other segment of the economy. It advertises, it transports, it finances, it restructures, it repositions itself, and it produces all the associated trappings of any business. What's more, it is populated and managed by skilled, educated people from a multiplicity of backgrounds, including foreign language majors in ever-increasing numbers.

Pharmaceuticals, machine-tooled parts, automobiles, plastics and polymers, and countless subcontracted component parts are constantly bought and sold around the world. Whether in South America, the Pacific Rim, Eastern Europe, or at an import/export desk here at home, foreign language majors will find they do not want to ignore manufacturing.

Help in Locating These Employers. Manufacturing firms are listed in *Moody's Industrial Manual, America's Corporate Families, Directory of Manufacturers* for states you are interested in, *Ward's Business Directory, Directory of Corporate Affiliations, Business Rankings Annual,* and *Hoover's Handbook of American Business*. Manufacturers may be listed by industry or by SIC code; if you are not familiar with these classifications, don't hesitate to ask the librarian or career office resource person on duty to help you with locating companies.

POSSIBLE JOB TITLES

Market Analyst
Import/Export Coordinator/Expediter
Pharmaceutical Representative
Manufacturer's Representative
Program Director
In-Country Representative
Income Generation Specialist
Tour Director
Overseas English Language Media Staffer
Collaborative Projects Program Officer
International Banking Loan Officer
Management Consultant
Training and Development Specialist
Salesperson
Customer Service Manager

PROFESSIONAL ASSOCIATIONS

A wide range of types of employers have been described, and a correspondingly wide range of professional associations is provided here. Examine the list to see which groups you might contact to get additional information about career choices, job opportunities, or professional development assistance.

American Association of Advertising Agencies
405 Lexington Ave.
New York, NY 10174
Website: www.aaaa.org
Members/Purpose: To foster, strengthen, and improve the advertising agency business; to advance the cause of advertising as a whole; to aid its member agencies to operate more efficiently and profitably.
Journal/Publication: Bulletin, *401(K) News*; media newsletter; New York and Washington newsletter; roster.

American Association for Leisure and Recreation
1900 Association Dr.
Reston, VA 20191
Website: www.aalr.org

Members/Purpose: Teachers of recreation and park administration, leisure studies, and recreation programming in colleges and universities; professional recreation and park practitioners; people involved in other areas of health, physical education, and recreation with an interest in recreation.

Journal/Publication: *AALReporter*; *Journal of Physical Education, Recreation and Dance*; *Leisure Today*.

Job Listings: Maintains placement service.

American Bankers Association

1120 Connecticut Ave. NW
Washington, DC 20036
Website: www.aba.com
Members/Purpose: Commercial banks and trust companies; combined assets of members represent approximately 95 percent of the U.S. banking industry. Seeks to enhance the role of commercial banks as preeminent providers of financial services through a variety of efforts.
Training: Offers educational and training programs.
Journal/Publication: *ABA Bankers Weekly*; *ABA Banking Journal*; many other publications.

American Council on International Sports

817 23rd St. NW, Room 109
Washington, DC 20052
Members/Purpose: Public-supported organization that attempts to enhance international cooperation and understanding through sports and physical education. Organizes demonstration teams for foreign assignments in physical education and sports programs; develops international sports exchanges and events with emphasis on third world countries.
Journal/Publication: Newsletter.

American Health Care Association

1201 L St. NW
Washington, DC 20005
Website: www.ahca.org
Members/Purpose: Federation of state associations of long-term health-care facilities.
Training: Conducts seminars.
Journal/Publication: *AHCA Notes*; *Provider: For Long Term Care Professionals*.

American Hospital Association
One North Franklin
Chicago, IL 60606
Website: www.aha.org
Members/Purpose: Individuals and health-care institutions including hospitals, health-care systems, and pre- and postacute health-care delivery organizations.
Training: Conducts educational programs.
Journal/Publication: *AHA News*; *Guide to the Health Care Field*; *Hospital Statistics*; *Hospitals*.
Job Listings: Provides weekly job listing for members.

Computer and Business Equipment Manufacturers Association
1250 Eye St. NW, Suite 200
Washington, DC 20005
Members/Purpose: Manufacturers of information processing, business, and communications products. Serves as a secretariat for information processing standards groups.
Journal/Publication: Directory; *Issues & Policies*; *Issue Brief*.

Hotel Sales and Marketing Association International
1300 L St. NW, Suite 800
Washington, DC 20005
Members/Purpose: Sales executives, managers, owners, and other hotel and motor inn executives; people from allied fields; other individuals and firms.
Training: Conducts seminars, clinics, and workshops.
Journal/Publication: Directory; *Marketing Review*; *Update*.

International Sports Exchange
5982 Mia Ct.
Plainfield, IN 46168
Members/Purpose: Participants include university teams. Promotes international goodwill and cultural exchange through sports. Organizes and sponsors international sports competitions and tours between North American and European teams.

Magazine Publishers of America
919 Third Ave., 22nd Floor
New York, NY 10022
Website: www.magazine.org
Members/Purpose: Publishers of 800 consumer and other magazines issued not less than four times a year.
Training: Sponsors seminars.
Journal/Publication: *Magazine Newsletter of Research*.

National Association of Environmental Professionals
6524 Ramoth Dr.
Jacksonville, FL 32226-3202
Website: www.naep.org
Members/Purpose: Persons whose occupations are either directly or indirectly related to environmental management and assessment.
Training: Conducts professional certification program.
Journal/Publication: *Environmental Professional*; newsletter.
Job Listings: See bimonthly newsletter for placement service.

National Association of Manufacturers
1331 Pennsylvania Ave. NW, Suite 1500N
Washington, DC 20004
Website: www.nam.com
Members/Purpose: Manufacturers. Represents industry's views on national and international problems to government.
Journal/Publication: Briefing; bulletin; directory of officers, directors, and committees; *NAM's Small Manufacturer: Issues and Information That Affect Your Business*.

National Newspaper Association
1010 Glebe Rd., Suite 450
Arlington, VA 22201
Website: www.nna.org
Members/Purpose: Representatives of weekly, semiweekly, and daily newspapers.
Journal/Publication: *National Directory of Weekly Newspapers; Publishers' Auxiliary*.

National Radio Broadcasters Association
1771 N St. NW
Washington, DC 20036
Members/Purpose: Representatives of radio and TV stations and TV networks.
Journal/Publication: Broadcast engineering conference proceedings; *Radio Week*; *TV Today*.
Job Listings: Offers employment clearinghouse.

National Sporting Goods Association
1699 Wall St.
Mt. Prospect, IL 60056
Members/Purpose: Retailers, manufacturers, wholesalers, and importers of athletic equipment and sporting goods and supplies.
Journal/Publication: *NSGA Market; NSGA Sports Retailer; Sporting Goods Market; Sports Participation*.

Nonprofit Management Association
315 W. 9th St., Suite 1100
Los Angeles, CA 90015
Members/Purpose: Individuals who directly manage or provide management or technical assistance to nonprofit groups.
Journal/Publication: Bulletin board; membership directory.

Public Relations Society of America
33 Irving Pl.
New York, NY 10003
Website: www.prsa.org
Members/Purpose: Professional society of public relations practitioners.
Training: Offers professional development programs.
Journal/Publication: *PRSA News*; newsletter; *Public Relations Journal*; *Public Relations Journal Register*.
Job Listings: Job listings contained in journal; provides job hotline telephone number.

Software and Industry Association
1730 M St. NW, Suite 700
Washington, DC 20036
Website: www.siia.net
Members/Purpose: Microcomputer software companies, software manufacturers, and other firms involved in the software and information industry.
Journal/Publication: International resource guide and directory; membership directory; *SIIA Newsline*.

Telecommunications Industry Association
2001 Pennsylvania Ave. NW, Suite 800
Washington, DC 20006
Members/Purpose: Companies that manufacture products for or provide services to the telecommunications industry.
Training: Sponsors seminars.
Journal/Publication: *Industry Pulse*.

Travel Industry Association of America
1100 New York Ave. NW, Suite 450
Washington, DC 20005
Website: www.tia.org
Members/Purpose: Travel industry executives; officials of federal, state, and local governments; chambers of commerce; and association executives.
Journal/Publication: Annual report; *International Travel News Directory*; newsletter; newsline; directory of membership and services.

United States Telephone Association
1401 H St. NW, Suite 600
Washington, DC 20005-2164
Members/Purpose: Local operating telephone companies or telephone holding companies.
Training: Conducts educational and training programs.
Journal/Publication: *Phonefacts*; statistical volumes; *Teletimes*.

ADDITIONAL RESOURCES

ABI/Inform on Disk
UMI-Data Courier, Inc.
620 South Fifth St.
Louisville, KY 40202

America's Corporate Families
Dun & Bradstreet Information Services
399 Eaton Ave.
Bethlehem, PA 18025

America's Federal Jobs
JIST Works, Inc.
720 N. Park Ave.
Indianapolis, IN 46202
Website: www.jist.com

America's Top Medical, Education, and Human Services Jobs
JIST Works, Inc.
720 N. Park Ave.
Indianapolis, IN 46202
Website: www.jist.com

American Bank Directory
McFadden Business Publications
6195 Crooked Creek Rd.
Norcross, GA 30092

American Jewish Year Book
Jewish Publication Society
1930 Chestnut St.
Philadelphia, PA 19103
Website: www.jewishpub.org

Best's Insurance Reports
A.M. Best Co.
Oldwick, NJ 08858
Website: www.ambest.com

The Boston Globe
The Globe Newspaper Co.
135 Morrissey Blvd.
P.O. Box 2378
Boston, MA 02107
Website: www.thebostonglobe.com

The Career Guide: Dun's Employment Opportunities Directory
Dun & Bradstreet Information Services
899 Eaton Ave.
Bethlehem, PA 18025
Website: www.dnb.com

Career Information Center
Macmillan Publishing Group
866 Third Ave.
New York, NY 10022
Website: www.mcp.com

Careers Encyclopedia
VGM Career Books
NTC/Contemporary Publishing Group
4255 West Touhy Ave.
Lincolnwood, IL 60712
Websites: www.vgmbooks.com
www.ntc-cb.com

Careers in Government
Careers in Health Care
Careers in Social and Rehabilitation Services
VGM Career Horizon
NTC/Contemporary Publishing Group
4255 Touhy Ave.
Lincolnwood, IL 60712
Websites: www.vgmbooks.com
www.ntc-cb.com

Careers in State and Local Government
Garrett Parks Press
Garrett Park, MD 20896

Catholic Almanac
Our Sunday Visitor, Publishing Division
200 Noll Plaza
Huntington, IN 46750
Website: www.osv.com

The Chronicle of Higher Education
1255 23rd St. NW
Washington, DC 20037
Website: www.chronicle.com

The College Board Guide to Jobs and Career Planning
Joyce Mitchell
The College Board
P.O. Box 866
New York, NY 10101
Website: www.collegeboard.org/index.html

College Placement Council Annuals
62 Highland Ave.
Bethlehem, PA 18017
Website: www.naceweb.org/about/

Community Jobs:
The National Employment Newspaper for the Non-Profit Sector
ACCESS: Networking in the Public Interest
50 Beacon St.
Boston, MA 02108
Website: www.accessjobs.org

The Complete Guide to Public Employment
by Ronald Krannich and Caryl Krannich
Impact Publications
4580 Sunshine Ct.
Woodbridge, VA 22192
Website: www.impactpublications.com

The Complete Mental Health Directory, 1999/2000
Grey House Publishing
Pocket Knife Square
Lakeville, CT 06039
Website: www.greyhouse.com

Credit Union Directory and Buyers Group
United Communications Group
11300 Rockville Pike, Suite 1100
Rockville, MD 20850
Website: www.ucg.com

Your Criminal Justice Career: A Guidebook
Prentice Hall
Upper Saddle River, NJ 07458
Website: www.prehall.com

Current Jobs for Graduates
Current Jobs for Graduates in Education
Current Jobs in Writing, Editing & Communications
Plymouth Publishing, Inc.
P.O. Box 40550
5136 MacArthur Blvd. NW
Washington, DC 20016

Dialing for Jobs: Using the Phone in the Job Search (video)
JIST Works, Inc.
720 North Park Ave.
Indianapolis, IN 46202
Website: www.jist.com

Dictionary of Occupational Titles
U.S. Department of Labor
Employment and Training Administration
Distributed by Associated Book Publishers, Inc.
P.O. Box 5657
Scottsdale, AZ 86261
Website: http://stats.bls.gov/oco/ocodot1.htm

Directory of Adventure Alternatives in Corrections Mental Health and Special Populations
Association of Experiential Education
2885 Aurora Ave., No. 28
Boulder, CO 80303
Website: www.aee.org

Directory of American Firms Operating in Foreign Countries
World Trade Academy Press
50 E. 42nd St.
New York, NY 10017
Website: www.iteams.org

Directory of Bond Agents
Standard and Poor's Corp.
25 Broadway
New York, NY 10004
Website: www.standardpoor.com

Directory of Public School Systems in the U.S.
Association for School, College, and University Staffing (ASCUS)
c/o High School
1600 Dodge Ave., No. 5-300
Evanston, IL 60204
Website: www.ub-careers.buffalo.edu/AAEE

DISCOVER
American College Testing
Educational Services Division
P.O. Box 16
Iowa City, IA 52244
Website: www.act.org/discover/

Effective Answers to Interview Questions (Video)
JIST Works, Inc.
720 North Park Ave.
Indianapolis, IN 46202
Website: www.jist.com

Encyclopedia of Associations
Gale Group
P.O. Box 33477
Detroit, MI 48232
Website: www.gale.com

Environmental Opportunities
Environmental Studies Department
Antioch/New England Graduate School
Keene, NH 03431
Website: www.antiochne.edu/prospects/esm/esmdept

Equal Employment Opportunity Bimonthly
CRS Recruitment Publications/Cass Communications, Inc.
60 Revere Dr.
Northbrook, IL 60062

Federal Jobs Digest
Breakthrough Publications
P.O. Box 594
Millwood, NY 10546
Website: www.jobsfed.com

Foundation Grants to Individuals
The Foundation Center
79 Fifth Ave.
New York, NY 10003
Website: www.fdncenter.org

Government Job Finder
by Daniel Lauber
Planning/Communications
7215 Oak Ave.
River Forest, IL 60305

Graduate Management Admission Test
Graduate Management Admission Council
P.O. Box 6108
Princeton, NJ 08541
Website: www.gmat.org

Graduate Records Exam
Graduate Records Examination Board
Educational Testing Services
P.O. Box 6000
Princeton, NJ 08541
Website: www.gre.org

Guide to Healthcare Market Segment
SMG Marketing Group, Inc.
1342 N. Lasalle Dr.
Chicago, IL 60610
Website: www.smg.com

Handbook for Business and Management Careers
VGM Career Books
NTC/Contemporary Publishing Group
4255 West Touhy Ave.
Lincolnwood, IL 60712
Websites: www.vgmbooks.com
www.ntc-cb.com

The Handbook of Private Schools
Porter Sargent Publishers, Inc.
11 Beacon St., Suite 1400
Boston MA 02108
Website: www.portersargent.com

Harrington-O'Shea Career Decision Making
American Guidance Service
4201 Woodland Rd.
P.O. Box 99
Circle Pines, MN 55014
Website: www.agsnet.com

Harvard Gazette
Harvard Office of News & Public Affairs
Holyoke Center 1060
Cambridge, MA 02138
Website: www.news.harvard.edu

The Helping Professions: A Careers Sourcebook
Brooks/Cole Publishing
511 Forest Lodge Road
Pacific Grove, CA 93950
Website: www.brookscole.com

Hoover's Handbook of American Business
The Reference Press
6448 Highway 290 E, Suite E104
Austin, TX 78723

Hospitals Directory
American Business Directories, Inc.
5711 S. 86th Cr.
Omaha, NE 68127

How to Prepare Your Curriculum Vitae, Second Edition
Acy L. Jackson
VGM Career Books
NTC/Contemporary Publishing Group
4255 West Touhy Ave.
Lincolnwood, IL 60712
Websites: www.vgmbooks.com
www.ntc-cb.com

How to Write a Winning Personal Statement for Graduate and Professional School
by Richard Stelzer
Peterson's Guide
P.O. Box 2123
Princeton, NJ 08543
Website: www.petersons.com

Human Service Career Connection
372A Broadway
Cambridge, MA 02139

Index of Majors and Graduate Degrees
College Board Publication
P.O. Box 2123
New York, NY 10101
Website: www.collegeboard.org/index.html

Infotrac CD-ROM Business Index
Information Access Co.
362 Lakeside Dr.
Foster City, CA 94404
Website: www.gale.com

Internships 2001
Peterson's Guide
P.O. Box 2123
Princeton, NJ 08543
Website: www.petersons.com

Job Bank Series:
Atlanta Job Bank
Boston Job Bank
Chicago Job Bank
Dallas–Ft. Worth Job Bank
Denver Job Bank
Detroit Job Bank
Florida Job Bank
Houston Job Bank
Los Angeles Job Bank
Minneapolis Job Bank
New York Job Bank
Ohio Job Bank
Philadelphia Job Bank
San Francisco Job Bank
Seattle Job Bank
Washington, DC Job Bank
Bob Adams, Inc.
260 Center St.
Holbrook, MA 02343

The Job Hunter: The National Bi-Weekly Publication for Job Seekers
Career Planning and Placement Center
University of Missouri-Columbia
100 Noyes Building
Columbia, MO 65211
Website: http://career.missouri.edu/

Job Listings in Jewish Community Centers and YM-YWHAs
JCC Association of North America
15 East 26th St.
New York, NY 10010
Website: www.jcca.org

Job Seekers Guide to Private and Public Companies
Gale Group
P.O. Box 33477
Detroit, MI 48232
Website: www.gale.com

Manufacturing Directories
Tower Publishing
588 Saco Rd.
Standish, ME 04084
Website: www.towerpub.com

Medical and Health Information Directory
Gale Group
P.O. Box 33477
Detroit, MI 48232
Website: www.gale.com

Million Dollar Directory: America's Leading Public and Private Companies
Dun & Bradstreet Information Services
899 Eaton Ave.
Bethlehem, PA 18025

Moody's Manuals
Moody's Investors Service
99 Church St.
New York, NY 10007

Myers-Briggs Type Indicator
Consulting Psychologists Press, Inc.
3803 E. Bayshore Rd.
Palo Alto, CA 94303
Website: www.cpp-db.com

National Ad Search
National Ad Search, Inc.
P.O. Box 2083
Milwaukee, WI 53201
Website: www.nationaladsearch.com

National Business Employment Weekly
Dow Jones & Co., Inc.
P.O. Box 300
Longmont, CO 80502
Website: www.dowjones.com

The National Directory of Children, Youth, and Family Services
Marion L. Peterson, Publisher
P.O. Box 1837
Longmont, CO 80502

National Directory of Churches, Synagogues, and Other Houses of Worship
Gale Research, Inc.
P.O. Box 33477
Detroit, MI 48232
Website: www.gale.com

National Directory of Private Social Agencies
Croner Publications, Inc.
34 Jericho Turnpike
Jericho, NY 11753
Website: www.croner.com

National Directory of State Agencies
Cambridge Information Group Directories, Inc.
7200 Wisconsin Ave.
Bethesda, MD 20814

National Human Service Employment Weekly
13137 Pennadale Ln.
Fairfax, VA 22033

National Job Bank
Adams Media Corp.
260 Center St.
Holbrook, MA 02343
Website: www.careercity.com

National Job Hotline Directory
Planning/Communications
7215 Oak Ave.
River Forest, IL 60305
Website: http://jobfindersonline.com

National Trade and Professional Associations of the United States
Columbia Books Inc.
1212 New York Ave. NW, Suite 330
Washington, DC 20005
Website: www.columbiabooks.com

Occupational Outlook Handbook
Occupational Outlook Quarterly
U.S. Department of Labor
Bureau of Labor Statistics
Washington, DC 20212
Website: www.dol.gov

O'Dwyer's Directory of Public Relations Firms
J.R. O'Dwyer Co. Inc.
271 Madison Ave.
New York, NY 10016
Website: www.odwyerpr.com

The 100 Best Companies to Work for in America
by Robert Levering and Milton Moskowitz
A Currency Book published by Doubleday
Bantam Doubleday Dell Publishing Group, Inc.
666 Fifth Ave.
New York, NY 10103
Website: www.randomhouse.com

The 100 Best Small Towns in America
Houghton Mifflin Co.
222 Berkley St.
Boston, MA 02116
Website: www.hmco.com

Opportunities in Banking Careers
Opportunities in Gerontology and Aging Careers
Opportunities in Government Careers
Opportunities in Health and Medical Careers
Opportunities in Insurance Careers
Opportunities in Journalism Careers
Opportunities in Law Enforcement and Criminal Justice Careers
Opportunities in Occupational Therapy Careers
Opportunities in Sport and Athletics Careers
Opportunities in Television and Video Careers
VGM Career Books
NTC/Contemporary Publishing Group
4255 West Touhy Ave.
Lincolnwood, IL 60712
Websites: www.vgmbooks.com
www.ntc-cb.com

Patterson's American Education
Patterson's Elementary Education
Educational Directories, Inc.
P.O. Box 199
Mount Prospect, IL 60056
Website: www.edudirectories.com

Peterson's Grants for Graduate and Post Doctoral Study
Peterson's Four-Year Colleges 2000
Peterson's Guides
P.O. Box 2123
Princeton, NJ 08543
Website: www.petersons.com

Places Rated Almanac (6th edition)
IDG Books Worldwide
919E Hillside Blvd., Suite 400
Foster City, CA 94404-2112
Website: www.idgbooks.com

Professional Career Series:
Careers in Advertising
Careers in Business
Careers in Communications
Careers in Computers
Careers in Health Care
Careers in High Tech
VGM Career Books
NTC/Contemporary Publishing Group
4255 West Touhy Ave.
Lincolnwood, IL 60712
Websites: www.vgmbooks.com
www.ntc-cb.com

Professional's Job Finder
Planning/Communications
7215 Oak Ave.
River Forest, IL 60305

Security Dealers of North America
Standard and Poor's Corp.
25 Broadway
New York, NY 10004
Website: www.standardpoor.com

The Skills Search (Video)
JIST Works, Inc.
720 North Park Ave.
Indianapolis, IN 46202
Website: www.jist.com

Sports Marketplace
Sportsguide
P.O. Box 1417
Princeton, NJ 08542

Standard Directory of Advertising Agencies
Reed Reference Publishing
P.O. Box 1417
Princeton, NJ 08542
Website: www.redbook.com

Standard and Poor's Register of Corporations
Standard and Poor's Corp.
25 Broadway
New York, NY 10004
Website: www.standardpoor.com

Strong Interest Inventory
Consulting Psychologists Press, Inc.
3803 E. Bayshore Rd.
Palo Alto, CA 94303
Website: www.cpp-db.com

The Tough New Labor Market of the 1990s (video)
JIST Works, Inc.
720 North Park Ave.
Indianapolis, IN 46202
Website: www.jist.com

**Volunteerism: The Directory of Organizations, Training, Programs &
Publications**
R.R. Bowker
121 Chanlon Rd.
New Providence, NJ 07974
Website: www.booksinprint.com

Wards Business Directory of Corporate Affiliations
Gale Research, Inc.
P.O. Box 33477
Detroit, MI 48232
Website: www.galegroup.com

What Can I Do with a Major In. . . ?
by Lawrence Malnig with Anita Malnig
Abbot Press
P.O. Box 433
Ridgefield, NJ 07657

World Chamber of Commerce Directory
P.O. Box 1029
Loveland, CO 80539

Y National Vacancy List
YMCA of the USA
101 North Wacker Dr.
Chicago, IL 60606
Website: www.ymca.com

Yearbook of American Canadian Churches
Abingdon Press
P.O. Box 801
201 Eighth Ave. S
Nashville, TN 37202
Website: www.abingdon.org

INDEX